Being Muslim in Hindu India

Praise for the Book

'Provocative, sharp and searing, Ziya Us Salam's *Being Muslim in Hindu India* is a sobering reminder of how Hindu majoritarianism has marginalized India's largest minority community. A must-read for every Indian who stands for a diverse, plural and inclusive idea of India.'

—**Dr Shashi Tharoor**
Member of Parliament for Thiruvananthapuram, Lok Sabha

'A searing exploration of what it means to be relegated to being an outsider, always the other. The author presents a melancholic yet courageous lament about the challenges of loving a country when it appears not to love you back. This is a must-read for anyone who cares about justice, empathy and human dignity.'

—**Manoj Jha**
Member of Parliament, Rajya Sabha

'As a journalist with many years of experience behind him, anything Ziya Us Salam writes is always of value. But when it is a book about what being a Muslim in India today means, we really need to sit up and take notice.'

—**Siddharth Varadarajan**
Founding Editor, The Wire

'The thousand-year-old Muslim community in India has shown remarkable strength of spirit and character in standing against a tsunami of caustic hate and vicious violence unleashed against them by state and non-state actors in the last thirteen years. Senior journalist Ziya Us Salam is an erudite and courageous chronicler of this historic struggle against Islamophobia and xenophobia, not seen since Hitler's storm troopers painted their targets on the doors of innocent neighbours. His work is a must-read.'

—**John Dayal**
Author and Christian leader

Being Muslim in Hindu India

A Critical View

ZIYA US SALAM

HarperCollins *Publishers* India

First published in India by HarperCollins *Publishers* 2023
4th Floor, Tower A, Building No. 10, DLF Cyber City,
DLF Phase II, Gurugram, Haryana – 122002
www.harpercollins.co.in

2 4 6 8 10 9 7 5 3 1

Copyright © Ziya Us Salam 2023

P-ISBN: 978-93-5699-584-0
E-ISBN: 978-93-5699-585-7

The views and opinions expressed in this book are the author's own
and the facts are as reported by him, and the publishers are not in
any way liable for the same.

Ziya Us Salam asserts the moral right
to be identified as the author of this work.

All rights reserved. No part of this publication may be reproduced,
stored in a retrieval system, or transmitted, in any form or by any
means, electronic, mechanical, photocopying, recording or otherwise,
without the prior permission of the publishers.

Typeset in 11.5/15.7 Bembo Std at
Manipal Technologies Limited, Manipal

Printed and bound at
Manipal Technologies Limited, Manipal

This book is produced from independently certified FSC® paper to ensure
responsible forest management.

Dedicated to
Dr Nirmala Lakshman
For her endless grace, silent strength and unmatched patience

The detailed notes pertaining to this book are available on the HarperCollins *Publishers* India website. Scan this QR code to access the same.

Contents

	Preface	xi
Part I	**Political Marginalization**	**1**
1.	The Disappearing Muslim	3
2.	The Missing Muslim Voter	16
3.	Reconstituting Constituencies	26
Part II	**Rubbishing Medieval History**	**35**
4.	Samrat Prithviraj and the Myth of the Hindu Ruler	37
5.	Raziya Sultan: The Forgotten Queen Who Dwarfed the Kings	44
6.	Khilji, Now Playing the Villain	50
7.	Akbar–Aurangzeb Parallel	58
8.	Changing Names of Cities	66
9.	Demolishing the Empire Builders	77

Part III Kill a Muslim a Day — 87

10. Lynching the 'Others' — 89
11. Jai Shri Ram — 109
12. Bilquis Bano: Remission and Felicitation of Convicts — 117
13. (A)Dharam Sansad: A Call for Genocide — 124
14. Bulldozers for Muslims — 135

Part IV Wrath on Houses of Worship — 145

15. Targeting Mosques — 147
16. Felled Like a Pack of Cards — 165
17. Namaz, the Art of the Impossible — 176
18. Following the Babri Template — 183
19. 'Jai Shri Ram', Again — 198
20. All Things Muslim — 205

Part V Matters of Love, the Jamaat and the Hijab — 213

21. Tablighi Jamaat as a Metaphor for Muslims — 215
22. Kumbh Mela, the Superspreader — 230
23. The Politics of Love Jihad and Ghar Wapasi — 236
24. Hijab and Hindutva — 250
25. Of Halal Meat and Food Fascism — 257

Part VI Looks and Beyond **265**

   26. 'You Look Like a Muslim'   267

   27. Firoze Khan, the Sanskrit Man   274

Part VII Finding Their Voice **279**

   28. Jihad at Every Step   281

   29. The Shaheen Bagh Women Show the Way   289

   30. Muslims Move Past Their Clerics   300

   Acknowledgements   309

   Notes   311

Preface

TO BE A MUSLIM IS to be an orphan. Born shortly after the death of his father, Prophet Muhammad was brought up by his grandfather for a few years before he too passed away. It was left to his uncle to provide him with a protective shield in his early years, long before he received the first revelation from the angel Jibrail at the age of 40. Muslims in India, though, have had to come to terms with orphan-hood slowly, painfully—in fact, the realization has only now begun to sink in, many decades after the loss of the Father of the Nation in 1948. It took a long time, maybe more than 60 years, and a succession of leaders of various political parties, but the realization dawned on the community that it had no godfathers in independent India. By 2014, there were no politicians willing to use the word 'Muslim' from a public platform, the word being avoided almost like an abuse in civil discourse and replaced with the more euphemistic 'minorities'. In the same country, Muslims and Hindus were once called the two eyes of the nation by Syed Ahmad Khan, the founder of Muhammadan Anglo-Oriental College in 1875, from which grew the Aligarh Muslim University.

The largest political party, the Bharatiya Janata Party (BJP), steadfastly marginalized the community. In 2014, it gave only 7 tickets to Muslims out of the 482 seats the party contested, the percentage of representation coming to an abysmal 1.45 per cent for India's largest minority; three of the seven tickets were given in Jammu and Kashmir, leaving only four for the rest of India! For the first time since Independence, the ruling party had no Muslim Member of Parliament (MP) in the Lok Sabha.[1] The states of Rajasthan, Uttar Pradesh, Gujarat and Madhya Pradesh, besides Delhi, did not send a single Muslim candidate to Parliament in 2014. In 2019, the BJP fielded only seven Muslim candidates. By July 2022, the Government of India, for the first time ever, had no Muslim minister. Indeed, by the end of the third year (summer of 2022) of Narendra Modi's second term as the prime minister, the BJP had no Muslim minister, no MP in either House of Parliament, and not one Muslim Member of the Legislative Assembly (MLA) among its over 1,000 MLAs across the country. Far from the days when the community's vote was sought by almost all political parties, in January 2022, a BJP MLA, Rajkumar Thukral, from Rudrapur in Uttarakhand felt emboldened enough to abuse the community in public and ask the police to frame its members with charges of sedition. The video of his vitriolic discourse went viral after it was shared on Twitter. 'Amid tension over recovery of a cattle carcass from a residential area in Uttarakhand's Udham Singh Nagar district, local BJP MLA Rajkumar Thukral was on 11 January was seen hurling abuses at Muslims and asking police to frame them under "false cases",' The Quint reported.[2] India, it seemed, had chosen the politics of exclusion and persecution with respect to its largest minority.

The rising tide of majoritarianism meant a marginalization of the minorities in general and Muslims in particular. To be a votary of Hindutva was synonymous with being a nationalist; to use the word 'Muslim' in public discourse began to be dubbed communal, even separatist. Muslims were supposed to merge with the mainstream to the extent of losing their identity. In fact, that was the whole idea. With a population estimated at 20 crores, aiming for mass displacement, as in the case of Rohingyas from Myanmar, seemed implausible. Instead, the attempt was to invisibilize the community—as veteran sociologist Imtiaz Ahmed wrote on social media, much like a tributary loses its identity when it meets the river, except that for centuries the rivers had run parallel and merged happily into the Indian Ocean. Not anymore. During the 2022 Vidhan Sabha elections in Uttar Pradesh, no party was seen addressing the concerns of the community, and the chief minister openly talked of the elections being a fight of '80 per cent versus 20 per cent'. In the state where 19 per cent of the population is Muslim, the thinly veiled hint was lost on no one. The Muslim 'merger' with the whole was different from what was chalked out for the Sikhs, the Jains and Buddhists. The latter were muffled with affection, the Hindutva umbrella seeking to draw under it all faiths originating in the subcontinent. The Muslims were different. They traced their faith to the desert of Arabia, counted their pilgrimage centres outside the country and, except for a significant influx in Kerala and some notable Sufi khanqahs, many had arrived as invaders in 712 CE. That despite countless battles for personal aggrandizement, brutalities and bloodshed they did not go back added to the heartburn of a few; the Muslims made India their home and over the centuries enriched its life, happily assimilating what they deemed necessary. They fought many of the local kings and stitched up alliances with some of them. Once able to carve out their space, they married the locals, settled with them, adopted their culture and added to it a dash of Islamic values. So much so that the 'Indian Muslim' became a separate category in the world of Islam. They were Muslims, yes, but clearly distinct from those of the Arab world in their language, attire, customs and even their interpretation of Islam. Many of their religious practices too were derived from Hinduism as were the social customs and traditions. As the community has realized over the past few years, that was not good enough for some.

The leaders of the Congress party, which had led India's freedom struggle and cut across barriers of religion and region, now vied with their saffron counterparts from the BJP in a naked exhibition of Hindutva. Even as Rahul Gandhi hopped from one temple to another with the press in his trail before the General Elections in 2019, the senior party leader Ghulam Nabi Azad cooled his heels at home for much of the campaigning period. A few months before the General Elections, he expressed his anguish:

> Today we are divided, society is divided, friends are divided. I will give a small example. Since the days of the Youth Congress, I have been campaigning across the country from Andaman and Nicobar to Lakshadweep. Around 95 per cent of those who used to call me were Hindu brothers and leaders and just 5 per cent were Muslim brothers. But in the last four years, I have observed that the figure of 95 has dropped to just 20 per cent.[3]

Muslims became an invisible minority, pariahs in their own land, identified on the basis of their clothes during the anti-Citizenship Amendment Act (CAA) movement and shunned for their appearance. For the first time in living memory, one heard the prime minister talk of recognizing a community by its clothes.[4] That the prime minister did it while referring to the clothing of protesters was a clever political ploy to stigmatize the 'other'.

A little before the attire-as-identity remark, every fourth Muslim had found his or her name missing from the electoral rolls in Karnataka, Telangana, Tamil Nadu and Delhi. Neither given tickets to contest elections nor allowed to vote in elections, the Muslims had become the new outcasts of India, the orphans nobody cared for.

In November 2019, the Supreme Court of India held out hope when in the long-pending Babri Masjid–Ramjanmabhoomi dispute it held that it had 'kept individual faith aside' in pronouncing on a land dispute. But in the end the site of the demolished mosque was given to the votaries of the temple. As journalist Nilanjan Mukhopadhyay writes:

> The objective of the petitioners claiming to represent Hindu sentiments indeed came a long way from 1885, when Mahant Raghubar Das demanded that he be allowed to build a temple over the Ram Chabutra, to the fateful day in November 2019, when the five-judge bench of the Supreme Court ruled in favour of the Hindu parties and directed the Centre in one voice to facilitate establishment of a board of trustees to build a Ram temple that would sprawl beyond the 'inner and outer courtyards' of the contested site. It was forgotten that the original demand was not for such a gargantuan-sized piece of land… In their collective verdict, the judges spoke in one voice undoubtedly but in the process ended up addressing only one community and their aspirations. If what the Chief Justice stated actually implied that the judges had unanimously agreed to be mindful of the majoritarian 'societal' sense on the issue, it carries worrying portents not just for the independence of judiciary, but also for the future character of the republic.[5]

In a nutshell, aggressive triumphalism prevailed. From the Somnath Temple in 1951 to the Ram Temple in 2019, Indian secularism has travelled a long way though not necessarily in the right direction. When Dr Rajendra Prasad agreed to inaugurate the newly renovated Somnath Temple in May 1951, the then prime minister, Jawaharlal Nehru, reminded him that the president of a secular nation had no business involving himself in religious matters. Prime Minister Modi seems untouched by such compunctions, though, as we were to discover in August 2020 during the bhumipujan (land worship) of the proposed Ram Mandir at Ayodhya, where he attended the ceremony despite being oath-bound to not discriminate between Indians on the basis of religion. In December 2021, he seemed to be reiterating his lack of concern for the oath by associating with the revamped Kashi Viswanath corridor. In Ayodhya, he felt no need to refer to the upcoming mosque in his address after the Supreme Court judgment. Here, it is pertinent to recall that the apex court in its verdict had asked the government—either the Centre or Uttar Pradesh—to allot a 'prominent and suitable' five-acre plot in Ayodhya to the Sunni Central Wakf Board, for the construction of a mosque. This was to be done simultaneously with the transfer of the property to the proposed trust for the temple to be constructed at the site of the Babri Masjid.

In Kashi, neither did he mention the mosque adjacent to the temple nor did the local municipal authorities deem it necessary to give a facelift to the path leading to the mosque even as huge sums were spent in sprucing up the temple corridor.

The supremacy of the Hindu faith in the country had already been reiterated a few months after the Babri judgment when the apex court allowed the Jagannath Rath Yatra to go ahead in June

2020, at a time when lakhs of Indians were battling the dreaded coronavirus disease. Popular news portal The Wire commented,

> The Indian Supreme Court has come under recent criticism, for its perceived favouritism towards the Hindu religious majority in general and the ruling party specifically. This decision is unfortunately not the only time when the apex court's impartiality was called into question. The Union home minister Amit Shah has credited the reversal of the Supreme Court's decision to Prime Minister Narendra Modi's actions. This remark has only amplified the allegations of a pro-majority bias of the court. The response of the court to the Delhi riots, its refusal to stay the implementation of the controversial Citizen (Amendment) Act and its decision in the Babri Masjid dispute, amongst others, have highlighted a possible slant against the religious minorities in the country.[6]

In a recurrence of the age-old conflict between individual faith and public health, the apex court ruled, 'We find, in one of the present applications, an affidavit filed on behalf of the State of Orissa stating that it might be possible to conduct the Rath Yatra at Puri "in a limited way without public attendance". Indeed, if it is possible to ensure that there is no public attendance, we see no reason why the Rath Yatra cannot be conducted safely along its usual route from temple to temple,' the court said in its written order.

That this ruling came weeks after the Indian media came up with a deadly concoction of half-lies and utter falsehoods to malign the largest Muslim organization in the world, the Tablighi Jamaat, which had held a congregation in Delhi between 13 and 15 March that allegedly resulted in the spread of Covid-19, did not assuage frayed nerves at all. It was not meant to. Many Tablighi Jamaat volunteers were left to languish in jails in Uttar Pradesh, Karnataka and Tamil Nadu for no fault of theirs except attending a religious congregation at Markaz, the Jamaat's headquarters in Delhi. Even as the media came up with a series of fake videos to malign the Jamaat, a small detail was deliberately brushed aside: when the Tablighi Jamaat held its conference in Delhi—in which men from across the country as well as valid visa holders from countries such as Malaysia, Indonesia, Thailand, Sri Lanka, Ghana and Kuwait participated—there was no ban on religious congregations in Delhi. No mosque, temple, church or gurdwara was instructed to discontinue sermons. Prayer services were held as usual. Only stadia, gyms and spas were ordered to close. The order barring religious congregations came on 16 March 2020, a day after the Jamaat's conference ended. But to a section of the nation drunk on Islamophobia, such details were avoidable extras. Even as media portal AltNews repeatedly exposed the malicious videos and news items as false, the damage had been done. In Himachal Pradesh, a man who had attended the Jamaat meeting in Delhi took his life after being subjected to the relentless taunts of people from his village. In Uttar Pradesh, two legislators of the BJP were seen driving out Muslim vegetable vendors from a locality, reminding one of what we read in history books about the lowest caste people in ancient India being shunned (for even their shadow was considered polluting). During the pandemic, to be a Tablighi Jamaat volunteer was no longer about representing the organization but about being the representative of the larger Muslim community. And in the eyes of a large section of our media, to be a Jamaat volunteer, unfortunately, became synonymous with being a Covid-19 spreader. Whether they were the political leaders of the ruling dispensation or a big section of the media, the voices reeked of prejudice. Muslims were their favourite punching bags, and they punched them with relish. As journalist Maya Mirchandani argues in her book *Politics of Hate*, 'They were painted as Muslims who deliberately plotted to spread a disease in Hindu-majority India.'⁷

The brazen vilification of the largest minority by a sizeable section of the majority community did not stem from Covid-19, nor was it limited to it. The deliberate marginalization of Muslims has been going on for the better part of a decade, as has the rehearsed erasure of their presence in public life. The attempt to thwart teenage hijab-wearing girls from attending school in Karnataka in early 2022 was never aimed at emancipating them from supposedly stifling social mores, although that's what Hindutva's supportes would like us to believe. It was more an attempt to wipe out hijab-clad women from the public eye—much like the multiple FIRs filed against Muslim men for praying in parks, pavements, metro stations, malls, hospitals and even in their homes, as was the case in a village in Moradabad.⁸ The idea was to make the largest minority invisible: Men could not be seen praying in public, women could not be seen wearing the hijab in school or college; mosques could not issue the azaan (prayer call) on loudspeakers, meat shops could not sell their ware during the Hindu community's sacred days. The climate of hate prevailed, and winds of fear blew over the largest minority community in an increasingly Hindu India.

A few years ago, many of the symbols of their association with the nation were removed—Mughal Sarai became Deen Dayal Upadhyay Station, Allahabad became Prayagraj and eventually, even Emperor Akbar came to be the new-age Aurangzeb. The renaming of Aurangzeb Road in New Delhi after the former President APJ Abdul Kalam seemed, to some, a classic case of pitting the 'good Muslim' against the 'bad Muslim'. It was followed by demands to rename Akbar Road in the vicinity. The message was that there were no good Muslims; maybe, just maybe, Kalam was an exception. Otherwise, all Muslims were foreigners who indulged in pillage and plunder. Those drunk on the potion of 'One Nation, One Leader, One Religion, One Language' or in other words, Hindi, Hindu, Hindustan, in the name of the unity of the country had no patience for pluralism of faith, food or dialect. The government ultimately resisted the temptation to rename Akbar Road, but demands were made by the BJP's Delhi Chief Adesh Gupta to rename 40 villages of 'Mughal Delhi'. Asking Chief Minister Arvind Kejriwal to issue orders for renaming the villages, Gupta said, 'Delhi is no longer "Mughalon ki Sarai" (resting place of the Mughals) but the capital of the country. The youth of these villages no longer want to carry on with symbols of slavery. They want their villages to be known after the great sons of the country and eminent personalities.' Of course, Gupta did not understand the difference between being a Muslim and being a Mughal. For him, they were interchangeable. It was a shrill reminder of the days of the Babri Masjid–Ram Janmabhoomi stir between 1989 and 1992 when some Hindutva leaders often referred to Muslims as Babur ki aulad (Babur's progeny). Thirty years later, the canvas has become more expansive. All Mughals, and not just Babur, formed the baggage that contemporary Muslims had to carry! Incidentally, most of the 40 villages of 'Mughal Delhi' Gupta wanted renamed predated the arrival of the Mughals in the 16th century. The party higher-ups ignored the cry but instead hit where it hurts more.

In school textbooks, the sections detailing the contributions of Muslims in general and the Mughals in particular were curtailed and amended. So much so, that Akbar was presented as the loser against Rana Pratap at the famous battle of Haldighati. So acquiescing was society that nobody asked, 'If Rana Pratap did actually win the battle of Haldighati, why did Akbar and his successors continue to rule for the next 300 years?' Those questions, obviously, are for a society still wedded to reason and logic.

That the Haldighati episode was not the sole concoction of minds drunk on blind hatred became evident when Mughal monuments were targeted next: they were derided and even denuded of their past. History was not being rewritten; it was being fabricated. Akbar Fort, built in 1570, was renamed Ajmer Fort in 2017. This was not just an attempt at erasing Akbar's name; this was an endeavour to wipe out the contribution of an entire civilization. In September 2020, the Uttar Pradesh Chief Minister, Yogi Adityanath, wondered 'how Mughals can be our heroes' as he renamed the upcoming Mughal Museum (yes!) near Agra![9] He named the museum after Chhatrapati Shivaji, insisting, 'The very name of Shivaji will invoke a feeling of nationalism and self-esteem.'

A couple of years earlier, the matchless Taj Mahal, which attracts six million tourists every year, was removed from the Uttar Pradesh tourism brochure titled *Uttar Pradesh Tourism: Its High Potential*. It was not the only insult to the white marble tomb, one of the seven wonders of the world. Chief Minister Adityanath's party colleague Sangeet Som called it 'a blot on Indian culture' and a monument built by 'traitors'. Though the party spokesperson dissociated himself from the statement, Som was neither penalized nor did the prime minister admonish him. It prompted All India Majlis-e-Ittehadul Muslimeen leader Asaduddin Owaisi to comment, 'Will [Prime Minister Narendra Modi] stop hoisting the national flag from a monument built by traitors (Red Fort)? I challenge them to say it to UNESCO that they should remove it from the list of world heritage sites.'[10] Owaisi spoke loudly. But his words were drowned out by a conspiracy of silence by the ruling party; the top leaders never said a word, the foot soldiers were let loose. And they ran amok.

By 2022, this zeal to fabricate history had taken on a new dimension: In January 2022, the Government of India's Press Information Bureau (PIB) came up with a publication titled *Amrit*

Yatra of New India. It outlined plans to celebrate epochal moments in Indian history, such as the birth anniversary of Netaji Subash Chandra Bose; it also claimed, 'The Bhakti movement heralded the freedom struggle in India. During the Bhakti Yuga, the saints and mahants of this country, whether Swami Vivekananda, Chaitanya Mahaprabhu or Ramana Maharishi, were concerned about its spiritual consciousness. It served as the precursor to the revolt of 1857.' If linking the Bhakti movement to the First War of Independence was a bit far-fetched, it was the height of desperation to link Vivekananda and Maharishi to the Revolt, as the former was born in 1863 and the latter in 1879. Though the PIB rectified the error shortly afterwards, the message was conveyed: In the zeal to undermine the Muslim contribution to India, anything was deemed acceptable.

By 2023, all pretension to neutrality had been dropped. In April of that year, the National Council for Educational Research and Training (NCERT) decided to drop entire chapters on the history of the Mughal courts from school textbooks for class XII students. Some 250 historians from India and abroad expressed concern at the decision, stating, 'There has been no attempt to consult members of the teams that had prepared the textbooks, which included historians and schoolteachers, apart from members of the NCERT... The selective deletion reflects the sway of divisive politics over pedagogical concerns.'[11] The government went ahead with the excision anyway.

Then the polity hit even harder: the industries employing a large number of Muslims—zardozi, karchob, kite-making, brassware, slaughterhouses—began to be closed. Reported *The Wire*, 'In India's "Brass City", an overwhelmingly Muslim workforce stares at a looming crisis... Industries that once offered socio-economic mobility for local Muslims are now being targeted across UP, albeit silently, some believe.'[12]

Days after the prime minister gave his infamous shamshaan–qabrastan (crematorium–cemetery) speech,[13] one realized we had been silent too long. We had not made enough noise when sundry elements sought to ban books, when they did not want a Muslim artist to paint a Hindu goddess, as was the case with MF Husain or when a Muslim politician, Congress leader Ahmed Patel, was derided by labeling him a 'mian' in an election campaign in 2017. Each time we dismissed these as the actions of a lumpen few or as meaningless utterances made in the heat of the moment during election campaigns, the fanatics came back with renewed strength. Now, they called the shots in the country and decided on matters of life and, indeed, death. While death, in the Indian context, is regarded as a great leveler, the dead could be divided and used for a political harvest: a shamshan here, a qabrastan there!

A couple of years after the crematorium–cemetery speech, many in the Muslim community started believing that their sentiments were important, but the sentiments of the majority community were more important. Thus, despite the court admitting to attacks on the Babri Masjid by members of the majority community thrice over, in 1934, 1949 and 1992, the monument was handed over to those very attackers (who believed Lord Ram was born there). Muslims could pray elsewhere. After all, what was a Muslim prayer! Soon, Muslims were to realize they were second-class citizens in their own country. Another instance where the legal stance became clear was in the case of the contentious Triple Talaq law, which came into force around the same time, having been instituted without any consultation with community elders. The court held that the word 'talaq' uttered thrice over by a Muslim man resulted in no divorce.

The new law, though, called it a crime—a crime that resulted in the practical breakdown of the family and a possible jail term for the man. No man of any religion had to face a jail term for a divorce, or a non-divorce as in instant triple talaq, except Muslim men. Also, Article 370, which conferred a special status on the only Muslim-majority state of India, Jammu and Kashmir, was stripped away. Now the whole of India had no Muslim minister, no Muslim chief minister and no Muslim-majority state. It was the darkest time the community had experienced since Independence; the time Muslims of India had no godfather to turn to.

Every now and then, sundry politicians and ruling party members took leave of their constitutional responsibility to ask the Muslims of India to go to Pakistan. The provocations ranged from opposition to the Ram Temple in Ayodhya to a ban on beef consumption and apprehensions about safety at a time when many Muslim men were being lynched in full public view. By August 2020, the community had completely lost its voice. As the prime minister participated in the foundation of the upcoming Ram temple in Ayodhya, nobody raised any objections about the head of the government openly standing with one community. The breathless media fawned over the powers that be and genuflected before them. Nobody, absolutely nobody, asked this simple question: What if the court had ruled in favour of the Muslim community in the Babri Masjid–Ram Janmabhoomi issue? Would the construction of a mosque have been allowed in the middle of a pandemic? Would the media channels have fallen over each other to celebrate the moment? Nobody asked how an event that was termed the 'nation's shame' in 1992, as *India Today* had put it when Babri Masjid was demolished, became a nation's pride in 2020. Was the Hindu Rashtra already upon us? Or had fascism dug in its heels in our courtyard without a whimper of protest from the nation?

Had we, as a nation, said goodbye to the principle of the state not discriminating between citizens on the basis of religion? Well, the answer had already come on 11 December 2019 when the CAA was passed by the Parliament. The Act clearly discriminated between refugees and immigrants on the grounds of religion. Those from Afghanistan, Pakistan and Bangladesh were welcome as long as they were not Muslims, the sovereign, socialist, secular, democratic republic of India declared loud and louder. That the Act got direct or tacit support from some of the MPs of parties like the Samajwadi Party, NCP and the TMC[14] spoke eloquently about how Muslims had been jettisoned by parties that were supposed to be their own! To be a Muslim was to be on your own.

After the darkest moment though, dawn could not be too far away. The CAA galvanized the community into action. This much and no further, the members felt. The community was no longer willing to retreat into a cocoon. It wanted its own space in the polity, society and economy. The community upheld the Constitution and retrieved the tricolour that had been used by hooligans to send fellow members cowering away after the Kathua rape case.[15] Suddenly, the Indian Muslim was no longer invisible. Holding aloft the tricolour, pledging to uphold the Constitution, Muslims were neither shy about their religious identity nor ready to cede space in a secular society. They wore their beards and hijabs with pride, used Urdu with finesse. They talked about the interests of the community and of the Constitution. They ushered in the New Year with a rendition of Jana Gana Mana at a hundred places across the country, raising the tricolour atop masjids, atop homes and places of business. The tricolour could no longer be used to browbeat the community; the community had snatched it back from those who hoisted it in marches to defend criminals, who tied it to their motorbikes as they rode through Muslim-dominated localities screaming 'Jai Shri Ram!' The tricolour belonged to Muslims as much as anybody else in the country. Muslims had found their voice. On the one hand, Muslims had looked fascists in the eye, on the other, they had marginalized the age-old imams known for conservatism—the ubiquitous maulanas—and banished them from confabulations within the community. And they came out smiling using the tools of democracy.

The violence in north-east Delhi (38 Muslims and 15 Hindus died) shook the lives of the Muslims, but not their faith. The attacks on mosques increased: many were charred, an idol was sneaked into a mosque in Delhi during the 2020 violence and another mosque in the National Capital Region (NCR) was attacked by a 200-strong mob during Isha prayers. On the last day of July 2023, two mosques were charred in Haryana's Gurugram and Sohna townships. Around the same time, there was increasing noise concerning the age-old allegations about the Kashi–Mathura mosques having been built after the demolition of temples was revived. Elsewhere, such as in Gurugram, the majority community-led mob could overrule the state, and Muslims were again denied the opportunity of holding Friday prayers despite having the local administration's permission to do so. As the 'Religious Minorities in India Report' published by the Council on Minority Rights in India said in November 2022, 'Post 2014, majoritarianism has been democratized. Mobs in the National Capital Region can veto the state. Muslim migrants from northern India into Delhi had no access to mosques for congregational prayer and had been given designated areas for this. Hindu mobs blocked the practice, showing up to harass them, and leading the state to undo the permission.'[16] The report also noted, 'A law in Gujarat that effectively ghettoizes Muslims was tightened further in 2019 to keep neighbourhoods segregated. A Muslim may not buy or lease property in Hindu neighbourhood even if the buyer and seller were willing... It was for the government to decide whether the sale could go through. Foreigners can buy and rent properties in Gujarat where Gujarati Muslims cannot.'[17]

Simultaneously, old ruses of Hindu–Muslim conflict gave way to allegations of 'love jihad', wherein Muslim men were accused of marrying Hindu women with the intention of increasing the Muslim population. Young Muslim men were roughed up and put in jail just for daring to love Hindu women. Parallel attempts were made to deplete their stock with Ghar Wapasi, the conversion of Muslims to Hinduism under the pretext of bringing 'Hindus who had gone astray' back into the fold. The state watched. The media played the handmaiden of the government. A pall of fear and helplessness hung low over and was ominous for the Muslims of India. Marriage and mosques, food and dress, even citizenship, nothing remained beyond rebuke and reproach. Laws were framed to bar Muslim men from marrying Hindu women, mosques from using loudspeakers to give the prayer call, and the community's men were either accused of beef consumption or transporting cattle for slaughter. Either way, many were lynched in full public view. On Eidul Azha in June 2023, a Muslim family was attacked for merely taking a goat home in Mumbai: the majority community attempted to decide whether or not a Muslim could celebrate her festival according to the tenets of Islam.

Will the Muslims fight one more round, for their lives and dignity, for the idea of India, knowing that the man who always fights one more round is never whipped? Will they be allowed to raise their voice? The answer came from the experience of the doughty women of Shaheen Bagh. For more than a hundred days, they staged an entirely peaceful protest against the CAA, singing songs of defiance, raising the tricolour, standing up for the national anthem many times a day. Among them were women well into their seventies and eighties, women who had never been known to raise their voice on any public issue. They found that the volume of their voices made those around them listen. But the government made no effort to speak to or negotiate with them. The Shaheen Bagh protesters kept waiting with the banners reading, 'Modi, tum kab aaoge? (Modi, when will you come [to speak]?)' At worst, the women were vilified through non-state organs, at best ignored by the state. The underlying message was that no matter what a Muslim woman (or a man) did, the government would not be moved. And to think these were the Muslim women about whose welfare and secure matrimonial life the government had made much brouhaha with the triple talaq law! The women of Shaheen Bagh continued undeterred, unfazed by the steep challenge, the studied indifference and the mounting abuse. Each morning brought with it possibilities of a new beginning, each evening helped build bonds of sorority. Only Covid-19 sent them home.

Barely a few months after the women's struggle against the CAA was halted by the pandemic, the farmers of Punjab, Haryana and other places took to occupying strategic entry points to the city of Delhi. Beginning November 2020, they wanted three agrarian laws repealed, the laws they believed helped corporate houses instead of the small farmer. Even when faced with tens of thousands at Delhi's entry points blocking the way, hardly anybody talked of the trouble in reaching the capital. Not many talked of the right to use a road, in total contrast to the arguments used to ask for a forcible removal of Shaheen Bagh protesters merely a few months earlier. The government engaged the farmers in talks almost on a daily basis, never giving up the option of a dialogue. This stood in stark contrast to the attitude of the same government to the Muslim women who had stood up in peaceful resistance against the CAA. What mattered, probably, in determining the official response was the identity of the protester. One had her citizenship under cloud, the other her livelihood in danger. The former's sacred land was abroad in Mecca and Medina, the latter's (or at least most of their) sacred land was in the country; the latter also did not look like Muslims from their attire. The difference in the government's attitude stemmed not from contemporary politics, but from Golwalkar's definition of an Indian. To be a Muslim was akin to being a foreigner, 'deserving of no rights, much less citizenship or equality'—that was the spirit of Golwalkar's teaching. The government obviously set store by this. A state government put up the photographs of those who took part in the CAA protests on public squares, pledging to recover from them compensation for any damage to public property. Later, many a state government went a step further, this time sending bulldozers to raze the houses and shops of those who dared to protest the provocative remarks about the Prophet made by Nupur Sharma, a BJP spokesperson, as part of a televised debate in the summer of 2022.[18] Whether in Delhi, Prayagraj or Khargone, bulldozers became the new weapon of triumphal majoritarianism.

Many summers ago, we had been warned about this day by the irrepressible Khushwant Singh. In *The End of India*, Singh wrote,

> These are dark times for India. The carnage in Gujarat, Bapu's home state, in early 2002 and the subsequent landslide victory of Narendra Modi in the elections will spell doom for the country. The fascist agenda of the Hindu fanatics is unlike anything we have experienced in our modern history… India is going to the dogs, and unless a miracle saves us, the country will break up. It will not be Pakistan or any other foreign power that will destroy us; we will commit hara-kiri.[19]

That was in 2003. Things have changed since then. The odds are even steeper now. Since 2014, there has been a descent into rampant majoritarianism, and India seems to have chosen the path of exclusion and persecution of its largest minority. What has happened to the lowest castes in India for centuries now seems to be happening to Muslims too: They are being told don't live here, don't worship there, don't eat this, don't sell that; the dos and don'ts are endless, as is the daily humiliation. Unlike in 2002, the danger today is not confined to Bapu's home state but has spread to the whole of Bapu's Bharat, the Bharat that still prints his photograph on its currency notes. The future will be decided when, if ever, India retrieves the spirit of the Mahatma and consigns the fascists to the dustbin of history. The Muslim cannot fight this battle alone. Being a Muslim amidst the ever-unfolding chapters of Islamophobia is not easy. India will have to speak up.

PART I
Political Marginalization

1

The Disappearing Muslim

MOVING THE MUSLIM WOMEN'S (PROTECTION of Rights on Marriage) Bill for passage in the Lok Sabha in June 2019, Union Law Minister Ravi Shankar Prasad claimed the bill was not against any community, religion or belief, rather it would ensure justice to women. Specifically, Muslim women, he meant.

His party colleague, the indomitable Meenakshi Lekhi, in a well-reasoned debate challenged the opponents of the bill to produce one Surah, one verse from the Quran in favour of instant triple talaq. 'It is not He versus She. Women are the largest minority in this country,' she said.[1]

Also speaking on the bill for the government in the Lower House was the former Human Resource Development Minister Smriti Irani, who later went on to be the minister for minority affairs. For the Congress, the principal Opposition party, Sushmita Dev, Mallikarjun Kharge and Ranjeet Ranjan spoke on the bill, which proposed a three-year jail term and a fine for any Muslim man found guilty of pronouncing a triple talaq in one go. A lot of noise was made on the subject with both the treasury benches and the Opposition speaking energetically and even vociferously about the bill. There was, however, one voice that was missing. That of the Muslim woman, the one directly impacted by instant triple talaq and the one who stood to gain or lose the most, depending on which side of the political divide you stood in relation to the proposed law. In the absence of any Muslim woman's voice, the debate on the pros and cons of the bill ran shallow, much like a third-person dialogue or as they say in Urdu, 'Begani shaadi mein Abdullah diwana'.

The absence of a Muslim woman speaker within the BJP's ranks was not incidental, though. It stemmed from its age-old policy of exercising extreme economy in giving tickets to Muslims. And as women, to quote Lekhi, 'are the largest minority', tickets given to Muslim women were fewer still. In its history of existence, from 1980, when the party was founded to take over from the erstwhile Jan Sangh to the day Narendra Modi became the prime minister in 2014, the BJP had given tickets to only 20 Muslim candidates to contest the Lok Sabha elections. In the sixteenth Lok Sabha, in which the talaq law was framed, the BJP had 282 members in the Lower House. The Muslim representation was zero. The party that rode to power on the slogan of 'Sabka Saath, Sabka Vikas' (Everybody's support, everybody's progress) had the dubious distinction of becoming the first winning party at the Centre with zero Muslim representation.

Interestingly, Muslim fortunes are proving to be inversely proportional to those of the BJP in General Elections. In 1980, the year the BJP came into existence, the Muslim representation to the Lok Sabha was the highest ever at 49. It was still 46 when Rajiv Gandhi rode a sympathy wave in the wake of the assassination of his mother, Indira Gandhi, to come to power as prime minister in 1984.

The BJP had only two members in the Lok Sabha then. The Muslim MPs numbered 30 in 2009 when Dr Manmohan Singh began his second innings as the prime minister. It declined to merely 22 in 2014, the lowest ever, even as the BJP notched up its highest tally till then with 282 Lok Sabha members. Muslims, who accounted for a little more than 14 per cent of the country's population made up only a little over 4 per cent of Lok Sabha MPs, down from 5.5 per cent and 30 MPs in 2009. The Muslim representation improved marginally to 25 in the General Elections in 2019 with the BJP once again romping home. By July 2022, the Narendra Modi government had the dubious distinction of becoming the first one since 1947 to not have a Muslim minister. India's largest minority was not visible in the corridors of power anymore.

The decline in Muslim presence in the Lok Sabha can best be seen in the context of the soaring fortunes of the BJP in the Hindi-speaking belt, specifically, Uttar Pradesh, Bihar, Madhya Pradesh, Delhi and Rajasthan. For instance, there were 10 Muslim MPs across parties from Uttar Pradesh in 2004 and 7 in 2009. The number of Muslim MPs dropped to zero in 2014, as the BJP, against all expectations, won 71 of the 80 seats in the state, besides 2 seats for its allies. The fact that it did it without fielding a single Muslim candidate clarifies the picture. The Muslim vote was no longer needed to win elections, as was proven emphatically by the BJP's success saga. The state has around 20 per cent Muslim population yet failed to send a single member to the Lok Sabha! The figures changed a wee bit when in 2018 Tabassum Hasan won by-elections as a representative of the Rashtriya Lok Dal from Kairana in western Uttar Pradesh, barely a year before the House was dissolved.

A little under five years after the 2014 verdict, seasoned commentator Harish Khare wrote in The Wire,

The total obliteration of Muslim representation from the largest state in the country was so stunning that neither the Muslim leadership nor the secular groups have got around to talking about it, even after five years. On the other hand, the BJP had cockily concluded that it could win national power without making even a token gesture, leave alone making any concession, to the largest minority in the country. The Bharatiya Janata Party won 73 out of 80 seats in Uttar Pradesh, and it was this UP tally that decisively catapulted Narendra Modi to authoritarian heights.[2]

The numbers in Uttar Pradesh were the result of an attempt by the BJP to say goodbye to any pretensions of taking the minorities along. As Khare commented, 'The 2014 UP outcome was a spectacular rebuff to our constitutional pretensions and commitments, and to the Muslims' sense of constituting a crucial voice in the national power sharing arrangements. A Gujarat-like marginalization of Muslims in Uttar Pradesh got neatly consecrated in the 2017 assembly elections. The tremors have been felt beyond Uttar Pradesh.' He added on a note of warning, 'No political party or leader—with the possible exception of the AIMIM's Asaduddin Owaisi—wants to be seen as speaking up for the Muslims, their concerns and anxieties, their insecurity and their sense of helplessness, lest they be accused of "minority appeasement".'

No one seems prepared to protest, leave alone contest, such brazen political marginalization of fellow Indians. By the time the next Assembly elections came around in Uttar Pradesh in 2022, the principal Opposition in the state, the Samajwadi Party—which had since the days of the Babri Masjid–Ramjanmabhoomi controversy in the late 1980s and early 1990s built up a reputation for relying on the Muslim–Yadav social component for electoral success—virtually dropped the mention of the Muslim community from its electoral discourse.³ As the party leader and former chief minister, Akhilesh Yadav hopped from one Assembly seat to another, conspicuous by their absence at most places were the party's Muslim MLAs and other leaders; the party needed the Muslim vote, but it seemed its top brass was keen not to be seen with Muslims on stage. The sole significant exception occurred at Rampur, the bastion of the party's Muslim face, Azam Khan. The Bahujan Samaj Party (BSP) did hand out tickets to more Muslim candidates; but with this silver lining came the cloud of candidates being put up to wean away the Muslim vote from the Samajwadi Party and indirectly help the BJP to edge ahead. As for the BJP, it repeated its policy of not fielding a single Muslim candidate in the state, something it did in the neighbouring Uttarakhand too (the hill state went to polls at the same time).

The picture remained dismal for Muslims. In the face of a Hindutva surge, it was becoming increasingly difficult for Muslims to win elections. Golwalkar's 'Others' became political pariahs, the new Untouchables. In the Assembly elections held between 2013 and 2018—the years of the beginning and peaking of the Hindutva electoral triumph story—the Muslim candidates' success rate was reduced significantly from 35 per cent to 20 per cent. Even this reduced percentage was possible only because of the surprising victory of the Congress in the Assembly elections in 2018 in Rajasthan, Madhya Pradesh and Chhattisgarh, the three states under the BJP, where Muslim representation in the government was at best nominal in the previous years. The three states combined to produce 11 Muslim MLAs in the new governments. In the Madhya Pradesh Assembly elections in 2018, only 14 Muslims were nominated by all parties combined: 1 by the BJP, 3 by the Congress, 9 by the BSP and 1 by CPI. The one ticket that the BJP gave to a Muslim (to Fatima Rasool) made the party's tally better than that of the Assembly elections in the state between 1993 and 2008, when the party did not field a single Muslim candidate. In the 2008, 2013 and 2018 Madhya Pradesh Assembly elections, the party nominated one Muslim each time. While the BJP's decision was on predictable lines, it was the decline in the number of the Congress tickets for Muslims that was disconcerting. The party, which put up 10 Muslim candidates in the state in 1980, has since been giving tickets to fewer Muslims. For three Assembly elections in 1993, 2003 and 2018, the Congress put up Muslim candidates only in six, five and three seats, respectively. Unsurprisingly, veteran Congress leader Aziz Qureshi lashed out at his own a few days before the Vidhan Sabha polls in 2023, stating 'Muslims are not slaves who will act as per their orders. Congress leaders are chanting "Jai Ganga Maiya", "Jai Narmada Maiya", "Garv se kaho Hindu hain," taking out religious yatras and installing idols at the Madhya Pradesh Congress office.' Muslims comprise a little under 7 per cent of Madhya Pradesh's population, and the proportional representation of Muslims in Parliament and the State Assembly should have been 2 and 15, respectively.

Things are not too different in Rajasthan, Gujarat, Telangana and Bihar. In Gujarat, since the 2003 Assembly elections, the BJP has not fielded a single Muslim for Assembly or Lok Sabha elections. In Telangana too Muslims struggled to make an impact on the electoral map. The young state has a 120-member Assembly in which are represented 15 constituencies where Muslims account for over 40 per cent of the population. In the last Vidhan Sabha polls in 2018, the BJP put up two Muslim candidates in these constituencies with sizeable Muslim populations, and the Congress five. As the Scroll commented, 'The bar for giving tickets to Muslims tickets is set sky high.'[4] Any talk of 'Sabka Saath, Sabka Vikas' rang hollow by then.

Not one person talked of minority appeasement anymore. Muslims had almost disappeared from the states' electoral landscape.

In the Bihar Vidhan Sabha elections in 2020, the BJP formed the government along with its major partner Janata Dal (United) (JD-U), notching up 74 seats compared to JD-U's 44 seats. It's success story translated into a wipe-out of Muslims from the government. Neither the BJP nor the JD-U had a single Muslim MLA in its final tally. All 11 Muslim candidates of the JD-U lost the elections, largely as a result of the JD-U's support of the CAA in Parliament. When the new cabinet was sworn in under Chief Minister Nitish Kumar, there was representation of Brahmins, Bhumihars, Rajputs, Yadavs and Dalits. Conspicuous by absence were Muslims, who form 16 per cent of the electorate in the state. In the same Assembly, however, there were eight Muslim MLAs from the Rashtriya Janata Dal (RJD), four from the Indian National Congress, five from the All India Ittehadul-e-Muslimeen and one each from the Bahujan Samaj Party and the Communist Party of India (Marxist–Leninist) (CPIML). The Muslim representation in the government improved significantly when the JD-U dumped the BJP and formed a new government in alliance with the RJD and the Congress in August 2022. Yet, there was no overlooking the fact that the number of Muslim MLAs had come down to 19, from 24, in the outgoing Assembly in 2015, in which the RJD–JD-U–Congress had fought the elections in an alliance against the National Democratic Alliance (NDA) led by the BJP. The success of RJD–JD-U–Congress had given a fillip to the prospects of Muslim candidates winning in elections. Wherever the BJP made conspicuous gains, Muslim representation became almost invisible. Wherever and whenever the lotus bloomed, Muslim voices and faces withered away.[5]

In Rajasthan, where the BJP reigned after the 2013 Vidhan Sabha elections, there were only two Muslim MLAs till 2018. This changed with the defeat of the BJP in the 2018 Vidhan Sabha elections, and the number of Muslim MLAs rose to eight, seven of them being from the Congress and one from the BSP, who too later joined the Congress.

Though the rise of the BJP and the increased popularity of Hindutva severely dented the prospects of Muslims either in getting election tickets or in winning their seats, it would be unwise to blame the BJP alone for the nosedive in their fortunes in the various Vidhan Sabha or Lok Sabha polls. In the 2014 General Elections, the Muslim candidates, cutting across party lines, accounted for less than 10 per cent of the overall tally. There were 320 Muslims in the fray, and 22 of them came out successful. The BJP fielded only 7 Muslims; the Congress was only a shade better with 27. Yet, the parties both notched up shameful success rates for these candidates, of 2 and 6 per cent respectively, a far cry from the community's numerical strength… There are 14 Lok Sabha constituencies where Muslims form most of the electorate. Then there are 13 more constituencies where Muslims comprise more than 40 per cent of the population. This takes the total number of seats with Muslim population predominance to 27. It may be reiterated that according to many estimates, India has the highest number of Muslims in the world after Indonesia.

The regional parties fared better. The RJD, the SP and the CPI(M) fielded between 15 and 20 per cent Muslim candidates.

Back in 2009, when the United Progressive Alliance (UPA) was riding high, there were 832 Muslim candidates contesting the General Elections. Importantly, nearly half of them were independents, often marking nothing more than a token presence in the hustings. The mainstream political parties had not shown any overweening enthusiasm in fielding Muslim candidates back then either. This lack of enthusiasm turned into reluctance in 2014, and now, political parties in general, and not just the BJP and its allies, are often too afraid to put up Muslim candidates in seats where the community does not have a strong presence. Commented The Wire in the run-up to the Uttar Pradesh Vidhan Sabha elections in 2022, 'Leaders in the (Samajwadi) party say they are ring-fenced by the BJP's aggressive religious polarisation, meaning the party may not field as many Muslim candidates as it usually does.'[6]

While a lot has been said about the political marginalization of Muslims since 2014, what often slips under the radar is the reality that since the 1980 elections, Muslim representation in the Lok Sabha has either been declining or at best stayed stagnant even as the community's share in the general population went up from 11.1 per cent in 1981 to 14.2 per cent in 2011, and possibly became marginally higher in 2023. At the same time, the number of Muslim MPs in the Lok Sabha declined by around half, from 49 in 1980 to 23 in 2014 and 25 in 2019. Writing in *Modi's India: Hindu Nationalism and the Rise of Ethnic Democracy*, Christophe Jaffrelot, professor of Indian politics and sociology at King's College London, described the issue as follows:

> The gap between the share of Muslims in the Indian population and their share in the Lok Sabha (which dropped from 9 to 4.2 per cent) increased fivefold, jumping from 2 to 10 percentage points between 1980 and 2014. Responsibility for this trend lies primarily with the BJP, which has never endorsed more than a few Muslim candidates, and this in constituencies where the party had a slim chance of winning, even as its group in parliament continued to increase in numbers.[7]

Indeed, in Gujarat, the BJP did not give even a single Muslim a ticket to contest elections in 2022 for the Assembly elections. The last time a Muslim contested an election, though unsuccessfully, with BJP's backing in Gujarat was back in 1998. Likewise, in Rajasthan, where Muslims account for 11.2 per cent of the population, the party did not enter a Muslim candidate in any Lok Sabha election 1980 onwards. In fact, since way back in 1952, Rajasthan has sent a Muslim to the Lok Sabha only twice—Ayub Khan being the sole representative, winning twice in 1984 and 1991 from Jhunjhunu on the Congress ticket. This descent into political majoritarianism is better expressed through the vicissitudes in the relationship of the Congress with Muslims. Steering away from the community in the face of Hindutva, the Congress put up only 31 Muslim candidates in the 2009 General Election. In 2014, the number declined further to 27, though the figure improved to 35 in 2019. 'Not only did parties of all political stripes field fewer than 10 per cent of Muslim candidates for the Lok Sabha in 2014 and even fewer, 8.6 per cent, in 2019, but above all hardly any were elected. Muslim MPs ultimately made up about 4.2–4.5 per cent of elected representatives in the lower house,' stated Jaffrelot.[8]

What is even more disturbing than the limited representation of Muslims in various Assemblies and the Lok Sabha is the emerging reality that fewer non-Muslim voters are likely to support a Muslim candidate. Even a seasoned politician like Ghulam Nabi Azad, for long a popular campaigner, expressed his disappointment at being considered extra baggage by many party candidates at the time of elections: Fewer Hindu candidates of the Congress invited Azad, a Kashmiri Muslim, to campaign for them. They felt his presence on stage itself affected their electoral prospects negatively. Things did not change with the formation of INDIA, a new alliance of

26 Opposition parties in July 2023. INDIA failed to project any Muslim leader outside Kashmir as its prominent representative. It left former member of Rajya Sabha Mohammed Adeeb disappointed. Without putting it in so many words, a Muslim face beyond the Kashmir old guard of Farooq Abdullah and Mehbooba Mufti was not considered a viable electoral option. It is the same lack of the winnability factor that is often cited by the BJP as the reason for giving fewer tickets to Muslims. In other words, the party felt that a Muslim candidate was not likely to get non-Muslim votes with the same strength when compared to a Hindu candidate.

In *Whole Numbers and Half Truths: What Data Can and Cannot Tell Us About Modern India*, Rukmini S wrote,

> When a Muslim politician is elected in India, the odds are that her constituency is overwhelmingly Muslim... there are only fifteen constituencies that actually have a population that is more than 50 per cent Muslim. Thirteen of them elected Muslim MPs in 2019 Lok Sabha elections. But in the rest of the country, the odds of getting elected decline sharply for a Muslim hopeful; if a constituency had fewer than 20 per cent Muslims, the odds of a Muslim winning went down to under one in a hundred in 2019.[9]

The point was reinforced in the 2022 UP Assembly elections where the SP struck a pre-poll alliance with the Rashtriya Lok Dal (RLD), which has its core base among the Jat voters. The idea behind the alliance was a consolidation of Jat and Muslim voters. Matters didn't quite work out that way on many seats where Jats failed to vote for the Muslim candidate fielded by the alliance. In the analysis of News Nine, 'Muslim–Jat unity remained a theoretical concept, it failed to work in favour of the SP–RLD alliance in West UP. The alliance won only 12 of the 58 seats that voted in phase one in West UP; Jat votes seem to have gone to the BJP, leaving Muslims in the lurch.'[10] Significantly, this Jat vote for the BJP came close on the heels of the farm law agitation, where the community leaders were ranged against the ruling party. But at the time of elections, many found it unthinkable to join hands with Muslims to vote against the party. Rukmini's point was reinforced when the Delhi-based Institute of Policy Studies and Advocacy and the Muslim Intellectuals Forum found, in April 2023, that the situation was no different even at the level of the local municipal elections. They stated: 'The number of Muslim MLAs in Delhi remains static at around 5.5% while the Muslim population is three times the number. The representation in the MCD is even lesser. Most political parties seem averse to giving tickets to Muslim candidates to contest elections from seats with a non-Muslim majority.'[11]

Interestingly, though the BJP did not deem it necessary to give tickets to many Muslims, it did not steer clear of mentioning the community in its election campaign. In the Uttar Pradesh Assembly elections in 2017, Narendra Modi himself levelled the qabrastan–shamshanghat comparison, insinuating that the previous state government led by the SP was more concerned about Muslims than Hindus, more likely to supply regular electricity on Eid than Diwali. At the same time, Yogi Adityanath was at his acerbic best in election campaigns. Both in Telangana in 2018 and Uttar Pradesh in 2017, he talked of the fight between 'Ali and Bajrang Bali'. Muslims may not have been seen fighting the elections, but the fear of Muslims had to be invoked to reap an electoral harvest. And what a harvest it proved to be for the BJP! One cannot help recalling the words of Khushwant Singh, who wondered soon after Modi became the chief minister of Gujarat for the first time:

Ever since the BJP and its allies have come to power, a sinister dimension has been added to this feeling of separateness. It is hard to believe that elements of the Sangh Parivar have been able to convince a significant number of Hindus that they have been treated as second class citizens in a country where they form eighty-two per cent of the population...How have the likes of Narendra Modi...succeeded in persuading the Hindus that they are discriminated against when there is no evidence whatsoever to substantiate their claims?[12]

The Muslims of India could soon become an invisible minority on the political map of the country.

2

The Missing Muslim Voter

A LITTLE BEFORE THE LOK Sabha elections in 2019, the *National Herald* carried a screaming headline on its website: 'Lok Sabha Elections 2019: 3 crore Muslim, 4 crore Dalit among 12.7 crore voters missing from electoral rolls'.[1]

The first glance conveyed the picture of all-round apathy, society in general paying the price for a few individuals' or an organization's lack of attention to detail. It was possible that was the case, but it was probably much more than just that. Without stating it in so many words, the article conveyed the story of a systemic bias against Muslims and Dalits. Muslims constitute a little over 14 per cent of the general population but in the missing names from the electoral rolls, the percentage shot up alarmingly to 25 per cent. In other words, if a Muslim family had four voters, one was sure to find his name missing from the rolls.

The report quoted a study by Hyderabad-based software professional Khalid Saifullah, who created the Missing Voters app. Saifullah revealed that 15 per cent of all voters in the country, including 25 per cent Muslims and 20 per cent Dalits, found their names missing from electoral rolls till the end of February, barely a couple of months before the Parliamentary elections in April–May 2019.

Soon after the report became public, many mosques across India asked believers of Islam to check if their names were still on the electoral rolls. There was fear, even panic. Friday sermons often concluded with an impassioned plea to the worshippers to go the extra yard to find out if their names were still there on the rolls, even if they had been voting for 30 years. They saw in the missing names a conspiracy to disenfranchise Muslims and Dalits. After all, this is what Hindutva politics was all about, they reckoned—the marginalization and, preferably, the erasure of Muslims from the political map. In fact, when some constituencies went to Lok Sabha polls during Ramzan, the clerics asked the worshippers observing the fast to go and cast their vote as a duty to the nation first thing in the morning to avoid the soaring afternoon temperatures. Under no circumstances were they to skip voting. The community was desperate, doing all within its limited means to make its presence felt in India's politics. 'Voting in elections was part of nation building,' they were reminded at Jamiat Ulama-i-Hind's mosque in New Delhi. 'And nation building was part of a Muslim's duty,' the faithful were told by the imams. Such a sermon in normal times would have presented a beautiful fusion of Muslim identity and Indian democracy, one where there was no contradiction between being a good Muslim and a good Indian. But we are not living in normal times.

The concern did not stem from the imaginary fears of a minority. It stemmed from the experience of the Vidhan Sabha elections in states such as Karnataka, Gujarat and Uttar Pradesh. The prospect of political redundancy loomed large. In all these states, Muslims constituted the largest segment among the missing names from electoral rolls. In fact, in Karnataka, things were particularly bad before the state elections in 2018. The Delhi-based Centre for Research and Debates in Development Policy (CRDDP) found that there was an estimated exclusion of around 180 million people from the electoral process at the time. In an interview with this author, Abusaleh Sharrif, founder of CRDDP, had said:

> There is a huge exclusion of Indians at large from the electoral rolls, but the exclusion of Muslims is higher. It threatens to make a mockery of our democracy. It is estimated that there is exclusion of 150 to 180 million Indians from the electoral process. It is like excluding a whole country or even a hundred small nations. That in itself is a disgrace to India. For Muslims, I would say, in up to 50 per cent of the households in a State, there is at least one person who does not have a vote though he/she is otherwise eligible. Though we started with Karnataka, the pilot work is on in Gujarat, Telangana, Andhra Pradesh and Tamil Nadu. The trend is similar in all States. It is a cause for concern.[2]

Shariff's concerns remained unheard. In the 2023 Vidhan Sabha elections in Karnataka, many Muslims yet again found their names missing from the electoral rolls. Some, to their horror, discovered that they had been declared dead! As *Outlook* magazine said:

> Over 9,000 adults find themselves declared dead or (that they) have moved out of the Shivajinagar constituency when they are alive and at home… Javeed is one among hundreds of voters from minority communities in the constituency whose names were on the list of voters who had apparently shifted out of the constituency or were dead. He had voted in 2018 as well. 'Why do they want to remove our names?' the oldest woman

in the house asks Javeed. 'Ye sab government ka kaam hai (this is all the work of the government),' he responds. This is mainly happening to the Muslim community, adds Javeed... 'Everyone knows I live and work here. Why snatch our right to vote just because we are from one community?'[3]

A grave concern, indeed. The names of Muslims had been missing from electoral rolls for quite some time. It was not a one-off mistake made by some incompetent ground staff or clerk of the election commission. Matters were the same in 2018. And in 2014. In 2009, too, there were complaints on similar lines, albeit fewer in number. Back in the mid-90s, the author's mother, then less than 60, was declared to be 127 years old according to her voter ID! She was allowed to vote on showing her passport as proof of her date of birth and residence. But those were less problematic times. In New India things are different. Starkly different.

Saifullah, the engineer who founded the Missing Voters app, spoke on the same lines. As reported by the *National Herald*, 'Huge discrepancies came to my notice during the 2014 parliamentary elections when lakhs of Muslim names got deleted from the voter's list,'[4] Saifullah recalled, adding, 'It prompted me to undertake a study in Gujarat where names of lakhs of Muslims were dropped from the electoral lists in at least 16 Assembly Constituencies during 2017 polls. The BJP candidates won with slight margins of often 3000 *(or less)* votes from these seats.' His findings lent credence to the oft-repeated claim of many BJP leaders: Asked to explain the party's reluctance to give tickets to Muslim candidates, they talk of the winnability of the candidate, implying that the party does not get Muslim votes, and a Muslim candidate was unlikely to get the majority community's vote. What was unsaid was, it helped that some Muslims could not vote!

'When I was analysing the voter lists, I found, for example, there was only one registered voter each from over 1800 households in Godhra,' Saifullah told the *National Herald*, adding, 'Is it possible? Where did the rest of the voters go?'[5]

The problem ran across states. The names of Muslims were missing from electoral rolls everywhere—from Tamil Nadu to Delhi, Gujarat to Telangana. *Frontline* commented,

> If you are a Muslim in Uttar Pradesh with four voters in your family, chances are that only three will get to exercise their right to franchise granted by Article 326 of the Constitution. The fourth person's name would either be missing or excluded from the electoral rolls.
>
> In Tamil Nadu, too, every fourth Muslim person's name is found missing from electoral rolls. The situation in neighbouring Andhra Pradesh and Telangana is not any better... Incidentally, the number of Muslim voters has declined over the years, giving rise to fears about discrimination, political exclusion, total elimination and so on. In Karnataka, the names of 6.6 million people were reportedly missing from the electoral list (2018). The names of members of other communities also go missing, but the figures are significantly higher for Muslims—15 per cent for other communities and 25 per cent for Muslims.

One reason for the increased share of Muslims, and even Dalits, in missing names from electoral rolls could be the two communities' relative poverty and lack of education. People from these two groups frequently change jobs and residence as they strive to find new avenues of earning a livelihood and somehow stay afloat. A large percentage of Muslims, particularly in urban areas, do not own houses. Many are not educated enough to update the changes in their addresses for their official documentation online. But similar problems confront other communities too, though admittedly the percentage of higher castes surviving just above or below the poverty line is lower. According to a study based on the data from a primary survey collected by the Giri Institute of Development Studies (GIDS) to assess the social and educational status of OBCs and Dalit Muslims in Uttar Pradesh during 2014–2015, 'The lowest poverty levels were among the Thakurs (9%), followed by Brahmins (15.9%) and Other General caste groups (20%). Jats (15.3%) from Hindu OBCs have less poverty than Brahmins and Other Caste groups but higher than Thakurs.'[6]

That is understandable, but what explains a huge jump in the numbers when it comes to Muslims who find their names among the missing voters? One answer is probably that we live in Islamophobic times. Not just in India, but across the world since 9/11, there have been many instances of Islamophobia. In India, the rise of far-Right forces has accelerated the process, as these groups use all tools, fair and foul, to eliminate the community from the nation and even national discourse. Targeting the electoral process is the first step. In the first stage, a constituency is delimited in a way that marginalizes the Muslim vote, a Muslim organizations like Jamiat Ulama-i-Hind have often claimed. They claim that the reorganizing of constituencies is done in a way that divides the Muslim vote between the two new constituencies, thereby reducing the community's overall impact on electoral outcomes. The Sachar Committee revealed that certain constituencies and wards with a large Muslim concentration were declared as 'reserved', and only Scheduled Caste (SC) candidates could contest. As quoted by TwoCircles.Net, 'A number of Parliamentary and Assembly constituencies with substantial Muslim voter population are reserved for SCs while the SC population was not high there.

Contrarily, constituencies with comparatively lesser Muslim voter population remain unreserved even though they have sizeable SC population.'[7] With this move, Muslims were systematically denied political participation. And their winnability, which political parties do not tire of speaking about, went down.

In the next stage, the political parties either reduce the number of tickets given to Muslim candidates or stop giving them tickets altogether. In the third stage, many Muslim voters find their names missing from the rolls due to a combination of their own lack of education and the complete absence of familiarity of the electoral official with Muslim names (often manifested through the creation of half a dozen spellings of the same name), adding fuel to the prevalent atmosphere of prejudice. Then there is the question of the misuse of technology. As explained by Saifullah, 'The political activists working for a specific politician, or a political party, can go to the National Voters' Service Portal and apply Form 7 in their name. If I want that Naveed Saab's name must be dropped from the electoral list, I can go online and fill Form 7, stating that Naveed Hamid saab no longer lives here.'[8]

Saifullah sought to help those who find their names missing with the Missing Voters app and tens of thousands benefited from it. But clearly, a lot more needs to be done. A few months after the Lok Sabha elections of 2019, the Delhi Assembly elections were held in February 2020. Then too names of people of all communities were missing. Yet again, the Muslim share was higher.[9]

Popular weekly *India Today* wrote about several voters finding their names missing from electoral rolls despite having exercised their franchise as recently as the Lok Sabha elections in 2019. Significantly, the constituencies being reported on were either Muslim-dominated or had a sizeable Muslim population. The report stated,

At Shaheen Bagh, the epicentre of the anti-Citizenship Amendment Act (CAA) protest in the national capital, some voters complained about the deletion of their names from the voters' list. 'A few voters could not cast their votes in Shaheen Bagh under the Okhla constituency as their names were either found deleted or incorrect in the voters list,' said a poll staff on duty. In Seelampur constituency, a voter Waqil Malik, claimed that his mother Zarina (62) could not vote since her name was missing in the voters' list. 'My mother's name was there in the list during the last Lok Sabha polls. I have no idea why her name was deleted,' Malik rued. In Krishna Nagar constituency, a 34-year-old resident of Khureji Khas, Fallahuddin Falahi, also claimed that he could not trace his name in the electoral roll. 'I have a voter ID card. I had voted in the Lok Sabha elections (2019) and the last Delhi elections (2015). This is the first time I could not vote,' he said.[10]

A Muslim voter from Chand Bagh in north-east Delhi told this author, 'We have grown up with photographs of burqa-clad women standing in a long queue to exercise their franchise. However, the way things are going, in the years to come, the photographers may have to hunt for a lady or two in a burqa or a bearded maulana to convey the picture of a pluralist democracy.'[11] He too found his name missing from the rolls.

Things were more or less the same in Uttar Pradesh at the time of the Vidhan Sabha elections in 2022. As *Deccan Herald* reported a few days before the Assembly polls in February 2022,

> Four days before voting in Moradabad, Sher Mohammad, who has voted in every recent election, was deeply upset. In his advanced years, he had been compelled to negotiate the

internet as he was desperate to find his name in the lists, vote and assert his rights as a citizen. But his name had vanished from the electoral rolls, and even political workers of the leading opposition party in the state, the Samajwadi Party (SP), could not help him. Almost in tears was Wasim Akram, who had found only one name from his family of 10 in the voters' list.[12]

In a Muslim-dominated block, the newspaper reported, 80 per cent of the names had not been found four days before the commencement of voting. 'In 2019, a "No Voter Left Behind" campaign found that the names of 12 crore Indians were missing from electoral rolls, of whom four crore were Dalits and three crore Muslims. This suggests that some of the weakest sections of society are being systematically excluded from the democratic process,' the report stated.

The Muslim exclusion is not an inadvertent error or a mistake by somebody unfamiliar with Muslim names and their spellings but a lived reality in New India. The fact is we have political parties not actively seeking the Muslim vote just as we have political parties cutting down on giving tickets to Muslims, with the ruling BJP leading by example. However, it is not a party-centric issue. The marginalization of Muslims runs deeper.

We live in times when Muslim speakers, former chief ministers and union ministers from the community are no longer star campaigners for their respective parties. If people like MJ Akbar and Shahnawaz Hussain were hardly seen canvassing for votes for the BJP in the Bihar Vidhan Sabha elections, shortly after the Karnataka Vidhan Sabha elections in 2023, former MP Mohammed Adeeb said in a telephonic conversation with the author, 'A strong Congress is not possible without the Muslim support. It is important to clarify its stand on Muslims.'[13]

Even as Adeeb cooled his heels at home, most INDIA leaders feared that a Muslim leader on stage will reinforce the view that the alliance favoured the minorities. It was not advisable to be represented by a Muslim leader.

Indeed, it is the age of majoritarian appeasement. And Muslims, repeatedly but wrongfully accused of being appeased, are always the victim. But they are rarely collateral damage; usually, their victimization is orchestrated through a series of well-deliberated moves aimed at the community's marginalization. Political orphanhood may well be a beginning.

3

Reconstituting constituencies

EVEN AS ELECTIONS HAVE MOVED from paper ballots to electronic voting machines, there is an election-related practice harking back to the immediate years after Independence that has remained unchanged. Across the Gangetic plains and beyond to states such as Maharashtra and Madhya Pradesh, after every election, be it the polls to the state Vidhan Sabhas or the General Elections to form the government at the Centre, Muslim community elders sit with paper and pencil to jot down the names of successful Muslim candidates. Often, this is done in groups over a cup of tea; some of the elders though do it alone at home. Back in the 1960s and '70s, they were largely dependent on their transistor radios to relay the news, which they cross-checked with the morning papers the following day. Things did not change much in the '80s as Doordarshan was used more for watching popular soaps like *Hum Log* and *Buniyad* and the Ramayan. Prompt news dissemination was not the national television broadcaster's forte. With the coming of private news channels, things took an interesting turn: people frequently changed channels to know the result from a certain constituency where the community elders believed they stood a good chance of winning. They identified with a particular party or candidate; his or her victory was their victory. It was a sweet advertisement for democracy as masses, sitting hundreds of miles away from the polling booths, could rejoice in the victory of candidates they had probably never met. After the declaration of the complete results, the community elders counted the number of Muslim MLAs/MPs. The names and numbers were tallied and cross-checked. An increase in the Muslim representation was met with euphoria, tea parties and distribution of laddoos. A significant decline in the number of successful candidates was met with disappointment, even dismay.

While being strictly community-specific, it spoke eloquently of Muslims' faith in Indian democracy, and their keen desire to use its tools to improve the socio-economic condition of the masses. The success of a Muslim candidate was not about development alone; it gave the community a reference point, an icon of inspiration. The success told the community that they belonged here.

Of course, it did not necessarily mean they voted or identified only with Muslim candidates. A candidate who delivered on the front of economic development and social harmony was often preferred over a community member who failed to deliver: a case in point being the victory of SP candidate Jayaprada in the 2009 general elections from Rampur. She prevailed over the Congress candidate Noor Bano amidst allegations of the former's senior party leader Azam Khan conspiring against her. Khan regarded Rampur as his pocket borough, yet Jayaprada won because of her work as the sitting MP. After winning the 2004 Lok Sabha elections, she had nursed her constituency, particularly building bonds with the women voters. Muslims, incidentally, account for a trickle over 50 per cent voters in Rampur.

Thousands and thousands of community elders who rejoice at a community member's victory, however, are not much more than well-meaning but entirely gullible men. Though they rightly feel like an important part of the political system—that they are part of the national mainstream, and the nation cares for them—when more Muslim candidates emerge successful, what they fail to decipher is that they deserve better. With over 14 per cent of India's population being Muslim, they ought to have had around 74 MPs in the Lok Sabha if there was population-based representation in the House. Yet, the community has never come close to being represented by those many MPs: the highest was 49 in the 1980 General Elections, with the average being just a tad under 27 since then. The reason for this low representation of the community in the corridors of power lies in the fact that seats with a high percentage of Muslims are reserved for SCs. While attempts to ameliorate the lot of the SCs are laudable, they have often come at the cost of Muslims, who, according to the findings of the Sachar Committee, lag behind all communities (including SCs) on many parameters such as health, education, employment and political representation.

Following the suggestion from the Sachar Committee to delimit such constituencies, Zakat Foundation of India did a study of the constituencies where the population of Muslim percentage was high, and the SC population percentage was lower, but where the seat had been reserved for an SC candidate. This effectively put a full stop to the aspirations of any Muslim candidate who might have otherwise nursed hopes of getting elected from such a constituency.

According to the Sachar Committee,

> The data shows that constituencies which have been declared reserved for SCs by the Delimitation Commission...are by and large those constituencies where Muslims live in greater

numbers often more than 50 per cent as well as their proportion in the population is higher than that of the SCs. On the other hand, there are quite a large number of other constituencies where the share of SCs is large, often closer to or even more than one-half but these are declared as 'un-reserved'. Arguably, this can be seen as discriminatory and certainly reduces the opportunities that Muslims have to get elected to democratic institutions.[1]

This is not a new development; it has been going on since Independence. It means that in all 17 Lok Sabha sessions, the Muslim community could and should have had more representatives. And given countless members of the community in small towns and villages reasons to rejoice.

Back in November 2006, the Sachar Committee noted that the matter was within the purview of the Delimitation Commission and could be remedied. 'The Committee hopes that it would receive the attention of the Government immediately because the Delimitation Commission is at present engaged in this exercise and evidently any suggestion or any exercise to be done by it has to be undertaken during the current term of the present Delimitation Commission,' it observed.[2] Nothing moved.

In 2013, shortly after the Seventh Pay Commission was announced, Dr Syed Zafar Mahmood, who had worked with the Sachar Committee, met the then Prime Minister Manmohan Singh along with other leaders to urge him to set up a Delimitation Commission and end the widespread violation of Section 9(1)(c) of the Delimitation Act. Nothing moved again with the prime minister expressing his inability to set up a commission so close to the General Elections. Around the same time, Dr Mahmood made a power-point presentation before Narendra Modi, then the chief minister of Gujarat and a prime ministerial aspirant.

Dr Mahmood and his team from the Delimitation Cell pointed to a number of seats where the anomaly had subsisted, repeating to various political leaders, including Congress leader Rahul Gandhi, what the Sachar Committee had stated: 'The Justice Sachar committee pointed out that the political under representation of Muslims is substantially caused by illegal earmarking of electoral constituencies and wards to be reserved for SCs. Establish a delimitation procedure that does not reserve constituencies with high minority population for SCs.'[3]

For instance, the Karimganj Lok Sabha constituency in Assam has 52 per cent Muslim and 13 per cent SC populations. But the seat is reserved for the SCs. Likewise in Uttar Pradesh, the story is repeated in constituencies like Nagina and Bahraich. The Bahraich seat in the Assembly is reserved for SCs though their population is only 16 per cent whereas Muslims account for 35 per cent of the population there. In Raibareli, things are different. The SCs account for 30 per cent of the population but the seat is still in the general category.

News 18 reported:

> Citing an example from Uttar Pradesh, Mahmood said that the Nagina Lok Sabha constituency has 42.21 per cent Muslim population and 22 per cent Scheduled Caste population and it is reserved for the SCs. Similarly, the Nagina assembly seat has 56.8 per cent Muslim population and 26.7 per cent SC population and it is reserved for the SCs. On the other hand, Dhuarahra and Unnao Lok Sabha seats have more than 30 per cent SC population and much less Muslim presence, but these are not reserved for the SCs. Chail, Maholi, Manikpur, Sirathu,

Harchandpur, Hardoi, Purva, Marihan, Bakshika Talab, and other assembly constituencies have more than 30 per cent SC population and negligible Muslim presence, but these are not reserved for the SCs.[4]

In other words, many seats have been reserved for SC communities since 1950 despite a sizeable Muslim presence in those areas. To be clear, one is not advocating separate electorates for any community or seat reservation for Muslims; but when seats with a certain demographic profile are reserved, effectively denying Muslim candidates the right to contest from there, it does raise questions. More so when the fact of reservation does not always extend to the seats where communities other than Muslims have significant numbers. That reservation for other communities has always taken place in seats where Muslim candidates would have stood a realistic chance of winning has translated into lesser Muslim representation in elected bodies. Said Mahmood, 'The presidential order of 1950 denies to Muslims access to 15 per cent or more seats in every legislature. Justice Ranganath Mishra Report says it is a black law infused in the statute book from the back gate. Yet this anathema remains on the statute book mostly to the chagrin of Muslims who are a dominant minority.'[5]

Combine this deliberate enfeeblement of the Muslim voice with the emerging trend of political parties cutting down on giving tickets to Muslims and tens of thousands of Muslims missing out on the right to vote, and you get a picture of a community being eased out of the country's political map through a mix of legalities and crude politics. Worse, it is nobody's priority to set the house in order. The government has not spoken on the subject. The media stays quiet. Everything is brushed under the carpet. There is a conspiracy of silence; the cautionary note of the Sachar Committee and the voice of protest of Dr Mahmood have been drowned out by the silence of our polity.

In the years to come, the celebrations of community elders after each election are likely to get more and more muted. Unknown to them, for years, the Muslim community has been short-changed in a bid to raise fellow deprived countrymen. The rise of a historically deprived community has often come at the cost of another deprived bunch. Indian Muslims today are an alienated, vulnerable lot: a community under siege, a minority with vanishing political representation, Indians deprived of their voice. The 2014 General Elections, which returned only 22 Muslim members to the Lok Sabha, presented ominous signs for the community. The warning bells rang with renewed force in the Vidhan Sabha elections in Uttar Pradesh in 2017 and Gujarat in 2022; the General Elections in 2019 also continued the trend although the numbers improved marginally. With fewer candidates, fewer voters, and deprivation of winnable constituencies, the future looks bleak. Predictably, in the latest exercise to redraw the electoral map in Assam which started towards the end of 2022, the seats with the supposed Muslim influence came down, leaving the Opposition crying foul. As *The Hindu* reported, 'Assam will have fewer Muslim-majority constituencies… The Election Commission, in its draft proposal, has effectively limited the number of Muslim-majority Assembly constituencies to 22 from 29, say the AIUDF and the Congress.'[6] Without mincing words, *The Hindu* informed its readers, 'The poll body had announced the delimitation exercise on December 27, 2022. Barely four days after the delimitation was announced, on December 31, the Assam Cabinet decided to merge four districts with existing ones and redraw boundaries in 14 places, effectively reducing the number of districts to 31 from 35. Three of the districts —Bajali, Biswanath, and Hojai—which were merged with their parent districts had a sizeable Muslim population. But post-merger, the proportion of Muslims in the newly merged districts was altered and that, in turn, impacted the Election Commission's exercise as it considered these new districts for redrawing the boundaries of the constituencies. The leaders argue that there has been a concerted effort to either "scatter" or "ghettoise" the Muslim vote.[7] Following the delimitation exercise, the Election Commission notified the redrawn boundaries of 14 Lok Sabha and 126 Assembly seats in August 2023.

The pattern of denial and deprivation continues unabated.

PART 2
Rubbishing Medieval History

4

Samrat Prithviraj and the Myth of the Hindu Ruler

HINDI CINEMA HAS OFTEN BEEN happy to play the handmaiden of the predominant political dispensation of the day. Back in the 1950s when India's first prime minister Jawaharlal Nehru laid great emphasis on socialism, besides often harking back to our syncretic past, Hindi filmmakers were happy to come up with films that sought to propagate the same message of secularism and egalitarianism. So, we had films like BR Chopra's *Naya Daur* and Mehboob Khan's *Mother India*, which critiqued the ways of the private sector in India, along with larger-than-life medieval romances like *Anarkali*, *Mughal-e-Azam* and *Taj Mahal*, which showcased the syncretic culture of our land.

Cut to post-2014. Our filmmakers still listen and often dance to the political beat of the day. Many directors are happy to make films to further the policies of the government. It is a mutually beneficial relationship. There is one critical difference, though. Probably in a bid to appease a section of polity, which has its own distinct view of things past, they now often choose subjects which either trifle with history, subvert it or at least reduce an emperor to just one aspect of his reign. History is a prisoner of selective interpretation, even willful distortion. Often the past is used as a weapon for current political gains, with scarcely a thought for credibility or authenticity in the narrative. And many of our filmmakers are happy to be the propagandists of the powers that be, as long as there is that sweet sight of cash flowing in at the box office.

So, let's try to address that by beginning with the latest portrayal of Samrat Prithviraj, whose valour we all read about in our middle school history books as well as in some remarkable poems of our Hindi books. In recent years, it is a different Prithiviraj we are presented with on screen. Added to his valour and indefatigable courage are a fistful of half-truths…

In the summer of 2022, as cineplexes were just beginning to see audiences come back after a Covid-induced lull in business, an Akshay Kumar film titled *Samrat Prithviraj* was released. It was promoted as a saga based on the last Hindu emperor of India. Kumar, known for his proximity to Prime Minister Narendra Modi's government, went from city to city talking about how the film sought to give pride back to the nation by narrating the tale of the valour and gallantry of Samrat Prithviraj, 'the last Hindu emperor'. 'Unfortunately, our history textbooks only have 2–3 lines about Samrat Prithviraj Chauhan, but a lot has been mentioned about the invaders. There is hardly anything mentioned about our culture and our Maharajas… We should know about the Mughals but know about our kings also. They were great too,' he said, almost as a curtain raiser to a film which happily reveled in post-truth statements like 'Prithviraj killed Mohammad Ghori'. In reality, Prithviraj died in 1192 and Ghori lived till 1206, following which the latter's manumitted slave Qutbuddin Aibak laid the foundation of the Mamluk dynasty in Delhi. Prithviraj's son remained a vassal of Ghori. As for Prithviraj Chauhan being the last Hindu emperor, well, he lived more than 400 years before the time of Shivaji and was a king of the region that lay between Ajmer and Delhi. The emperors of India answered to the names of Ashoka, Chandragupta, Samudragupta, Rajaraja Chola, Akbar, Shivaji and Aurangzeb, etc.

While being factually inaccurate, the film continued the rather daft division of pre-modern history as an interplay of Hindu and Muslim kings fighting for their respective faiths. The truth is, in medieval India, wars were fought on political exigencies and alliances were formed to expand empires. Conflicts were seldom, if ever, about religion. If Prithviraj Chauhan fought Ghori, he fought the Chalukyas and the Chandelas too. The battle between Ghori and Prithviraj was one resulting from political ambition, not from civilizational conflict. And the Muslim fanatics who often quote Ghaznavi, Ghori and the rest with pride would do well to remember that the former was no crusader of Islam, setting out to slay the enemies of religion. He loved his wine, women and wealth. Not quite the traits expected of a 'good' Muslim! War was like a sport to him, an unending means to augment personal riches.

Kingship knows no kinship. Ghaznavi, better remembered for 17 attacks on India between 1000 and 1027 CE, defeated his younger brother Ismail to ascend the throne; the commonality of faith and the same blood running in his veins failed to prevent a war of succession. Though often hailed by some impressionable Muslims for laying the foundation of the Islamic empire in the subcontinent, Mahmud was no different from contemporary princes; he enjoyed similar pleasures, did not always refrain from vile pursuits, and certainly did not consider himself as a crusader. Greed and expedience characterized his military campaigns. Writing about him in *Studies in Medieval Indian Polity and Culture*, noted historian

Mohammad Habib expressed, 'He was morally neither better nor worse than most of the princes who had preceded and followed him. He shared their fondness for war and wine and women as well as their appreciation of poetry and music.'[1] Unlike most practising Muslims, contemporary gossip held that Ghaznavi lacked faith in the Day of Judgement! With such credentials, real or imagined, he certainly does not qualify to bear the mantle of 'warrior of Islam', which is placed upon him by some. Ghaznavi's military forays were characterized by his greed of wealth, opportunistic alliances and an overweening arrogance.

Though the inherent iconoclasm behind his well-documented attack on Somnath Mandir cannot be denied, what is significant to recall is that Somnath was an important centre of inland as well as maritime trade at that time. Its riches were much coveted. And Ghaznavid, a ruler who cared little for his own faith showed no scruples about attacking the place of worship of another religion. It was akin to Muhammad Ghori, in the 12th century, refraining from confiscating the property of Wasa Abhira, a Hindu merchant who owned properties in Ghazni. Business, not faith, was important. In the 14th century, a Jaina merchant, Jagadu, got a mosque constructed for his visiting trade partners from Hormuz in Iran. Again, economy, not faith, was the guiding light of relationships. Interestingly, contemporary Brahmin thinkers did not write about Ghazni's assaults or even the sacking of the Somnath Temple. As historian Audrey Truschke mentions in *The Language of History*, 'Mahmud of Ghazni sacked Gujarat's Somnath temple in 1025, and we know of no contemporary Brahmin-authored account of the episode, or specifically, in response to it, in Sanskrit.'[2] Back then the Muslims were not even called 'Muslims'; instead, they were often referred to as 'yavanas' or 'mlechhas'. The Hindus too were just 'Brahmins', 'Kshatriyas' or later 'Rajputs' and 'Marathas', never 'Hindu'! The social alliances, rifts, bonds and dissensions were all about political gains or losses.

For rulers ranging from Ghazni and Ghori to Khilji and the Mughals, alliances were stitched together or tossed aside based on political convenience. For instance, take the invasion of Babur in 1526. Babur was invited by Daulat Khan and Rana Sanga, both of whom had a common enemy, Ibrahim Lodi, and in Babur found a man strong enough to rid them of their common rival. If Daulat Khan's was an opportunistic move, Sanga's could not have been patriotic.

The story changed not a bit when Babur's son, Mughal king Humayun, having been expelled from Delhi, where the Afghan rulers held sway, sought refuge with Rana Parshad, the Hindu ruler of Amarkot, where, incidentally, Akbar was born. Akbar, born in the house of a Hindu ruler, was breastfed by a Hindu wet nurse, Daya Bhawal. Later, as an emperor, Akbar came to be regarded as an avatar of Vishnu by many. When Akbar himself was blessed with a son, he sent him not to maulvis to learn about Islam but to Jesuit priests (by then Christian traders had started arriving at the ports of his empire). Akbar came up with the policy of Sulh-i-Kul, which can be seen in many ways as a preceptor to the Constitution of India, which gives every citizen the right to equality and the freedom to practise and propagate any religion. In medieval India, where the faith of the emperor often determined the faith of the subjects, Akbar's was a revolutionary move. The Ibadat Khana he built in Agra was not a place for Muslim theologians alone to discuss and debate matters of religion. It encouraged discussion among proponents of various faiths, and clearly moved the basis of the empire away from a religion, any religion. While much of it would have to be credited to Akbar's liberal leanings, some of it, like his matrimonial alliances with Rajput princesses, had to do with the realities of the age. For a stable Mughal empire in the 15th century, the support of the Rajputs was critical. Hence, there were inter-faith marriages where political reality held paramount sway, and the matters of faith were secondary. And to think we had the Uttar Pradesh Chief Minister Adityanath say in 2020, 'How can the Mughals be our heroes?' Well, the answer was provided by Akbar through his policies and actions of Sulh-i-Kul, Ibadat Khana, and such others. In fact, among all the rulers from 1206 to 1857, only Aurangzeb, and before him Firoz Shah Tughlaq, stressed on the importance of matters of faith when it came to official policies. Even Aurangzeb, widely reviled for demolishing temples and imposing jizya (a discriminatory tax imposed on Hindus), gave grants to more temples than he demolished, and gave employment to more non-Muslims than any of his predecessors.[3] Every third mansabdar (administrative official) of his time was a non-Muslim. No medieval ruler, including Aurangzeb, worked actively to convert the local populace or even the kings they defeated to Islam. The wars they waged were all about the expansion of their empires and not about augmenting the ranks of Islam. As 13th-century Delhi Sultan Iltutmish said on a note of pragmatism, 'The ulemma say we must convert people to Islam. We are like a piece of salt in water. If the salt starts meddling with water, it will just disappear.'[4]

The clinching evidence of kingship being above faith and family for medieval rulers was provided by Balban and Aurangzeb; the former marched against his son Bughra Khan, and had his governor and supporters killed in the 13th century. He is then supposed to have said to his son, 'Do you see these corpses? This is what will happen to you if you think of a rebellion.' That was in the initial years of the foundation of the Sultanate. As for Aurangzeb, his battles with his brothers, notably Dara Shukoh and Murad, as well his treatment of his father Shah Jahan in the second half of the 17th century are too well known to need reiteration.

This dependence on temporary allies and bonds forged on commonality continued right till 1857 when Bahadur Shah Zafar, as the nominal Mughal emperor, led an alliance of Indian rulers, including the likes of Rani Lakshmi Bai of Jhansi, Begum Hazrat Mahal, and Tantia Tope, against the British. Though unsuccessful, the effort came to be referred to as the 'First War of Indian Independence'. That term says it all.

We have had Delhi Sultans, Rajput warriors, Maratha rulers and Mughal kings and emperors, but never quite Hindu kings or Islamic rulers. In fact, each ruler had plenty of support from the followers of another religion. That is the reality which a Bollywood film cannot change, no matter how lopsided its narration, how bigoted its motive.

5

Raziya Sultan: The Forgotten Queen Who Dwarfed the Kings

IN ANOTHER AGE, RAZIYA SULTAN would have been feted, celebrated, and presented as a feminist icon, a woman far ahead of her times. But we ceased to live in the age of justice, of recognition based on accomplishment, not long after the universally accepted icon from Sabarmati breathed his last. We may not be living in the age of Godse yet, the increase in noises favourable to him notwithstanding, but ours is an era characterized by half-truths, falsehoods and blatant lies. Myths and fantasies are replacing history, and facts are often superfluous to popular narration.

Truth be told, Raziya is not the only one to suffer the sledgehammer of posterity, leading to a diminution in the projection of her worth. But, Raziya, more than many others, needs no brownie points to stand on a pedestal uniquely her own. Back in the 13th century, when she ruled with a mix of politically savvy and earthy honesty, she was the only woman to hold the reins of power all the way from the Himalayas down to Indore, from

Abbottabad to Kamrupa. In many ways, she was probably the only popular monarch who derived her strength from the support of the masses. She could as well have been celebrated as being almost a democratically elected ruler in the age of emperors and empires. And to think she was born to a former slave, Iltutmish, and was the granddaughter of another slave, Qutbuddin Aibak!

It may be recalled that Qutbuddin Aibak, the founder of the Delhi Sultanate, was once a slave of Muhammad Ghori. He was manumitted before Ghori's death. Aibak married off his daughter Turkan Khatun to Shamsuddin Iltutmish, his favourite slave. Iltutmish was sold and bought by many merchants before Aibak purchased him and proved to be a true benefactor for him. Iltutmish took over the reins of power after Aibak's death in 1210. He proved to be a wise ruler, religiously inclined, militarily powerful and astute in matters of administration. He was a patron of the ulemma (scholars of religion) and constructed many a mosque, raising Delhi to the status of a sanctuary of Islam. He was lavish in his grants for madrasas and founded the famous Nasiriya College in Delhi, named after his son Nasiruddin, who at the time was the heir apparent. Nasir, though, predeceased his father, passing away in 1229.

Like her male contemporaries, Raziya, despite being well educated, and worthy, did not have it easy when it came to the transition of power following the death of her father in 1236. She had proved her capability when Sultan Iltutmish was away on an expedition to Gwalior in 1231 and she oversaw the state affairs in his absence. So impressed was Iltutmish that upon his return he named her as his heir apparent. A daughter was nominated as a successor to a king ahead of her brothers! History was being made.

The nobles of the time, predictably, could not digest the decision. They asked, as reproduced by contemporary historian Juzyani: 'Why would the Sultan nominate his daughter as a "king of Islam" when he has several sons? Tell us the wisdom (hikmat) of your action,' they implored, 'for we do not understand it.'

Iltutmish responded, 'My sons are given to follies of youth: none of them is fit to be king and rule this country, and you will find there is no one better able to so do than my daughter... It will become clear to you after my death.'

The nobles remained unconvinced, making it easier for Iltutmish's other queen, Shah Turkan, to conspire with them upon his death and give the reins of power to her son, Ruknuddin. Interestingly, Raziya acquiesced to the decision, confident that her turn would come soon. Indeed, Ruknuddin lived up to his father's dire prediction. He was given to a life of unending pleasures even as his mother, Shah Turkan, virtually ran the state. The state's treasury began to deplete fast, and within six months of Ruknuddin taking over, Raziya made bold to go all the way to Mehrauli at the time of Friday prayers. Clad in red, the customary dress for one with a grievance, she addressed the crowd in a mind-boggling mix of emotion and reason. Raziya not only drew attention to the imminent danger to her life from the queen mother but also pledged to be better than any of the men if she was given the responsibility for running the Sultanate; she insisted that if she were not able to deliver on her promises, the people had the right to take the crown away!

Raziya's words, seeking the support of the nobles and the common man alike, were spoken at a public gathering at the Quwwatul Islam Masjid in Mehrauli near the Qutb Minar some 800 years ago. They could as well have been aired at an election rally in modern India! So far ahead of her times was Raziya Sultan! She even refused to call herself Sultana, the feminine of Sultan. Such was her confidence; such was her mindset. Her speech forced the Turkish amirs (nobles) to rethink their opposition to her. Meanwhile, the word spread in the Sultanate about her words and worth, and common people came out in her support. For the first time, royalty was seeking their support! They raided the royal palace, and Shah Turkan was taken into custody. On 19 November 1236, Raziya Sultan created history by assuming power. She owed the crown as much to her own astuteness as to the support of the common people of Delhi. She was almost a democratically chosen monarch!

Writing in *Lovers of God: Sufism and the Politics of Islam in Medieval India*, widely respected historian Raziuddin Aquil noted, 'Invoking the name of her father, she appealed for protection. In a rare example of sensitivity shown by the people of Delhi, the palace was attacked, Shah Turkan was seized, and Raziya was placed on the throne. The nobles and the soldiers pledged their allegiance to her.'[1]

The nobles' support did not last long. However, her popularity among the commoners, both Hindus and Muslims, soared, leaving the age-old Turkish nobles fuming. The power brokers had just had their power transferred to the man on the street. The times of ethnic superiority seemed to have been put on hold. And Raziya ruled. She is reported to have said, 'Everywhere people are my supporters because their welfare is my concern.'[2]

Of course, not all nobles had reason to sulk. Among the happy few was Ikhtiyar al-din Altunia, who rose to be a governor of Baran and later even married Raziya. Then there was Ikhtiyar al-din Aitgin, who rose to be a military chamberlain of sorts. And there was the much-celebrated Ethiopian slave, Jamal al-Din Yaqut, probably the only one of non-Turkish Shamsi origin among men of importance. His ethnicity, however, did not dissuade Raziya from conferring high honour upon him. Much to the chagrin of Turkish-origin nobles, this black slave became a trusted official of Raziya. Again, in an age when much was conferred, and indeed denied, by the accident of birth, the rise of a black slave in a court of Turkish men spoke eloquently of Raziya's ability to take independent decisions and reward merit irrespective of the colour of one's skin. Yaqut rose to be her confidant. It was this relationship which our Hindi film industry, often in search of drama at the cost of authenticity, loved and perpetuated in the film *Raziya Sultan*. Directed by Kamal Amrohi, the 1983 film came a cropper at the box office but managed to leave an impression on the common man's mind about the medieval queen being besotted with her slave. A little more than two decades before Amrohi's film, director Devendra Goel had directed *Razia Sultan* in 1961, wherein he showed a love triangle between the queen, Yaqut and Altunia, focusing on the Altunia's intense jealousy of Yaqut.

Lost amidst such accounts was the brilliance of Raziya Sultan. Forgotten was her military prowess—she used to ride her own elephant to the battlefield. Cast aside was her ability to take decisions that rankled the ulemma—she discarded the veil. Also forgotten was her ability to lead the army, to quell rebellion and quash any insurgency. She struck coins in her name too; some called her 'Bilqis-i-Jahan' (Queen of the World), others 'al-Sultan al-Azam Jalalat al-Duniya wa al-Din Raziyah' (the Glory of the Earthly World and the Faith). She was her own woman, neither cowed by her courtiers nor afraid of her military advisers. She defeated Nizam-ul-Mulk Junaidi, her father's wazir, who had opposed her elevation and led a rebellion of nobles. She sent an expedition to Ranthambhore to control the Rajputs and personally led an expedition to Lahore to compel the governor to submit to her.

Noted Aquil, 'Several important features marked Raziya's enthronement. She is reported to have given her tenure as sultan the form of a contract, with the people having the right to remove her if she failed in her duties. Further, her enthronement not only vindicated Iltutmish's choice, but also exposed the limits of Islamic orthodoxy.'[3] For instance, Minhaj-us-Siraj, a contemporary chronicler, called her sagacious, beneficent, just and a patron of the learned, yet not good enough to be an emperor merely because of her gender! Raziya cared not for such opinions and put on her cloak and cap to ride out in public, silencing her detractors with her actions rather than words.

A woman of such sterling character lies forgotten at a time when we are frequently reminded, 'Beti Bachao, Beti Padhao' (a scheme launched with much fanfare by the Government of India in 2015 to save the girl child from being killed in the womb, and later help her get education). Raziya was the daughter who deserved India's love and pride. She was the daughter who, in proving to her father that she could do what her brothers could not, set an example before the nation, which—more than 780 years after her death—is still struggling with a skewed sex ratio where many people still consider the girl child a liability and kill her in the womb. Raziya should have been on the billboards, in newspaper advertisements, in awareness campaigns on television, as an icon of what women can achieve. Instead, she lies forgotten, buried in the by-lanes of Old Delhi, flanked by Chitli Qabar (arguably named after a spotted goat) on one side and Bazaar Sitaram, where lies Haveli Haksar, the house where India's first prime minister came as a groom. The haveli is difficult to locate, the goat's grave is reduced to an amusing anecdote. And in a travesty of justice, Raziya rests between the two. (A woman who dwarfed the men in her age surely deserves better.) She was neither a romantic novelist's delight, as sold by Bollywood filmmakers, nor an accidental ruler, as projected by a section of the nation that seems to be afflicted by selective amnesia. Raziya Sultan of the 13th century, could, and should, have been a rallying point for Indian women. She fought and ruled as a woman.

6

Khilji, Now Playing the Villain

FOR YEARS, YOUNG IMPRESSIONABLE MINDS in India were fed information about Muslim invaders in the subcontinent. In school textbooks, chapter upon chapter discussed the likes of Mahmud of Ghazni and Muhammad Ghori, and how they ransacked India. The attackers, youngsters were told, destroyed kingdoms. They humiliated local kings, plundered their wealth and kidnapped their consorts. They attacked temples and looted all the gold accumulated there. There was barely a single redeeming point about these invaders. The Muslim attackers were barbarians who killed for pleasure, who looted for joy. Remember VS Naipaul's plaints of a wounded civilization, a pristine Hindu land subjected to repeated assaults by rapacious Muslim invaders, from Qasim to Ghori and beyond, a place where 'ruin lies upon ruin'?[1]

No nuances. No scope for presenting elements of grey in this watertight division of black and white—the locals were all clean and bound by principles, the invaders were all villains who shed blood out of habit. While the adventures of Subuktigin, the founder of the Ghaznavid dynasty, were seldom analyzed, the Kushan rulers of Afghanistan, who were neither Scythians nor Turks and whose language upon their entry into the portals of power was an Iranian dialect, were hailed for their administration. Students were taught about the Kushan Empire under Kanishka, an empire that included parts of northern India, Afghanistan and Turkestan. Thrown into the narration was the history of the spread of Buddhism. Anybody who attacked the Buddhist rulers of Peshawar and Afghanistan was considered to have attacked India. This was perhaps the earliest unwitting instance of the othering of Muslims and the assimilation of only those faiths that were founded in the subcontinent.

Interestingly, not a single positive feature about Subuktigin and Mahmud of Ghazni was related to youngsters in middle school. True, often there was bloodshed, loot and plunder during battles. But those instances cut across lines of religion when it comes to armed conflicts. But school students were seldom given the complete picture. It was left to illustrious historian Mohammad Habib, father of the equally illustrious historian Irfan Habib, to present a more rounded picture of the Ghaznavids. He wrote, 'The frontiers of Islam had been gradually pushed across the country, and now the two forces (Ghaznavid and Rai Jaipal's) stood opposite to each other in the province of Lamaghan on the southern side of the Kabul river.'[2]

No such space for a negative review was given to the other invaders of the Indian subcontinent such as the Aryans, the Hunas, the Greeks or even the early Europeans. They attracted a mere fleeting mention here, another small paragraph there. Back in the 1970s and '80s young Muslim boys and girls often hung their heads in shame as teachers elaborated on how Ghaznavi attacked India and deprived it of its wealth. The often curious, occasionally hateful, stares of classmates were enough to make a young Muslim student feel guilty and somehow responsible for the act of a man nearly a thousand years ago.

Fortunately, the sense of shame and guilt seldom lasted more than a few fleeting moments. Soon, in another class, one read about the Delhi Sultanate, how Qutbuddin Aibak rose to be the ruler of Delhi despite starting his life as a slave. A teacher with the skills of a raconteur presented Aibak as an idol for youngsters aspiring to upward mobility in life. Then there were feel-good moments when one heard about Iltutmish, Balban and the rest. And a few amusing moments came when the chapter on Mohammed bin Tughlaq unfolded. Teenage boys and girls exchanged smiles and a few laughs at the foolishness of the Sultan who shifted his capital from Delhi to Daulatabad. There never was a dull moment studying about Mohammed bin Tughlaq! The laughs were preceded by a much more serious discussion on Alauddin Khilji, his market reforms, his measures against hoarding and black-marketing in the days when terms like 'futures trading' had not been coined. Historians praised Khilji for ruling over a region that now essentially constitutes the entirety of modern India, barring the Northeast and parts of southern-most India. They also praised him for stalling the march of the Mongols and protecting India from their rampaging ways.

Khilji, we were told, believed in one principle: the burden of the strong will not be cast on the weak. With this single mantra, he sought to make life more livable, even equitable, for those times. He relieved the low-caste cultivators of the oppression of the higher-caste intermediaries. Not formally educated, Khilji could discern between the needs of the masses and the chosen few. For instance, trade in ordinary cloth was left to private enterprise under government supervision, but trade in finer textiles was assigned to traditional Hindu merchants of Multan. As the trade was expensive, they were given government subsidies. He also fixed tariffs on the prices of all things. In his own way, he gave a legal status to the earnings of dancing girls by fixing a fee for their services. An able administrator, he was ruthless in his pursuit of justice. He came down heavily against black-marketing and hoarding. And to think, he knew hardly anything about Islam! His sole objective was service to the people of God.

Habib called him the greatest ruler that the Musalmans of India produced. He neither fasted nor prayed. As Habib wrote,

> He never went to the Friday congregation. At the beginning of his career, he could neither read nor write Persian… He was hundred per cent Indian; he had never been to foreign lands… He knew nothing about the Shariat and did not care to go to it for guidance… He was neither afraid of meeting death nor reluctant in inflicting it… Of all the schools that have filled this earth with their chatter, Alauddin believed in one school only—the school of experience. The concrete problems of life had to be solved by the process of trial and error.[3]

Khilji regulated agricultural markets from Lahore to Allahabad and brought the land under the Khalisa. Land revenue was fixed at half the production cost and other duties were waived. He piloted the concept of initiating specialized markets for foodgrains, cloth, ghee, oil, dry fruits, cattle and the slave trade. This segregation of trade and formation of specialized markets was in many ways a precursor of the modern-day concept of separate wholesale markets for foodgrains, fruits and vegetables, besides cattle fairs.

In his dealings with peasants and landlords, he often sided with the peasants. Since both groups were Hindu, peasants being of the lower castes, there was nothing communal in his actions. As *Frontline* quoted Habib, 'After the tremendous Khilji adventure

...India would never again become the land of caste-privileges it had been for some centuries past. Alauddin assured one thing for all time. In all spheres of life, except marriage and personal laws, India would become what the Manusmriti so intensely hated—"a confusion of castes".[4]

So, Alauddin not only saved India from the rampaging Mongols, he also sought to protect the peasants from upper-caste landholders. He did not allow the rich to fleece the poor or for law and order to be compromised. He kept the Islamic clerics away from affairs of the state. He did not interfere in the personal laws of the populace but made sure that public life continued on an even keel. He punished without remorse and lived and worked according to the school of experience rather than the teachings of any school of Islam. In other words, Alauddin Khilji was a ruler way ahead of his times. His secular ways and egalitarian streak put him at least centuries ahead of his times. Reason enough for our hate-filled era to make a mockery of the ruler through contortions of facts and fictional narratives. And what better weapon to use than Hindi cinema with its enviable reach and a vice-like grip over the reasoning and thinking ability of the masses.

In a country where vast multitudes often fail to discern between the reel and real, it was easy to portray one Muslim ruler after another as blood-thirsty tyrants, not governed by the slightest scruples of conscience. Hindi cinema has rarely been reluctant to be the handmaiden of the ruling political dispensation. It lived up to this unenviable reputation with Sanjay Leela Bhansali's *Padmaavat*, a film that portrayed Alauddin Khilji as a cruel autocrat, the Hindu queen Padmavati as the heroine and the Rajputs around her as paragons of moral rectitude. Bhansali's *Padmaavat* related the saga of a Rajput queen first heard of in 1540 in Malik Muhammad

Jayasi's sufi masnavi of the same name. Jayasi's poem, on which Bhansali's film is said to be based, was written over 200 years after Alauddin Khilji breathed his last. The poet, who hailed from Jayas near Amethi in modern Uttar Pradesh, was in the employment of a Rajput chieftain. His hosannas to Rajput pride were probably inevitable and quite expected at a time when the benefactor's indulgence or lack thereof made or ruined many a life. Interestingly, Jayasi himself came up with a sort of disclaimer at the end of his allegorical work, calling it a story, a figment of his imagination, in what was otherwise a philosophical take on matters of life, death, the soul and salvation. These niceties did not interest the masses who accepted Bhansali's film with its over-the-top depictions of the central characters warmly; they cheered the Rajputs on loudly and jeered at the Sultanate king disdainfully, hatefully. The distance separating the alleged depravity of the 13–14th-century ruler and Muslims of the 21st century was traversed within a couple of hours. Bhansali was not alone in attempting to rewrite history to suit the needs of contemporary times. Ashutosh Gowariker's *Panipat* walked the same line in its depiction of Ahmed Shah Abdali. As did Om Raut's *Tanhaji. The Mint* analysed,

> Historical films allow directors to play up present-day beliefs while evoking past legends... Katherine Schofield, senior lecturer in South Asian music and history at King's College London, says these films are useful for understanding modern values. 'Film scholars talk about the historical film as providing a "heterotopia"—literally "another place"—in which to play out the political and social issues of the present day. We should be reading these films not for what they tell us about the past... but what they tell us about us, now, in the present day.'[5]

There is another interesting representation of Khilji, also in a work of fiction but met with a significantly different degree of acceptance. The second instance is Padmanabh's *Kanhadade Prabandh*, a 15th-century Marathi book, which has slipped under the radar of popular culture to the extent that most of us are completely oblivious of it.

In Jayasi's *Padmaavat* and Bhansali's film, Alauddin Khilji was shown as lusting for the Rajput princess, a point that has been used by a section of Hindutva proponents to drive home the message that the Muslim emperor had no morals and no conscience; he was simply driven by uncontrolled carnal desire. Padmanabh's fiction though relates to a Rajput prince of Jalore. Khilji attacked his kingdom a couple of years after attacking Chittor in 1303. In *Kanhadade Prabandh*, Khilji's daughter falls in love with the prince. As a father, the senior ruler tries to dissuade his daughter, but she remains determined. A battle thus ensues between the Sultanate king and the prince of Jalore, in which the prince is killed. On hearing the news, the distraught daughter of Alauddin immolates herself, committing sati. This engrossing story is completely ignored by Hindi film merchants and the Hindutva brigade. Noted historian Harbans Mukhia wrote about it in a piece in the *Frontline*,

> All the talk of love jehad being a challenge for Hindu society for a thousand years is part of a political project. Rani Padmawati falls into the political project, the Jalore prince does not. So that gets ignored.[6]

The lopsided and biased projection of Alauddin Khilji is part of a larger project of the selective use of history to score points in our modern-day polity. The message is: it was not just Ghaznavi or Ghori; most Muslim rulers, including Alauddin Khilji and much later Babur, adept at matters of administration and military, were all vain, bigoted barbarians. In these times of widespread Islamophobia, this narrative fits the bill. And nobody is complaining. Fictionalization of history is mere collateral damage in the heady days of majoritarianism.

7

The Akbar–Aurangzeb Parallel

TO THE VOTARIES OF HINDUTVA, all Muslim Indian rulers of medieval India are the same. Be it the rulers of the Delhi Sultanate, the Deccani sultans or the Mughals, their names are incidental, even superfluous. They were all *Muslim* kings! It does not matter that no Muslim king governed by the principles of Islam and most of their decisions were taken based on political needs. Their alliances and conflicts were all entered for personal aggrandizement. No king waged a jihad, a crusade. The fight was not to uphold the supremacy of any faith, but to expand fiefdom, kingdom or empire. To the rabble-rousing Hindutva brigade, it matters not that there were Muslim commanders of Hindu armies, and Hindu governors in charge of the so-called Muslim armies. For instance, Raja Jai Singh led Aurangzeb's armies against Shivaji, just as Raja Man Singh had led the Mughal forces against Rana Pratap in the time of Akbar. At the same time, Hakim Khan Sur led Rana Pratap's forces against the Mughals! Violence was a regular feature of premodern Indian kingship, and there were no religious divisions when it came to violence. All kings, all dynasties, were violent—right from the

Nandas and Mauryas to the Sultanate and Mughals, everyone. From Kalinga to Panipat, the story was the same.

However, these facts are for the discerning. For the Hindutva proponent with a clear agenda of 'we' and 'they', the important basis for distinction is the name of a Muslim king. It is under this light that persuasive attempts have been made to link up Aurangzeb and Akbar, the two Mughal emperors hitherto seen at opposite ends of the spectrum of religiosity and pluralism. The former has historically been projected as a bigot, the man who charged jizya, demolished temples and withheld state patronage to arts and culture. The latter has been hailed for the breadth of his vision, his ability to forge matrimonial alliances with the Rajputs—taking their princesses in marriage while they remained practising Hindus—initiating a dialogue with priests and practitioners of all faiths, even collecting the best principles of various religious denominations to come up with Deen-e-ilahi, a new faith that sought to appeal to the broader instincts of the educated. The faith died with Akbar, but the fact remains that Deen-e-ilahi and the underlying principle of Sulh-i-Kul were probably among the earliest attempts at finding a solution to inter-faith differences. 'Akbar supervised translations of Singhasan Battisi, Atharva Veda, Mahabharata, Harivamsa and other scriptures into Persian,' says historian Shireen Moosvi, professor at Aligarh Muslim University, adding that Sulh-i-Kul was the result of genuine considerations to suit the needs of a multi-religious country like India.[1] Much before the Indian Constitution made secularism the touchstone of democracy, Akbar had practised it.

Now, the difference between Aurangzeb and Akbar, clear as night from day, is being gradually blurred. No, despite serious attempts by historians, the polity is not looking at Aurangzeb afresh; in the mind of the common man, he continues to be a destroyer of temples, one guilty of regicide, patricide, fratricide and what have you. In

February 2023, the name of Aurangabad, the city where he is buried in a simple tomb, was changed to Chhatrapati Sambhaji Nagar, after Chhatrapati Shivaji's son, who was executed by Aurangzeb in 1689. Quoting Audrey Truschke from *Aurangzeb: The Man and the Myth*, *The Hindu* reported,

> Aurangzeb ordered Sambhaji, who had spent years fighting the Mughal state, along with his Brahmin adviser Kavi Kalash, to be publicly humiliated... He then had Sambhaji's eyes stabbed out with nails, and, in one historian's poetic words, 'his shoulders were lightened of the load of his head'. Interestingly, Aurangabad hosts the well-known Shivaji Museum which is an ode to the genius of the man who took on the mighty Mughal emperor with limited resources and astounding success.[2]

Repeated attempts are being made to nibble at Akbar's greatness, letting us know through an incident here, a rechristening attempt there, that Akbar was not so great after all! That the Rajputs were better, that Akbar was a Mughal and hence incapable of being our hero. The attempt is not only to rewrite history, but also to deprive contemporary Muslims of their heroes, in whose actions they could take pride, and icons they could quote in conversations as their contribution to the nation. The stray barbs about the Taj Mahal or the Ajmer Fort are actually not isolated or spontaneous utterings of a loose cannon, but a deliberate ploy to take the sheen off the accomplishments of the Mughals—and by extension, modern-day Muslims—who are now held accountable for all the battles and bloodshed of the past. In the grammar of Hindutva votaries, you see, every Muslim king was a Mughal, and every Indian Muslim of modern India is responsible for the failures and sins of the Mughals, even as he is no longer allowed to take pride in the good they did! The derogatory 'Babur ki Aulad', a term often heard since the Babri Masjid–Ramjanmabhoomi dispute, stemmed not just from a political mindset, but a much deeper and divisive ideology.

It is this ideology that refuses to take a dispassionate look at our past. It prefers rather to settle present-day disputes with the weapon of history, real or imagined. For instance, Aurangzeb, for all his perceived hatred of Hindus, had to confront certain mitigating factors. For instance, he did cut down on court expenditure by reducing patronage of proponents of art and culture, but his non-stop military expeditions made such a move almost inevitable. The only other option would have been to fleece the peasantry even more to make up for the deficit in money.

Catherine Asher argued in *Architecture of Mughal India*,

> The destruction of Raja Man Singh's famous Vishvanath temple in Benares was largely to punish Hindus, especially those related to the temple's patron, who were suspected of supporting the Maratha Shivaji. Many of these temples, desecrated by Aurangzeb, including the largest and most notable among them, had been built by Mughal amirs. In each case, Aurangzeb reacted to the violation of a long-established allegiance system binding the emperor and nobility by destroying property maintained previously with Mughal support. Thus in a sense Aurangzeb destroyed state-endowed property, not private works. Some of Aurangzeb's alleged destruction is more legendary than real.[3]

Not many will see matters with these same tools of dispassionate analysis today. Asher has also contended:

> Tradition still perpetuated in Benares blames Aurangzeb for destroying many of that city's temples, even though imperial

documents indicate that he long had been concerned with maintaining harmony between the Hindu and Muslim communities there. In fact, there is evidence only for his demolition in 1669 of the Vishvanath temple, built almost certainly by Raja Man Singh during Akbar's reign. Aurangzeb's demolition of the temple was motivated by specific events, not bigotry. One was rebellion of zamindars in Benares, some of whom may have assisted Maratha Shivaji in his escape from Mughal authorities. Another was reaction to recent reports of obstructive Brahmins interfering with Islamic teaching. The demolition of the Vishvanath temple, then, was intended as a warning to anti-Mughal factions, in this case, troublesome zamindars and Hindu religious leaders who wielded great influence in this city.[4]

Incidentally, back in 1659, shortly after ascending to the Mughal throne, Aurangzeb issued a firman (decree), wherein he pulled up Mughal officials accused of harassing the Brahmins of Varanasi. With faith in the goodwill of the Brahmins, who obviously held a high station in Hindu's society, Aurangzeb wrote: 'You must see that nobody unlawfully disturbs the Brahmins or other Hindus of that region, so that they might remain in their traditional place and pray for the continuance of the Empire.'[5] Around a decade later, he confirmed a land grant to the Umanand Temple in Guwahati in the east, and to the Jain community in Gujarat in the west. Continuing in the same spirit, Aurangzeb gave a piece of land near the ghats (riverbank) in Varanasi in 1687 to Ramjivan Gosain to build residential dwellings for Brahmins and holy faqirs.

Yet, the good that Aurangzeb did is not just being swept under the carpet, it is being buried with finality. Hindutva proponents treat Aurangzeb much like a political tool that can be employed to serve present-day interests of stirring up anti-Muslim sentiment in India. In a way, Aurangzeb suffers from the bigotry of the present. As Shashi Tharoor wrote in *Why I Am A Hindu*,

> Historical evidence suggests that Aurangzeb did not destroy thousands of temples as is claimed and that the ones he did destroy were largely for political reasons; that he did little to promote conversions, as evidenced by the relatively modest number of Hindus who embraced Islam during Aurangzeb's rule; that he increased the proportion of Hindus in the Mughal nobility by co-opting the Maratha aristocrats from the Deccan; that he gave patronage to Hindu and Jain temples and liberally donated land to Brahmins; and that millions of Hindus thrived unmolested in his empire. History is a complex affair: Aurangzeb was undoubtedly an illiberal Islamist... but he was not the genocidal mass-murderer and iconoclast many Hindus depict him as having been.[6]

If Aurangzeb has for long been seen a hateful ruler given to bigotry, a similar fate is being visited upon Akbar now. Since by no yardstick can he be called a bigot, attempts have been made to project him as a military loser, as evidenced in the repeated attempts to tell us that in the famous Battle of Haldighati, it was Akbar not Rana Pratap who came in second best. It is not the facts of history that matter to Hindutva politics, but binaries of religion. It is due to this same reason that one finds his name dropped from the title of the Akbar Fort in Ajmer! If we believe Abul Fazl's account, the structures within the fort were constructed in 1570 during Akbar's reign. It remained an important fort under Jahangir, who had also stayed there for long periods as Prince Salim before succeeding to the throne. In early 2017 an attempt was made to rename that fort to simply Ajmer Fort by erasing the name of the emperor from the gate of the fort. A new blue board was put up at the fort without mention of the emperor's name. That this move went against what the Gazette of India said seemed to matter little. The fort, it seems, sprouted after rainfall in monsoon.

Not quite satisfied with erasing Akbar's name from the fort in Ajmer, the Hindutva brigade enlisted the support of dubious historians to turn the good old Battle of Haldighati story on its head. Like a dishonest referee at the end of a bout, they declared in history textbooks in Rajasthan that Rana Pratap, not Akbar, was the winner of the conflict at Haldighati.[7] Professor KS Gupta of Mohanlal Sukhadia University in Udaipur claimed that the dominant view that Pratap lost the battle was not correct. That the claim flies in the face of historical evidence matters not a jot; it is perception rather than reality which holds sway. And in popular perception, bit by bit, there is a diminution in Akbar's stature, as evidenced by the demand to rename the Akbar Road in New Delhi after Rajput prince Raja Man Singh. Of course, New Delhi already has a Man Singh Road, that too in close proximity to Akbar Road. And to think Akbar idealized Ram as an ideal Indian monarch! He even had both the Mahabharat and Ramayana translated into Persian. It is believed, as Abul Fazl mentions in his preface to the *Razmnanah* or the Persian Mahabharat, that 'one major goal of that translation [and presumably others] was to prompt conservative Muslims to reconsider their beliefs'.[8]

But these are all inconvenient and avoidable little quibbles for Hindutva proponents. In their world of binaries, you are either with them or against them. No study of the Ramayana or *Razmnamah*, no grant to temples, no aid to Brahmins suffices in erasing the binaries in their world of 'we' and 'they'. That explains the complete absence of the mention of the likes of Begum Hazrat Mahal, Bakht Khan,

Zeenat Mahal and Maulvi Ahmadullah from any talk of the First War of Independence. Such has been the complete elimination of Muslims from a newlyfangled narrative of the country's history that when the Aam Aadmi Party MP Sanjay Singh spoke in Parliament about the contributions of Ashfaqullah and Bahadur Shah Zafar, not only did he surprise fellow Parliamentarians, his video went viral too. It was news to many in the new generation whose information about India's history came from forwarded WhatsApp messages! That something like Sanjay Singh's speech was needed in the first place to make the public at large aware of historical facts is a cause for concern and serious contemplation. India is in danger of erasing more than half a millennium of its past. The recycling of Hindutva mythologies is merely an attempt to fuel modern-day bigotry. Nuanced study, not sweeping generalizations, is the need of the hour. Teach a student about Aurangzeb's destruction of temples, but also teach her about the prayer space called Ibadat Khana where practitioners of all religions were equally welcome. Not too difficult, one would say.

8
Changing Names of Cities

DURING OUR FREEDOM STRUGGLE, THE Hindu Mahasabha and the RSS did not join hands with Mahatma Gandhi's non-violent struggle for freedom from British rule. As veteran historian Mridula Mukherjee writes in The Wire, 'The RSS… In the entire period from 1925 till 1947, it did not participate in any campaign or movement launched by the Congress or any other party or group. Nor did it initiate any movement against the British by itself. This is indeed remarkable for an organisation which claims nationalism as its creed. The mystery is solved very easily, however, if we realise that its creed is indeed nationalism, but not Indian nationalism. Its creed always has been and is Hindu nationalism. Its primary purpose therefore was to consolidate Hindu society against the perceived threat of Muslim domination.'[1]

VD Savarkar outlined as much in his book *Essentials of Hindutva*, which was published in 1923 and reprinted as *Hindutva: Who Is a Hindu?* in 1928. 'This ideology was a deeply divisive one which had the potential to distract attention from the British and cast it on Muslims instead. While he was careful to specify that Hindutva, or "Hinduness", was different from Hinduism and encompassed a wide range of cultures including, among others, the "Sanatanists, Satnamis, Sikhs, Aryas, Anaryas, Marathas and Madrasis, Brahmins and Panchamas"... Mohammedan or Christian communities, he argued, possess all the essential qualifications of Hindutva but one and that is that they do not look upon India as their Holyland.'[2] A cohesive nation, according to Savarkar, could ideally be built only by those people who inhabit a country which is not only the land of their forefathers, but 'also the land of their Gods and Angels, of Seers and Prophets'.[3] Savarkar's ideology was carried forward by MS Golwalkar, the second sarsanghchalak of the RSS. Noted author Jyotirmaya Sharma in *The RSS and India*, as cited in Humra Quraishi's work, observed, 'In Golwalkar's universe, there are two permanent enemies, the Muslims and politics.'[4] Incidentally, Golwalkar was the first person to present the concept of Hindu Rashtra.

The British did leave India in 1947. And the men of the RSS trampled over the new flag of India, our beloved tricolour. As First Post recalled, 'Shortly after Mahatma Gandhi's assassination, there were widespread reports of RSS activists trampling upon the tricolour. This greatly upset Prime Minister Jawaharlal Nehru. In a speech on the 24th of February 1948, Nehru spoke sorrowfully of how "at some places members of the RSS dishonoured the National Flag. They know well that by disgracing the flag they are proving themselves as traitors..."'[5] Nathuram Godse, the man who assassinated Mahatma Gandhi, owed allegiance to the RSS at one time. India's first home minister, Sardar Patel, banned the RSS and the ban was not lifted until the organization agreed to respect the national flag. It took the self-proclaimed nationalist cultural body another 50 years to hoist the tricolour at its headquarters. All along their cry was for a bhagwa dhwaj or saffron flag, not an inclusive flag denoting valour, peace and prosperity for all.

Anti-communalist publication Sabrang India writes:

> The first time that the RSS hoisted the Tricolour on its own headquarters was during the term of the first NDA government in power in New Delhi, in 2002! *Organiser*, the RSS English organ, in its third issue (July 17, 1947), disturbed by the Constituent Assembly's decision to select the Tricolour as the national flag, carried an editorial titled 'National Flag', demanding that the saffron flag be chosen instead. The same demand continued to be raised in editorials on the eve of independence (July 31 editorial titled 'Hindusthan' and August 14 editorial titled 'Whither'), simultaneously rejecting the whole concept of a composite nation. The August 14 issue also carried 'Mystery behind the Bhagwa Dhawaj (saffron flag)', which, while demanding the hoisting of a saffron flag at the ramparts of Red Fort in Delhi, openly denigrated the choice of the Tricolour as the national flag in the following words: 'The people who have come to power by the kick of fate may give in our hands the Tricolour but it will never be respected and owned by Hindus. The word three is in itself an evil, and a flag having three colours will certainly produce a very bad psychological effect and is injurious to a country.'[6]

Now with a Right-wing government ruling India, as well as a large number of states, there is a manifest saffronization of the country's public spaces. For instance, let's recall what the Uttar Pradesh chief minister, the firebrand Yogi Adityanath, did after assuming power in the state in 2017. The colours of hospital bedsheets, curtains and blinkers were all changed to saffron! As were the colours of buses and school bags provided to children. 'It started with a saffron towel being put on Chief Minister Yogi Adityanath's chair at his official residence and his car seat, before moving on to government booklets, school bags and even buses.

An *Indian Express* report reads, 'Adityanath flagged off 50 saffron-coloured buses of the State Road Transport Corporation, named "Sankalp Seva", to provide service in rural areas. The stage was decorated with saffron-coloured curtains, and the buses with saffron-coloured balloons..."[7] That was, in a way, a harmless indulgence of a personal whim of a new chief minister who knew no better; but the fact remains that when Right-wing politicians change names of cities and towns in New India, they seldom target colonial monikers. They go instead for Muslim names, seeking to erase the Muslim contribution to the nation's pluralist history. They are uncomfortable not with colonialism, but with the so-called Muslim rule in India between 1206 and 1857. Even Prime Minister Narendra Modi, when he first assumed charge of office in 2014, talked of the end of a thousand years of slavery. Maybe he counted together the years of the Sultanate, Mughal and British rule! As Rizwan Ahmad, a socio-linguistic expert, wrote, 'In 2014, Prime Minister Narendra Modi said India is troubled by "1200 years of slave mentality". He was clearly lumping together the hundred years of British colonial rule and the preceding medieval Muslim era as a long and undivided period of colonial suffering.'[8] For Modi, the British and the Muslims were both foreign rulers. Much like what Savarkar and Golwalkar preached when they talked of the concepts of pitrabhoomi and punyabhoomi (fatherland and sacred land, respectively).

Unsurprisingly, when a state comes under the sway of Modi's partymen, the only names they think of for striking off the map are those of the cities and towns founded by Mughal emperors,

Sultanate kings, nobles, saints and mansabdars. It seems India post-2014 is bent on erasing its own pluralist past, the contributions of various sections that make India what it is—a melting pot of cultures, a nursery of various faiths. In April 2023, *The Hindu* wrote,

> We are living in the Dark Age of Islamophobia. Full stop. Naked, ugly, disconcerting. A sad testimony to the moral squalor of our times… It manifests itself most clearly in this urgent, almost desperate, bid to rename places built by Sultanate and Mughal rulers. While some towns may have a direct relation to the name of the king or Sultan, in many cases the names of cities are either being changed or there is a demand that they be changed, solely because they are in Urdu. This is ironic, considering that Urdu was born in India. And till not long ago, it was not considered the language of adherents of a particular faith.[9]

The newspaper quoted the instance of Faizabad, which was built by Nawab Saadat Ali Khan in the 18th century. It was located on a busy trade route connecting east and central Awadh. Here, business flourished, and people made a lot of profit—hence the word 'faiz', meaning successful or victorious. *The Hindu* went on to note,

> For hundreds of years, there was no issue with Allahabad or Aurangabad. Or Aligarh and Osmanabad. Or even Mughal Sarai. The common citizen still does not have a problem. Go to Allahabad… people still refer to their city as Allahabad, except that the powers that be see everything through tinted glasses. It is immaterial that a city may have been built by a Sultan who saved the country from repeated assaults by the Mongols, or that a monument may have been built by a Mughal emperor who was born in undivided India, in Sindh or Gujarat, ruled

from Agra or Delhi, and never set foot abroad (not even to go on a pilgrimage to Mecca). Just the name is sufficient to rouse the Right-wing brigade.

Adityanath, not renowned for new building projects, had earlier decided to rename Mughal Sarai, one of the busiest railway junctions in India, after Pandit Deen Dayal Upadhyaya, the BJP ideologue who died there under mysterious circumstances in 1968. It also happens to be the birthplace of former Prime Minister Lal Bahadur Shastri. Earlier too in 1992, the BJP had tried to rename Mughal Sarai. However, with the demolition of the Babri Masjid and the following communal violence, there was little time for rechristening one of the oldest railway stations of the country. Adityanath had no such encumbrances. The Babri Masjid no longer stood there, and the chief minister also had a thumping majority in the State Assembly. He was free to do as he chose.

He then focused his energies on renaming Allahabad, which translates as 'Abode of Allah', to Prayagraj, the latter denoting a place of confluence of the rivers Ganga, Yamuna and the mythical Saraswati. However, as historical records will show us, the logic behind the decision to rename the city was at least questionable! The greatest Mughal Emperor Akbar had named the city 'Illaha-bad' or 'Illahi-bas'. 'Illaha' is considered a generic term to mean 'gods', and 'Illaha-bas' translated into 'abode of Gods'. Akbar regarded the place as the holy city of Hindus. According to the contemporary chronicler Badauni, when Akbar was informed about the devotion of the Hindus for the sacred site of Sangam and their wish to die there (as attaining death there, it was believed, would mingle their soul with the spirit of God), he instantly decided to rename the place as Illaha-bas, the abode of Gods![10] In other words, the Mughal emperor honoured Hindu sentiments by naming the place thus.

Importantly, he left the age-old name of Prayag, the area of the confluence in the vicinity, completely untouched. That was in the spirit of the tradition of our land.

As far as legend is concerned, 'Ila' is the name of the mother of Puruvas, the progenitor of the Aila tribe. The Mahabharata also mentions the name Ila as that of a river (variously identified) or as that of a king. 'Vas' again means abode. Yet again the meaning comes to be the 'abode of Ila'! In the age of the Mughals, Prayag and Allahabad coexisted. In New India, Allahabad had to be erased for Prayag to come to the fore! In a comic turn of events in December 2021, the name of popular Urdu poet Syed Akbar Hussain, better known as Akbar Allahabadi, was changed to Akbar Prayagraj on the website of Uttar Pradesh Higher Education Service Commission (UPHESC), an autonomous body under the Uttar Pradesh state government!

Similarly, in the case of Ayodhya and Faizabad, the former name was subsumed under the latter: Adityanath decided to rename the Faizabad district as Ayodhya, completely obliterating Faizabad, again a Muslim-sounding name, from the map. It was indicative of the non-pluralist mindset of medieval times. As Sharat Pradhan wrote in Daily O,

> Awadh's first nawab Saadat Ali Khan, who built Faizabad on the banks of the Ghaghra river in 1730, made no attempt to give any new name to Ayodhya that was always known as the birthplace of Lord Ram. The ancient temple town eventually became a part of Faizabad district, carved out by the British. The upkeep of Ayodhya's oldest temple—Hanuman Garhi—came from the Nawab's treasury. This healthy practice continued even after Saadat Ali Khan's grandson Asaf Ud-daula shifted the capital of

Awadh from Faizabad to Lucknow, soon after he inherited the throne in 1775. And significantly, just as 'Illahabas' meant 'abode of the divine', Faizabad meant a 'place for the good of all'.[11]

Such profundity of belief, such spirit of mutual respect! That is being replaced by a mantra of segregation and severance, one which focuses on exclusion rather than inclusion. A product of our divisive times, it seeks to sell us all over again, the myth of India's golden past, the time when our nation was a Sone ki Chidiya (golden bird) until the invaders took it all away. The name changes seek to fulfil that longing of walking back in time to the age when everything was golden, laudable and prosperous, to a utopia we never experienced. As well-known academic-activist Apoorvanand wrote,

> We fail to see in the excitement generated by the incessant renaming of towns and railway stations in India that the past, which these new old names allude to, is an imagined land that we are being invited to inhabit. We are not exactly recovering lost ground, because as the Hindi poet Bodhisattva wrote, there never was a Prayag that the Rashtriya Swayamsevak Sangh and the Bharatiya Janata Party (BJP) claim to be restoring now. What is being sold in the defence of capturing the glory of the past is an ideological construct.[12]

The ideological construct stemming from the value system of the Hindutva lobby, the one which reduces millions of fellow Indians to the level of 'others'.

As for our golden age, the time associated with the Gupta kings or the era when villages were governed like little democracies, even direct democracies, illustrious historian DN Jha characterized it thus:

During the freedom struggle, Indian historians indulged in an uncritical glorification of pre-Islamic India: the Indian state was described as a constitutional monarchy; tribal oligarchies were equated with Athenian democracy; the village assemblies (sabhas) in south India were portrayed as little democracies; the period of the Gupta rulers was treated as the golden age when the Indian people were happy and prosperous and lived in peace and harmony. This picture of ancient India supplied an ideological support to freedom fighters; but after India's Independence it served no such purpose though the Hindutva ideologues have clung on to these ideas... A scientific analysis of our sources amply proves that at no stage in history the common people of India witnessed a truly golden age. The history of India, like that of any other country, has been a story of social inequities, exploitation of the common people, religious conflict, and so on. The idea of a golden age has always been abused, in India as well as in other countries.[13]

The land of Allahabad and Prayagraj, Ayodhya and Faizabad, Mughal Sarai and Pandit Deen Dayal Upadhyaya Nagar is teeming with history, with places founded by Muslim rulers, each a reminder of the varied tapestry of this land. For instance, we have the brassware town of Moradabad in western Uttar Pradesh. The town was built in 1600 and is named after the Mughal prince Murad, son of emperor Shah Jahan. Murad, at one time, was in the fray to be emperor until Aurangzeb defeated him as well as his other brothers, notably Dara Shukoh, after whom is named the town of Shikohabad. Close to Moradabad is Ghaziabad, yet another Muslim-sounding city of Uttar Pradesh. It is named after its founder, Wazir Ghaziuddin. At one time, it was called Ghaziuddin Nagar. With the coming of the railways in the 19th century, it was renamed Ghaziabad for administrative ease. Close to Ghaziabad is the township of Muzaffarnagar, named after a Mughal chieftain Sayed Muzaffar Khan. Khan was gifted the place as a jagir (A grant for collection of public revenue from the place) by the Mughal Emperor Shah Jahan in 1633. The place was named after Sayed Muzaffar Khan by his son. Ditto for Shahjahanpur. The name is self-explanatory, the town being named after the Mughal emperor Shah Jahan, known in history for commissioning the construction of the Taj Mahal, Lal Quila and Delhi's Jama Masjid. Much more variegated is the history of Aligarh, the seat of Aligarh Muslim University. It has probably undergone more changes in its name than any other town in Awadh. It was once called Kol. Then it became Muhammadgarh in 1524–5, when Mohammad, the son of the area's governor during Ibrahim Lodhi's reign, renamed the city after himself. The reign of the Lodhis ended a couple of years later in 1526. And Aligarh underwent a name change too. It was once called Sabitgarh, named after its governor, Sabit Khan. Later, a Jat chieftain Surajmal named it Ramgarh. It derives its present name from a Shia commander, Najaf Ali Khan. He named it after Hazrat Ali, the son-in-law of the Prophet, and the last caliph. The Right-wing political dispensation, which has seldom shied away from wearing its predilections on its sleeve, has plans to name it Harigarh![14] Chief Minister Yogi Adityanath did not desist from making his preferences clear in 2019 during an election meeting before the first phase of polling for the Lok Sabha elections. 'Tumhe agar Ali par vishwas hai to hamey Bajrang Bali par vishwas hai (If you have faith in Ali, we have faith in Bajrang Bali),' he was reported as saying by the *Indian Express*.[15] What was disturbing here were not the words in themselves, but who said it. These were the words of a man bound by the Constitution not to discriminate between citizens on the basis of religion!

As evident from the cases of Allahabad, Mughal Sarai and the rest, many more places are in imminent danger of losing their identity, which constitutes a huge slice of their past. We have already heard of plans to rename more towns such as Mainpuri, Basti and Agra: there are whispers that Agra is to be renamed Agravan; Basti is to be named after Maharishi Vashishth, the guru of Ram. Bareilly is said to be next in line.[16] Then there have been periodic noises by the BJP leaders about the Taj Mahal being a Shiv temple! In October 2022, the Indian Railways decided to rename the widely used train Tipu Express as Wodeyar Express. Born in 1750, Tipu Sultan bore no ordinary name. He was named after Tipu Mastan Aulia, the saint of Arcot, who was widely revered. That did not matter. Neither did his sufi connection, nor his brave battles against the British. He had to give way to Wodeyar, who was a supporter of the British. Well-known columnist-critic Anna MM Vetticad tweeted, 'This is sick. Tipu Sultan fought the British colonisers, the Wodeyars allied with the British, but because Tipu was Muslim, he will be erased completely along with the truth.'[17] These are not isolated actions or aberrations, but part of a thought process that considers everything non-Hindu to be foreign, exploitative and hateful. And tries to erase this non-Hindu section of 'others' from history books, pushed out of the portals of power and from the cosmopolitan spaces in society. As society slips ever deeper into the clutches of Islamophobia, we get the picture of a nation trying to sever a part of its civilization, virtually one of the legs it stands on.

9

Demolishing the Empire Builders

IT WAS ALWAYS ON THE cards. For years, the leaders of the ruling dispensation had been airing unsubstantiated claims about medieval Indian history. If one leader, against all evidence, pronounced Maharana Pratap as the victor of the famous Battle of Haldighati against Akbar, many others lost no opportunity to dub the Mughals in general, and not just Babur, as invaders. The fact that right from Akbar to Aurangzeb and beyond all were born and died in undivided India was of no consequence for political leaders keen to use the past to score brownie points against their rivals. Initially, historians confined themselves to presenting the correct picture of the events as they unfolded post-1526, when Babur defeated Ibrahim Lodi to lay the foundation of the Mughal Empire in India. Noted historian and secretary of the Indian History Congress Syed Ali Nadeem Rezavi observed,

In understanding the past, we are not aided only by our imagination, fancy or wishes. We are guided by 'sources' which help us unveil the past. By sources, one means artefacts, written words, documents, chronicles, books, etc., which have survived the period under study. It is these which inform us of past happenings, good or bad… Any interpretation of past events not supported by evidential facts is not history but myth—wishful thinking… The study of the past based on written or material evidence is slowly but gradually being converted into myth—an imagined past not supported by any fact, weak or strong. We are busy tailoring history as per our wishful thinking.[1]

On the same lines, in an interview with *The Hindu* in March 2023, noted historian Amar Farooqui, who has been a fellow of the Nehru Memorial Museum and Library, discussing the Haldighati battle, stated, 'A lot that is being done I won't regard as history. These are just assertions. For instance, about Haldighati… But history is too developed a discipline for historians to be taken by these assertions. For a historian, dynasties are not important.'[2]

For the government, however, dynasties were not only important but a political goldmine when it came to the Mughals. For the academic year 2023–4, the NCERT decided to drop certain chapters on the Mughal Empire from the Central Board of Secondary Education (CBSE) Class 12 history textbooks. The dropped chapters from the book 'Themes of Indian History, Part II' included 'Kings and Chronicles; the Mughal Courts (C. 16th and 17th centuries)' and the topics 'Central Islamic Lands' and 'Confrontation of Cultures' were dropped from the Class 11 syllabus. The move was said to be an attempt at 'syllabus rationalization' to avoid 'overlapping' and 'irrelevant' portions.

Quoting Dinesh Prasad Saklani, director of NCERT, ABP reported, 'NCERT has been engaged in rationalising the content of the textbooks for many years... This involves a group of experts who are highly professional. It is important that we do not want to see this in a narrow manner and create unnecessary controversy.'[3]

Some of the most respected names in the discipline were appalled at the changes in the syllabus. They included, among others, professors Romila Thapar, Irfan Habib, Mridula Mukherjee, Aditya Mukherjee and Jayati Ghosh. Soon, there was a formal statement from the Indian History Congress: 'We are appalled by the decision of the NCERT to remove chapters and statements from the history textbooks and demand that the deletions be withdrawn. The decision of the NCERT is guided by divisive motives. It is a decision which goes against the constitutional ethos and composite culture of the Indian subcontinent. As such, it must be rescinded at the earliest.'[4]

The statement, signed by the Indian History Congress President Professor Kesavan Vekuthat and Secretary Syed Ali Nadeem Rezavi, added: 'As such, removing chapters/sections of chapters is highly problematic not only in terms of depriving learners of valuable content, but also in terms of the pedagogical values required to equip them to meet present and future challenges.'[5] The new syllabus 'tailored' for students will make them ignorant of mutual interactions that shaped India and divide citizens in ways even colonial masters couldn't, the historians felt.

The vociferous criticism and loud objections soon died down, and quietly but surely the new syllabus began to be implemented with teachers in schools quickly omitting the said sections on the Mughals in their classrooms lectures; the sole exception was Kerala, where a new handbook was introduced with the omitted lessons for the students of humanities stream. Other states, notably Uttar Pradesh and Uttarakhand, were happy to implement the changes brought in by the NCERT. The government's purpose was fulfilled.

Despite the selective deletions aimed at undermining the contribution of the Mughals—and through them that of Muslims in India's growth—they deserve much credit for not only providing India with political stability but also for giving the country pride of place on the world map. The glory of the Mughal Age was well summed up by Ebba Koch in her recent book.[6] Koch was quoted in the media stating, 'The Mughal dynasty was perhaps one of the most glamorous and charismatic in the history of mankind. It was a driving concern of the first six padshahs to construct their image for posterity and be remembered as great rulers.'[7]

Indeed, in a bid to be remembered for long, and to foster better relations between all subjects, the Mughals took to getting the Hindu scriptures translated in a big way. As Audrey Truschke wrote in *Culture of Encounters: Sanskrit at the Mughal Court*, 'In the 1580s, Emperor Akbar ordered the translation of the Sanskrit Mahabharata into Persian. The newly minted Mughal epic called the Razmnamah (Book of War), would prove a seminal work… The Mughals took up the Mahabharata as part of the larger translation movement that Akbar had inaugurated in the 1570s… As a prince, Jahangir commissioned a Persian Yogvashishta (Vashishta's Treatise on Yoga), a philosophical work.'[8]

Modern India is inconceivable without the progress made in medieval India. Shortly after the changes in the history syllabus were ushered in by NCERT, *The Hindu*, noting that most Mughals were as Indian as one gets, stated, 'It's hard to understand the history of modern India without the contribution of the Mughals, who, including Akbar, Jahangir, Shah Jahan and Aurangzeb, were all born in undivided India; and were buried here. None of them ever left the country, not even to go on a pilgrimage to Mecca.'[9] Quoting Rezavi, it asked,

> From legal system to legal jargon, we owe to the Mughal and Turkish Sultanate before them. Words like vakalatnama, kacheri, durbar, we owe them all to the Mughals. Today, when a large number of Indians consider Lord Ram as a major deity, we have to thank Tulsidas who wrote his version of Ramayana during the Mughal period. Also, Vrindavan, associated with Lord Krishna, developed thanks to Chaitanya saints who were given grants by Akbar, Jahangir and Shahjahan, and helped Vrindavan and Mathura emerge as a key centre of Krishna Bhakti.

These grants continued even under Aurangzeb, otherwise held to be a hateful iconoclast.

The culture of keeping records of everything, the modern practice of documentation, started in a big way with the Mughals. Except Sher Shah Suri, who reigned briefly in the first half of the 16th century, no Indian king had laid as much emphasis on keeping records of the things around them—a file of land revenue, land grants, and even the donations of some kings subdued in a battle and the courtiers. A descendant of Timur and Genghis Khan, Babur, who knew Turkish and Persian, started the practice of chronicling events and noting down his impressions of the landscape and the artists he met. He thus authored a unique document—the *Baburnama*—originally in Turkish, which was later translated into Persian. His successor Humayun took record-keeping to the next level. He had the best scientists to advise him. As Koch stated,

The scholar Muslih al-Din al-Lari from Shiraz was at Humayun's court in the 1530s; he wrote on cosmological concepts which would have been of interest to the padshah. A special favourite of Humayun's was Maulana Nur al-Din Tarkhan from Jam in Khurasan, who was distinguished for his knowledge of mathematics, astronomy, and the use of the astrolabe. Abu'l Fazl mentions the Hindu astronomer or astrologer Maulana Chand, who had 'great skill in and knowledge of the astrolabe and the details of the star catalogues and casting horoscopes'. He was placed by the padshah in his wife-consort Hamida Begam's entourage at Amarkot to cast the horoscope at Akbar's birth.[10]

That's not all for evidence of his unique mind. Back then, the demarcations of specific subjects like astronomy and astrology had not taken root, and his inquisitive mind often made space for both. Unsurprisingly, therefore, scholars such as Shaikh Abu'l Qasim Astarabadi and Maulana Ilyas al-Ardabili joined Humayun's court in Kabul. With them, the emperor studied astronomy and mathematics. Humayun himself wrote scientific treatises and is credited with a mathematical text for his son Akbar. 'Jahangir,' as Koch recalled, 'was proud to own a manuscript by his grandfather, which contained an "introduction to the science of astronomy and some other unusual matters, most of which he had experimented with, found to be true, and recorded therein". When Humayun returned to India, he planned to construct an observatory.'[11]

Humayun's successor Akbar, though not educated in the modern sense, gave developments in science and religion a whole new dimension with the building of Ibadata Khana where frank interactions and debates were encouraged between scholars of various faiths. The Ibadat Khana was constructed around the room of Shaikh Abdullah Niyazi Sirhindi, a disciple of Shaikh Salim Chishti, who later became a devotee of Lord Shiva. This, by itself, conveys a lot—the exchange of views on religion beginning from a sufi's room and the sufi, in turn, becoming a devotee of Shiva! It was a move way ahead of the times, one that may not be possible to replicate even today. Add to that the rousing progress made in the art of miniature painting during the reign of Jahangir and the stupendous architectural works, including the building of the world-famous Taj Mahal, accomplished during the time of Shah Jahan. One realizes that there is no history of at least 300 years, beginning 1526, without understanding and crediting the role of the Mughals. True, it was not all hunky-dory all along. Their influence, which peaked in 1556, when Akbar assumed power, soon faded after 1707—when Aurangzeb breathed his last—thanks to the succession of incompetent rulers, often driven by hedonistic pursuits. The last Mughal ruler, Bahadur Shah Zafar, was only a symbolic leader of the Revolt of 1857. However, in this symbolism lay a message: Common Indians, as evidenced by the uprising of the sipahis (soldiers), still considered the Mughals to be their kings and hence the leadership role offered to Zafar. This was the lingering effect of the golden era of the great Mughals; the latter Mughals, post-1707, had done nothing to earn that kind of trust of the people. Aurangzeb's prolonged battles in the Deccan had heavily affected the state's finances. Also, to augment the state's resources, Aurangzeb had imposed jizya, a tax solely on non-Muslims, which proved detrimental in the long run. Once Aurangzeb passed away, his successors proved incapable of ruling over a huge, unwieldy empire or replenishing the treasury. Their internecine battles didn't help. Many, like Mohammed Shah Rangeela, were given to a life of debauchery. Add to that the gradual advance of the East India

Company in India and the latter Mughals proved incapable of defending their empire. It all came to a sad end with the banishment of Bahadur Shah Zafar to Rangoon (now Yangon, in present-day Myanmar) after the 1857 revolt.

That last part takes away some of the glimmer from the history of the Mughals. But even then, the Mughals, in the heyday of their pomp and glory, not only built their own empire but also provided a lesson on how to effectively rule over a vast empire with disparate local rajas, nawabs and people of different religions and castes. The greatness of the Mughals, which is sought to be diminished today, would not have been possible without the staunch support of the Rajputs, who not only led Mughal armies in many a battle but also replenished the state treasury with their administrative acumen.

The grandeur of the Mughals was owed substantially to the Rajputs, sharers of power from the time of Akbar, who defeated Maharana Pratap in the Battle of Haldighati and co-opted them in his empire through matrimonial alliances. Most Mughal rulers after Jahangir were born to Rajput women. As a result, within the family, Hindavi was often the language of communication. Aurangzeb, incidentally, conversed in Hindi and composed in Braj bhasha.

Indeed, today, when objections are raised in social media and even political circles if a Muslim actor portrays the role a Hindu hero on celluloid, it is important to remember that during the time of the Mughals, Raskhan wrote of Krishna in Hindi and Balkrishan Brahman in Persian. That was a time of synthesis: Hindu practices of painting human bodies with tiger stripes were adopted to commemorate Imam Hussain; and the concept of the triple dome mosque architecture, popularized by the Mughals, is uniquely Indian, and unlike West Asia where most mosques had a single dome. Just like the Mughals.

Suffice to recall what Koch stated, 'What would our lives be without those fascinating Mughals!' She mentioned the globe-trotter and inter-culturalist Count Hermann Keyserling, who was in India in 1911–2, and who hailed the Mughals as the 'grandest rulers brought forth by mankind… they were men of action, refined diplomats, experienced judges of the human psyche and at the same time aesthetes and dreamers.'[12]

Reason enough for youngsters to read about the Mughals!

PART 3
Kill a Muslim a Day

10

Lynching the 'Others'

IN THE UK IN 2016, a white supremacist unleashed a 'Punish a Muslim a Day' campaign. The man, David Parnham, started a letter campaign targeting Muslims and their places of worship encouraging hate crimes and murder of members of the community. Parnham also shot off letters claiming Europe and North America would soon be overrun by Muslims. As a step to ward off this supposed demographic change, he encouraged the recipients of the letters to pull off the headscarves of Muslim women, butcher Muslims with knives and guns, bomb their mosques and maybe even attack Mecca. His call sparked several Islamophobic incidents in the UK. In 2018, the law caught up with him, and Parnham, who called himself a 'Muslim Slayer' with unabashed pride, was handed a 12.5-year jail term.

The Independent wrote, 'In December 2016, Parnham sent a fan letter to Dylan Roof, a white supremacist terrorist who murdered nine black victims at a church in Charleston, South Carolina', wherein he is reported to have expressed his gratitude to Roof for 'opening' his eyes. In this words, 'Ever since you carried out what

I'd call the "cleansing" I've felt differently about what you'd call "racial awareness". My main reason for disgust is Muslims. I hate these animals with a passion. After I sent letters with white powder to some mosques in London, they had to close down parliament because of it.'[1]

Parnham had earlier issued pamphlets and letters rewarding points to criminals who outraged the sensibilities of Muslims. Assuming all whites to be non-Muslims, possibly all Christians, he exhorted them to punish Muslims, 'Sheep follow orders, and are easily led, they are allowing the white majority nations of Europe and North America to be overrun by those who would like nothing more than to do us harm and turn our democracies into Sharia-led police states. Only you can help turn this thing around, only you have the power.'[2]

For every abusive incident perpetrated by someone, Parnham offered points: from 10 points for verbally abusing a Muslim and 25 for pulling off the headscarf of a Muslim woman to 500 points for butchering a Muslim using a gun or a vehicle, and, finally, 1,000 points for burning or bombing a mosque.

After the Parnham verdict, adult psychiatry consultant Shazad Amin, who helms the organization Muslim Engagement and Development, analyzed on TRT World: 'This is not happening in a bubble or a vacuum, these kind of comments or threats are made by people who are actually looking at, seeing and reading and thinking about all of the negative hatred and bile produced by right-wing organisations, the right-wing media against the Muslims.'[3]

Fortunately, the despicable offer Parnham made had few takers in the UK. One wonders though what would have happened had Parnham been an Indian, a bigoted practitioner of Hindutva, and made a similar offer in contemporary India. He could well have had a million followers in a short span of time and would have been leading the team of those who peddle hate against Muslims in the country. Not only would a majority of criminals have gone unpunished, some who may have been convicted, would perhaps have been feted like heroes by fawning multitudes on getting bail. Others, on arrest, would have been raised on the shoulders of their followers, all the way to the police station, to the accompaniment of garlands and slogans. The surrender to the police would have been celebrated as an accomplishment, as we saw with the arrest of Hindu Raksha Dal leader Pinky Chaudhary in New Delhi. Chaudhary had been accused of raising anti-Muslim slogans in a meeting at Jantar Mantar, barely a kilometre from Parliament House, and his anticipatory bail application had also been rejected. After evading arrest for weeks after the incident, he finally surrendered. His so-called surrender presented scenes similar to those seen when a hero is welcomed home after accomplishing a major achievement. 'Chaudhary reached Mandir Marg police station around 2:30pm on Tuesday, where over 100 of his supporters lifted him on their shoulders and took him inside the police station. The supporters stay put outside the station for around half an hour and chanted slogans, such "Jai Shri Ram", and "Pinki Bhaiya tum sangharsh karo, hum tumhare sath hain",' the *Hindustan Times* reported.[4]

Others may have entered the bedrooms of Muslim adults to make sure they do not marry the one they like or procreate the way they want. A little before we had frequent allegations of love jihad, or a supposed crusade waged by Muslim men to marry gullible Hindu women to increase the ranks of Muslims, we had many Hindutva leaders asking Hindu women to be more prolific. We must remember how within a few months of Narendra Modi being sworn in as the prime minister in 2014, his party colleague Sakshi Maharaj, with 'cases ranging from promoting enmity… criminal intimidation, robbery, dacoity, murder, forgery, cheating and criminal breach of trust' against him,[5] had advised Hindu women to produce four children each to protect their religion. Not to be left in the cold, the ever-acerbic Pravin Togadia went a step further. Addressing a gathering at Jambusar in Bharuch district in Gujarat to induct fresh blood into the RSS, Togadia, then the working president of the Vishwa Hindu Parishad, asked Hindu couples to have more children to counter the growing numbers of Muslims in India. He asked the Hindu men who had gathered to listen to him, to 'go home and worship your manhood' in order to have more children!

If Parnham had been an advocate of Hindutva he would have had seemingly endless reason to be happy in New India. He would have seen what happened with the attackers of Mohammed Akhlaq Saifi in 2015 in Dadri, which was easily the best publicized case of lynching resulting from the warped allegation of cow slaughter. A few weeks later, when Ravin Sisodia, one of the 18 accused in the Akhlaq lynching case, died in prison, his body was wrapped in the national tricolour in the presence of Union Minister Mahesh Sharma. This is an honour reserved for soldiers who sacrifice their life in combat with the enemy. Here, a man accused of lynching a Muslim man, a fellow Indian citizen, after dragging him out of his bedroom to the road, was being conferred this 'honour'. Sharma, who was also a practising doctor and ran a couple of popular hospitals in the NCR was seen paying his respects to the departed Sisodia. The draping of the tricolour on the body of a murder accused was a violation of the Flag Code of India 2002. It mattered little. Nobody pursued the case; the minister never had to account for his presence at the gathering 'honouring' Sisodia. Another accused in the crime, Rupendra Rana, was offered a ticket by the fledgling political body Navnirman Sena to contest the 2019 Lok Sabha elections from Dadri. Rana was hailed by Amit Jani, president of the Uttar Pradesh Navnirman Sena, as 'the perfect person to protect cows as he has spent two-and-a-half years in prison for the respect of gaumata [cows]'.[6] A prison term was said to be a qualification for excelling in cow protection!

The same thing happened with Shambhulal Regar, the alleged killer of daily wager Afrazul in Rajsamand in Rajasthan. Afrazul was lynched on camera by Regar on 6 December 2017, the date coinciding with the 25th anniversary of the Babri Masjid demolition. Regar invited Afrazul to meet him on the pretext of business.

> Once there on a barren piece of land with some cactus plants and a few wild shrubs, Shambhulal all but beheaded Afrazul. His mutilation of a live man made for a most macabre spectacle. He did not stop there. He then set a crying, wailing Afrazul on fire. For a few minutes, he breathed in agony. Afrazul was about to die but Shambhulal had to stoop to another level yet. He asked his nephew to film the gory murder to upload it on the Internet soon after. All along, Shambhulal ranted against the Muslim community, promising to eliminate them all. It was a textbook case of hate violence.[7]

As Regar was arrested and sent to the Jodhpur jail, more than 500 people from different parts of the country collected money and raised a sum of a little more than Rs 3,00,000 in support of the man who was seen beheading an unsuspecting and unarmed Muslim labourer without provocation. Eight days after the videographed killing, Hindutva groups took out a rally in support of Regar and signed various online petitions in support of him; the masses were exhorted to reach Udaipur for another rally, which forced the administration to impose Section 144 of the Indian Penal Code to bar any public gathering. It failed to prevent some protestors from unfurling a saffron flag at the entrance of a district and sessions court in Udaipur. More than 30 policemen were injured as they tried to control the Right-wing supporters of Regar, who had risen in status to become an instant idol.

Some nine months later in September 2018, Regar was offered a ticket by the Uttar Pradesh Navnirman Sena to contest the Lok Sabha elections in 2019. Life had come a full circle; a man caught murdering a labourer on camera was being considered as a prospective lawmaker!

Regar's popularity knew no bounds. Barely a few months after the lynching, he became part of a tableau in Jodhpur on Ram Navami, a festival celebrating the birthday of Ram, an avatar of Vishnu, the Preserver deity in the Hindu pantheon. In the pictures of the tableau circulated in Indian media, one can see a man with a striking resemblance to Regar sitting on a throne-like chair. Holding a pickaxe in his hand, he is dressed in clothes similar to what Regar wore on the fateful day. This was no show of piety but an arrogant celebration of a murder. To some, though, Regar was worthy of worship, a man who had eliminated a mlechha—a term used in India in medieval times to denote a foreigner who indulges in 'uncouth' behaviour. In New India, Afrazul was a mlechha.

The story of Akhlaq and Afrazul was repeated in 2018 in Ramgarh in Jharkhand where another union minister, Jayant Sinha, was on hand to garland and offer sweets to eight men convicted of killing 45-year-old Alimuddin Ansari. On getting bail, they were received like Olympic medal winners, escorted to a waiting car and driven straight to Sinha's residence. They could as well have touched down after bringing pride to the nation at the biggest sports meet on earth! As the foot soldiers celebrated each new catch, Prime Minister Narendra Modi, never short of words otherwise, maintained a studied silence. The man, who famously told a journalist interviewing him about the pogrom of 2002 in Gujarat, if 'someone else is driving a car and we're sitting behind, even then if a puppy comes under the wheel, will it be painful or not? Of course, it is. If I'm a chief minister or not, I'm a human being. If something bad happens anywhere, it is natural to be sad' seemed to have suddenly run out of words.[8] His silence spoke eloquently.

Acclaimed author Arundhati Roy did not miss the significance of this. In her book *Azadi* she wrote,

> In its latest report, released in October, the National Crime Records Bureau has carefully left out data on mob lynchings. According to the Indian news site The Quint, there have been 113 deaths by mob violence since 2015. Lynchers, and others accused in hate crimes, including mass murder, have been rewarded with public office and honoured by ministers in Modi's cabinet. Modi himself, usually garrulous on Twitter, generous with condolences and birthday greetings, goes very quiet each time a person is lynched. Perhaps it is unreasonable to expect a prime minister to comment every time a dog comes under the wheels of someone's car. Particularly since it happens so often.[9]

The prime minister was silent again in 2020 when Kapil Bainsla, a resident of Kondli in east Delhi, on 1 February, 'set out for Shaheen Bagh with a pistol. He fired two rounds in the air, nobody was injured before he was nabbed by the police. While being taken into custody, he shouted, "Jai Shri Ram" and blurted out, "Hamare Desh mein kisi ki nahin chalegi, sirf Hindu ki chalegi" (Nobody but Hindus shall rule our country).' He raised slogans in support of the Hindu Rashtra too. His words bore an eerie resemblance to senior BJP leader LK Advani's slogan during the tension-ridden days of the Babri Masjid–Ramjanmabhoomi stir, 'Jo Hindu hitt ki baat karega, wohi desh par raj karega (He who speaks in favour of Hindu interest shall rule the country).'[10]

Barely a month after Bainsla's arrest, a Delhi court granted him bail on a bond of Rs 25,000 and a surety of a similar bond. He walked out to a hero's welcome on 7 March 2020. 'Kapil Bainsla, who opened fire in Delhi's Shaheen Bagh area on February 1, was greeted with cheers, hugs and music from his sympathizers after he was released on bail by a Delhi court on Saturday,' reported the *National Herald*.[11]

The residents of the area, singing, dancing and cheering, garlanded him, called him a 'lion' and lifted him on their shoulders. For the crowd, he was that brave warrior who entered the enemy's den and came out unscathed. Even if he did not manage to kill, at least he tried to intimidate. Bainsla, on his part, was humility personified, calling himself a mere follower of Modi![12] Nobody argued with the description. No debate was needed. His actions had spoken loudly enough of his affiliation. His political masters remained quiet. Very quiet.

The Dadri, Ramgarh and Shaheen Bagh incidents were part of a pattern meant to pulverize India's largest minority; the assailants had the reassurance that the police either would helpfully turn a Nelson's eye to their crime or would, in many cases, act as enablers. The perpetrators were also confident that, if captured, they would not be behind bars for long, a faith largely justified as none of those who attacked Muslim men after accusing them of cow slaughter have since been handed their final sentences. Most of them have spent short periods in jail and many have walked out, as in Delhi and Ramgarh, like victors. Some have received help to find new jobs!

This strike-and-rejoice, intimidate-and-revel campaign started barely a month after Narendra Modi first took oath as prime minister back in May 2014. Then 24-year-old Mohsin Sheikh, an IT professional, was lynched in Pune by 21 men allegedly owing loyalty to the newly formed Hindu Rashtra Sena (HRS). Sheikh was coming back after offering Isha, the last prayers of the day, to pick up his dinner at a takeaway joint when he was attacked. He was to succumb to his injuries shortly after, the day's last prayers proving to be the last prayers of his life. His father, Sadiq Sheikh, waited for four years for justice before breathing his last in December 2018, but by then all the 21 accused men had walked out on bail. For peace to prevail, justice had to wait. And wait long.

What started with Sheikh in Pune has since spread across India, with Muslims now being attacked for no reason except their faith. A little over 17 years ago, while reviewing noted film director Govind Nihalani's film *Dev*, I began the piece with the words, 'They judge everybody by the foreskin.' It was enough to outrage the sensibilities of an editor. The sentence was deleted from the review. But today, as I review the Muslim killings, the truth of the words comes back to haunt me. In the initial years after Modi's elevation, a fig-leaf allegation or suspicion of cow slaughter or transportation of animals for possible slaughter was enough to trigger a mob to vent its fury on a helpless man. None of the allegations of animal slaughter was substantiated. Worse, none needed to be. At least not in public perception. Neither did the dead come back to life. By 2019, even these flimsy excuses were done away with. Being a Muslim was enough to be vulnerable to murder, to one's house being set on fire or bulldozed. Not every instance was as gory or gruesome as the ones we have read about till now. But there were instances when a clean-shaven shopkeeper with no visible sign of his faith—no beard, no skullcap, no amulet, no tehmat—was murdered on a whim! In some cases, the man was asked to 'pull down trousers'—the attackers, you see, judged by the foreskin, its absence being a life-threatening condition, as Imran Khan, a street hawker, discovered in the north-east Delhi violence. In others, the victim was asked to say 'Allah-u-Akbar' by goons. The ability to pronounce the first line of the Muslim call for prayer was deemed sufficient for them to unleash the most macabre violence in full public view.[13] Thrashing a Muslim was no longer a crime furtively and hurriedly carried out in the dingy by-lanes of small-town India. It had become a public administration of violence, even death. It was a spectacle to be viewed by scores of passive but not necessarily non-approving observers at the site and was to be later devoured and even celebrated by thousands and tens of thousands on the Internet, after the video of the attack was uploaded by the 'brave defenders' of sanskriti (culture). The murder of innocents had become a ritual. Muslims in modern India could as well be the cattle of ancient India! It forced noted legal eagle Dushyant Arora to tweet in October 2020, 'To be a Muslim in today's India is to fear for your life 24X7.'[14]

Dushyant's words were in response to a series of fatal attacks on Muslim men. In June 2019, a young man in Jharkhand was caught by a group of violent, sword-wielding men; fearing for his life, he mouthed, 'La Ilaha Ilallah', the first tenet of Islam. He was taunted by the attackers to say 'Jai Shri Ram' instead, if he wanted to live. Overpowered and fearing he would die if he didn't comply, he did as asked. The rampaging mob continued, tied him to a lamp post and beat him with anything that was on hand, from iron rods to batons, tyres and belts. The man bled from his head, hands and face. His legs were swollen, many of the bones were broken and his hands were bleeding. He could barely stand. He sought forgiveness. His crime? He was a Muslim in New India.

The police took him away. Not to the hospital to get his wounds the urgent medical attention they required, but to the police station. He was booked on charges of theft. The police initially preferred not to press charges against the men who had attacked him. Presented to a magistrate as an accused, the Muslim man was sent to four days' police custody. He died. He was Tabrez Ansari, the new Mohsin Sheikh, the best publicized victim of lynching in Modi's second innings as prime minister. It was not until four years had passed that the Seraikela Court of Jharkhand pronounced 10 years imprisonment to the 10 accused in June 2023. They were sentenced under Section 304 of the Indian Penal Code, which concerns culpable homicide not amounting to murder. Other laws under which they were sentenced include IPC Sections 323, 325, 341, 295 (A) and 149. Additional District Judge (One) Amit Shekhar pronounced the sentence and imposed a fine of Rs 15,000 each on all the convicts. The verdict came too late for his wife who alleged her husband was lynched because he was Muslim. The only solace she may have had was that there was no dearth of company for her husband. Scores of men before him had met a similarly violent, terrifying and hate-filled end. And many more joined him soon after. The way he was murdered after being compelled to chant 'Jai Shri Ram' became a template that many others copied in the days to come. A little more than two years after his death, similar slogans were raised at Jantar Mantar in New Delhi where the goons screamed, 'Jab mulle kaate jayenge, Ram-Ram chillayenge (Muslims will chant Ram-Ram when they will be slaughtered).' Supreme Court lawyer and former spokesperson of Delhi BJP Ashwani Upadhyay, Pinky Chaudhary and noted actor Gajendra Chauhan were in attendance.

Ansari was in many ways luckier than others. His ordeal ended with his life. Unlike Akhlaq in Dadri or Pehlu Khan in Alwar, who was waylaid and killed by cow vigilantes in April 2017 and his sons Irshad and Aarif charged under the Rajasthan Bovine Animal (Prohibition of Temporary Migration or Export) Act, there was no posthumous FIR filed against him or his family members. The cause of his death, at least initially, was not attributed to the injuries inflicted on his person but to cardiac arrest. In other words, Ansari was not murdered. He died naturally. Lynching was not just the new normal in New India, it was the new natural.

Like any movement, this new pattern of events in India—full of hate, blood and bigotry—started slowly. There was a 30 per cent increase in hate crimes against Muslims between 2014 and 2017. Then, there was an exponential rise of such crimes after Modi won a second term as the prime minister in 2019. The crimes of the previous five years had seemingly got an endorsement of sorts. Criminals masquerading as foot soldiers of Hindu nationalism got free run. And they ran amok.

In a column in the *Medium*, CJ Werleman wrote, 'Hate crimes against Muslims in India have exploded since Narendra Modi's party came to power in 2014, with religious-based hate crimes surging nearly 30% in the 2014 to 2017 period, and then doubling since his landslide re-election in 2019, culminating with the murder of more than 50 Muslims over the course of six bloody days in New Delhi during February 23–29, 2020.'[15]

Tracking hate crimes against India's 200 million Muslims, he quoted Amnesty International India as saying, 'For India to be committed towards ending hate crimes—where people are targeted because of their identity stemming from race, religion, caste and gender amongst others, it is essential for the country's penal laws to first recognize the bias behind the commission of such crimes and document the occurrence of such incidents—both of which remain conspicuously absent currently.'[16] In a move not entirely unrelated, Amnesty International was made to shut down its India operations shortly after.

Werleman was on sound footing when he talked of the bias and the country approaching a genocide. Importantly, he did it more than a year before Gregory Stanton, president of Genocide Watch, went public with a similar warning about the groundwork being done to create a possible genocide of Indian Muslims. Speaking at a US Congressional event in January 2022, Stanton stated, 'We are warning that genocide could very well happen in India.' As reported by Al Jazeera, 'Stanton said genocide was not an event but a process and drew parallels between the policies pursued by Indian Prime Minister Narendra Modi and the discriminatory policies of Myanmar's government against Rohingya Muslims in 2017.'[17] Significantly, Stanton had accurately warned about a genocide in Rwanda some 30 years ago.

Sample this: The day is 16 September 2020. Four Muslim men, hailing from the Tablighi Jamaat, the largest Muslim organization, are viciously assaulted with bricks and clubs by a Hindu mob in Maharashtra. Most mainstream newspapers prefer to either ignore the case or report it as a routine crime with no hate or community angle to it. It was left to popular New Delhi-based site TwoCircles. net to report that the assailants had said to their victims, 'Tum Hindustan mein rehne ke laayak nahi ho, tum yahan nahi reh sakte (You are not worthy of living in India. You cannot live here).' These were the words of the assailants who allegedly beat Suhail Tamboli, Aslam Ather, Sayyed Layak, Nizamuddin Qazi on the night of 16 September in Beed's Hol village in Maharashtra.'[18] Not too long after the passage of the CAA in December 2019, the mob had started to decide who was worthy of living in India. A Muslim could be deemed unworthy of citizenship not just by a whimsical Foreign Tribunal officer but also by a group of men blinded by hate and driven by violence.

The Tablighi Jamaat members told the TwoCircles correspondent that they were travelling to Ambajogai village from Dharur to attend their friend's funeral when their car developed a glitch. Suhail Tamboli and Sayyed Layak went to get water for coolant and parked the car. 'Meanwhile, two men on a bike arrived at the spot where their car was parked and for no reason started verbally abusing Aslam and Nizamuddin, and as per them, "used filthy language against our community." The men were wearing skull caps and kurtas.'[19] The attackers threw away the caps of the victims, pulled their beards, and allegedly smashed their heads with a brick. 'It felt like we were their enemies for a long time. We were clueless for why they were constantly hitting us,' Sayyed Layek told the media outlet, adding, 'They were not ready to listen to us at all. Before we could speak anything they started hitting us with bricks.'[20] This animosity towards the 'Other' runs rampant in many places in the country now. In some instances, men were attacked because they sported a skullcap and beard, at others because of their missing foreskin. At still others, mosques were burnt down. All symbols of the 'Other' were smashed. In the minds of the hateful men, India was divided between the Conquerors and the Conquered.

Incidentally, the men from Dharur escaped only because after a point the attackers assumed they were dead. An FIR was registered at Yusuf Wadgaon police station, and two of the assailants, namely, Narayan Dhanraj Ghuge and Rahul Tukaram Ghuge were arrested and charged with attempt to murder under Section 307 of the Indian Penal Code.

Yet Sayyed Layek's words, 'It felt like we were their enemies for a long time', shall haunt the conscience of the nation for a long time.

Here we had two groups of total strangers. One group attacked the other because they looked like the 'Other', were not people 'like us'. It was a classic case of Islamophobia reaching the hinterland of India.

A few days before the Maharashtra incident, a teenage Muslim girl was allegedly gang-raped, then murdered in Palamu in Jharkhand. The news was largely ignored by the media—the girl did not evoke even a tenth of the media interest that befell the unfortunate Dalit victim in Hathras less than a couple of weeks later.

Incidentally, precisely two days before the Hathras tragedy, a Muslim man called Shabir was lynched in Jammu, allegedly by a history-sheeter in the habit of teasing and tormenting Muslim women in the region. Shabir was targeted because he had dared to raise his voice against the harassment of women. As reported by IBTimes, 'With an increase in attacks against minority groups in the country, another case of mob lynching has surfaced. A 42-year-old farmer identified as Shabir Chaudhary was lynched by an alleged gang near his home in Phalian Mandal village in Satwari Police limits on the outskirts of Jammu city.'[21] A little later, FreePress Kashmir covered the incident, stating, 'The family said that the accused person Mahesh is a history-sheeter and had recently been to jail on charges of teasing and harassing women from the Gujjar Muslim community, a minority in Jammu in his locality. In the past, the community had on several occasions raised complaints about Mahesh's misbehaviour. And a couple of weeks ago, he was caught by people and handed over to police. "He came out after spending 15 days in police custody," said Naseeb Ali Chaudhary, who identified himself as a cousin of Shabir. According to him, Mahesh and his gang started threatening Shabir for whistle-blowing and sending him to jail. "They targeted Shabir because he had raised objections about Mahesh's actions," Naseeb said.'[22]

The lynching failed to make national headlines; the media had lost the zeal it had shown in ample quantities at the time of the attack on Akhlaq in September 2015. Back then, practically every newspaper made Akhlaq's lynching page-one news. However, as repeated instances of lynching started occurring, the reports about such tragedies were usually wrapped up in a few sentences and buried in the inside pages. Meanwhile, Akhlaq's family, unable to go back to its traditional house in Dadri, awaited justice. In 2023, even eight years after the crime, hearings were going on in a sessions court with only charges being framed. Many years after the Dadri killing, too many Muslims were being lynched for anybody to retain their sense of horror. Unsurprising, considering the annual floods in Bihar and Assam evoke a similar indifference from most Indians.

September 2020 was a particularly daunting month for Muslims. A barber, whose earnings had reduced to a trickle due to the Covid-19 lockdown and the pandemic, ventured out in search of livelihood in Haryana. On 8 September, he was lynched by a Hindu mob as he stopped to ask for a glass of water. The mob cut his arm with a chainsaw. A couple of days later, he was discovered lying on a cot in his drawers, his right arm, cut off from below the elbow, heavily bandaged. Once again, this was no ordinary attack. If in Beed the men were attacked because of their manifest religious identity, in Panipat the barber was sought to be deprived of his livelihood for a lifetime by cutting off his hand—the distance of 1,444 kilometres between Beed and Panipat failing to enfeeble Islamophobia.

A few days before the Panipat assault, on 4 September, a 32-year-old Muslim man was tied to a tree in Aonla in western Uttar Pradesh, and, as reported by the *South Asia Journal*, 'beaten' for sheer 'fun'.[23] Even as the victim, Basid Khan, was being thrashed, in the background, young men posed with their mobile phone camera! Once again, a hapless Muslim was treated like booty captured in war.

Khan was later handed over to the police, who discovered he was an alcoholic, not a thief. The police handed him over to his family. The next day he died of internal bleeding. There were no obituaries for him, no commissions of inquiry.

Around the same time Khan was subjected to the worst communal taunts and torture, Aftab Alam, a Muslim cab driver in the state, was forced to drink alcohol and chant 'Jai Shri Ram'. His family claimed that when Alam was attacked by three passengers and forced to say 'Jai Shri Ram', he dialled his son, who recorded the conversation on his mobile phone. The police claimed Alam was found injured in his car in Greater Noida's Badalpur area and then admitted to a private hospital where he breathed his last during treatment.

Alam's son Sabir told the media, 'My father noticed something unusual with the activities of the three [passengers]. He made a phone call to me and placed his mobile phone by the side without uttering a word. I recorded a 41-minute audio. At 8:39 minutes, the three persons asked my father to utter Jai Shri Ram.'[24] The family first called up Delhi Police as they live in Trilokpuri in East Delhi. The attackers' call was traced to Greater Noida as the vehicle was there at the time of the assault. The police reached the spot and took Alam to the hospital, where he later passed away. Sabir insisted his father was lynched by the passengers and wanted the police to add the audio recording to the FIR filed in the case, but the police assured him that they would investigate the audio and add it later.[25] The police also claimed that the passengers were asking a vendor to say 'Jai Shri Ram'!

Predictably, the case made no headway. A month and a half later, Sabir started an online campaign to get justice for his father.

On Twitter he wrote, 'I am Mohammad Sabir, son of Aftab Alam, who was lynched to death on September 6. It has been one and a half months, there has been no arrest, no update given to us by the police. We are on a twitter campaign #AftabAlamKoInsaafDo. I request all of you to join us. Please share this, pin it on your page. Please help me get justice for my father.'[26] These murderous attacks on the innocent followed similar ones in August: An imam in Karnal in Haryana was attacked by sword-wielding proponents of Hindutva; a man was targeted in Jodhpur by cow vigilantes; another man was attacked in Delhi for merely criticizing Modi;[27] a Muslim man was arrested in Madhya Pradesh for criticizing the RSS on his Facebook page;[28] and a journalist was hassled and attacked for speaking up on the harassment of Muslim women in violence-torn north-east Delhi.

Things remained as brutal in 2021. Across India, there were instances of Muslim men being lynched, attacks on Muslim shrines—ranging from Nemuch in Madhya Pradesh to Himachal Pradesh to Delhi—and attacks on Muslim businesses (in Gujarat, Uttar Pradesh and Madhya Pradesh). Of all the crimes, the best documented was the killing of Moenul Haque in Sipajhar village in Assam's Darrang district. The visuals of photographer Bijoy Baniya stomping on the dead man went viral. *The Independent* reported in September 2021, 'Horrific visuals of police brutality emerged from India's northeastern state of Assam as the police opened fire at protestors during an eviction drive. A photographer with the administration was caught on video stomping on the body of a man who lay motionless, probably dead, on the ground.'[29] Baniya was later arrested.

The prime minister felt it unnecessary to talk or to tweet about any of this. His, by now customary, silence spoke eloquently. The home minister of India did not react to the debasement of the dignity of Muslims nor to the threat to their lives. The media stayed silent. Muslims continued to be abused, assaulted and killed; some were attacked for wearing skullcaps or hijabs, others for running a dosa restaurant by the name of Srinath; in still other cases, the police shot them in the leg for alleged cow smuggling in Uttar Pradesh in November 2021. The *Siasat Daily* carried a piece titled '2021: The Year of Atrocities on Muslims', commenting, 'Anti-Muslim hate crimes in India increased exponentially in 2021, with every month at least five major cases erupting in various parts of the country.'[30] The din that was raised following Akhlaq's lynching in 2015 had died down. That too only because some English news portals and Urdu dailies had still not made peace with the continued chicanery and brutal assaults. Elsewhere, killing a Muslim no longer made news. For many, it ceased to be a crime.

By the time, Nasir and Junaid were brutally thrashed, then set on fire in Bharatpur in early 2023, the attacks had even ceased to be covered by mainstream media on a daily basis until some news portals pushed the case to the forefront. The Wire reported, 'In what is being described as yet another case of cow vigilantism leading to the loss of life, merely 100 kilometres from the national capital, two Muslim men from the Rajasthan-Haryana border were allegedly attacked and abducted by a mob that later set them ablaze, alive while they were inside their car. This is said to have happened after accusations of cow smuggling were made against the victims. The dead have been identified as Junaid and Nasir, both residents of Ghatmeeka village in Rajasthan's Bharatpur district… Junaid's family maintains that the bodies had been badly charred due to the burning and could be only identified because of the car's license number. Junaid is survived by a family of 12, including his wife and daughter and the family of his mentally ill older brother.'[31] Less than six months later, the main accused Monu Manesar, said to be absconding by the police, was moving around freely near the village of the victims. In New India, the killers are not afraid of the law; it is the victims' kith and kin who have often had to relocate for their safety.

By April 2023, the sustained attacks forced some Muslim intellectuals to seek redressal of grievances from the home minister. 'A 16-member delegation of Muslim leaders, led by Jamiat Ulama-i-Hind president Maulana Mahmood Madani, met Union Home Minister Amit Shah to raise concerns about "violence committed against Indian Muslims" in various parts of the country on the occasion of Ram Navami… "unabated hate campaign and Islamophobia" in the country; growing incidents of mob lynching, etc.,' reported *The Indian Express*.[32] The home minister assured all help. Didn't quite work out that way though. And Muslim men continued to be lynched for the mere accident of their birth in a particular religion.

11

Jai Shri Ram

During the Bhumi Pujan on 5 August 2020 for the Ram temple in Ayodhya, the main priest exultantly proclaimed, 'Jai Shri Ram.' Prime Minister Narendra Modi in his address said, 'Jai Siya Ram.' He remembered and invoked Sita and Ram both. With the building of the temple now a certainty, the Hindu Hriday Samrat as the prime minister is known, gave Sita her rightful place. But for decades since the Ram temple agitation started, a vast section of Hindu society virtually forgot Ram's wife. In the late 1980s, it was not unusual to find middle-class men greet each other with 'Jai Shri Ram' every morning. This was different and new, because earlier, the devout greeted each other with 'Namaskar' or 'Jai Siya Ram'. Even in a manifestly patriarchal society, Sita was not forgotten. It all changed with BJP leader LK Advani's famous Rath Yatra in 1990. The improvised Toyota rath was hailed everywhere from Gujarat to Uttar Pradesh with cries of 'Jai Shri Ram'. In many towns, supporters woke up at dawn to greet Advani as he arrived and reiterated his pledge to construct the Ram temple at the very site of the Babri Masjid. 'Mandir wahin banayenge,' he said, stubborn as ever. The determination was in part an assertion that his endeavour was above the law. No matter what the court decided, the temple would be built at the very site of the Babri Masjid. This was the message of Advani, who had read Adolf Hitler's *Mein Kampf* when in jail during the Emergency. His party's ideologue MS Golwalkar would have approved of his reading taste. Often, a young man dressed as Ram sat in the middle of Advani's cavalcade. In the endeavour to add another Ram temple to Ayodhya, Sita was all but forgotten. Until Modi sought to restore the balance a little in 2020.

Ram himself has become a tool to further a political party's ambition. For years, Indians, cutting across all faiths, had grown up with depictions of a beatific Ram as a family deity. Temples always had a Ram durbar, with Ram in the centre, Sita to his left, his brother Lakshman to his right and Hanuman at his feet in supplication. Ram, always, without exception, wore a saintly expression, seemingly at peace with the world, happy to bless all. Hindi cinema, often happy to please the ruling dispensation, came up with a song, 'Ram ji nikli sawari…ek taraf Lakshman, ek taraf Sita, beech mein jagat ke palanhari'. Sung by ace playback singer Mohammed Rafi, the song became a raging hit in the late 1970s. For the common man, it denoted love and obeisance. The notion, however, changed as the campaign for the Ayodhya Ram temple gathered momentum. The ubiquitous Ram durbar gave way to a much more muscular imagery of Ram, who was now flaunting rippling muscles, holding an archer's pose, ready at a moment's notice to strike. Suddenly, he no longer appeared to be the avatar of Vishnu, the Preserver.

Many years before he joined the BJP, noted editor-columnist MJ Akbar wrote about the phenomenon with a tinge of forewarning in his book *Riot After Riot,* which was published at the height of the Babri Masjid–Ramjanmabhoomi conflict.

This latest political religion must have its own language, of course... 'Namashkar' or 'pranam' are now passe; they are the salutations of the old culture... In the court of Advani, or in the armies of Advani, you do not greet one another with 'Namashkar' or 'pranam' anymore: you say 'Jaya Sri Ram' or 'Jaya Siya Ram'. This is not true merely of the bazaars of Aligarh or Kanpur or Varanasi or Meerut; this is equally true of a posh dinner hosted for Advani at the residence of one of the richest and most famous industrialists of the country.[1]

What Akbar wrote about was not a mere usurpation or mutilation of a salutation. It was an invitation to replicate the brutal days of Hitler's Germany. The invocation 'Jai Shri Ram' in the hands of the Hindutva votaries of the late 1980s and early 1990s was not just an expression of faith or an announcement of intent. It was a weapon to demonize Muslims; those from the community in the 20th century somehow were held responsible for the alleged destruction of a temple in the early 16th century, when Mughal emperor Babur set foot in the Awadh region. The vicious attempt at vendetta stretched the limits of credulity, but it was bought by the restless youth. Advani had found his target. As Akbar wrote, 'Hitler had the Jews. Advani has the Muslims. The Jews were rats choking the pristine Aryan youth. The Muslims are snakes crawling across the body of Mother India. Kill, kill, kill...'[2]

Kill. Kill. Kill. That is exactly what goons have been doing with impunity since the General Elections in 2019. Once again, they are using the slogan 'Jai Shri Ram' as a weapon to intimidate helpless Muslim men, the 'snakes crawling across the body of Mother India', on the streets of the nation. The slogan about the glory of Ram is now being used as a cry for intimidation of the opponent, an announcement of hate for the Other. What was used by Hanuman as a war cry against Ravan, became a rallying cry against Muslims and a slogan to humiliate the minorities. It happened in the well-documented cases of Tabrez Ansari and Aftab Alam, both in Uttar Pradesh. It happened in the much lesser known cases of Sikar in Rajasthan and Champaran in Bihar. It happened in the Delhi violence shortly after the city's 2020 Vidhan Sabha elections.

In August 2020, in Rajasthan's Sikar district, a 52-year-old Muslim autorickshaw driver was assaulted, allegedly after he refused to shout 'Modi zindabad' and 'Jai Shri Ram'. Hailing the deity and the prime minister seemed interchangeable for the attackers! *The Indian Express* reported that an FIR was filed by Gapphar Ahmad Kacchawa, who was left with broken teeth, a swollen eye and bruises on his cheek. He also claimed that he was robbed of his wristwatch and money. '"One of the men asked me to chant the slogan 'Modi zindabad' and I refused… Then he slapped me hard. I took my taxi and tried to flee towards Sikar. But they followed me in their car and stopped my vehicle near Jagmalpura. They forced me to descend from the vehicle and they badly beat me up…The men abused me and forced me to chant 'Modi zindabad' and 'Jai Shri Ram'", Kacchawa said in his complaint,' *The Indian Express* report revealed.³

Earlier, during the first wave of the Covid-19 pandemic, when state governments were still deliberating about the consequences of extended lockdowns, news came from Champaran in Bihar about a Muslim man being forced to chant 'Jai Shri Ram' merely because he had stepped out to charge his mobile phone. Mohammad Israil from Mehsi alleged that not only did some people compel him to chant 'Jai Shri Ram', but also tried to slit his throat.

Narrating the incident to media personnel, he said that due to heavy rainfall in his village, there was no electricity, which is why he had gone to his friend's house to charge his mobile phone. 'I had gone to a friend to get my phone charged. Some people surrounded me and told me to say "Jai Shri Ram". When I protested, they attacked me with a knife on my head and neck. They were beating here and there like a football,' Israil told The Quint.[4]

He was only left alone when the attackers thought he was dead. His brother Tahir revealed, 'When the attackers thought that Israel had died, they ran away. Israil was then lodged in a government hospital in Mehsi. Because he was found in critical condition, he was referred to Muzaffarpur.'[5]

In July 2019, barely a couple of months after the Lok Sabha results were declared, two men were forced to chant 'Jai Shri Ram' in Aurangabad city by some unidentified persons.[6] Here two boys were abused, attacked and threatened as they waited for an autorickshaw to go home. Shaikh Amer, a delivery boy working with the food delivery app Zomato, and his friend Shaikh Nasir were waiting to hire an autorickshaw when four or five men in a car intercepted them, abused their religious identity and threatened to kill them if they did not say 'Jai Shri Ram'.

Amer and Nasir did as asked. However, this happened in the presence of other people who were moving around nearby, and this probably saved their lives. The assailants fled on seeing the passersby, but the incident was captured on a CCTV camera.

About a month before Amer and Nasir were attacked, a similar incident took place in the same state. Three men allegedly beat up Faizal, a Muslim cab driver, and later asked him to chant 'Jai Shri Ram'.

A case under the Indian Penal Code sections 295 (hurting religious sentiments) and 392 (robbery) was registered by Mumbra police against Faizal's assailants. Faizal, it was found on investigation, had taken some passengers to Divas town in Maharashtra. While returning, the inebriated passengers got into a quarrel with him and beat him up. When they realized he was a Muslim, he was asked to say 'Jai Shri Ram'.

Sikar, Champaran, Aurangabad and Divas were part of a chain of events where goons used Ram's name to humiliate Muslim men. The slogan was used not as a greeting but as a statement of hatred. In Delhi, the situation was no different. The words 'Jai Shri Ram' were used when committing hate crimes, and the city witnessed 53 deaths in such incidents in February 2020. Many cases were reported of men being hauled up in different parts of strife-torn regions in the city and being forced to say 'Jai Shri Ram'. In some cases, the assailants were not satisfied with merely the slogan and asked their victim to recite a few mantras to ascertain their Hindu identity. In most cases, men were asked to lower their trousers even if they chanted the slogan. It was far worse for those who did not chant it.

In July 2020, news portal Scroll.in reported,

> The Delhi Police have said that a group of men killed nine Muslims after they refused to chant 'Jai Shri Ram' during the large-scale communal violence that broke out in the North East district of the Capital in February. The accused used a WhatsApp group to coordinate their activities and offer manpower or ammunition when required. The WhatsApp group—Kattar Hindu Ekta—was created on February 25 at 12.49 pm 'to take revenge on Muslims,' the police said in a chargesheet. The members bragged about 'killing Muslims' and 'dumping their bodies in the sewer', according to *The Indian Express*. Initially the group had about 125 members. By March 8, a total of 47 members had exited the group, as per the chargesheet. The police plan to use the WhatsApp conversations as 'extrajudicial confessions'.[7]

The portal reported in detail about the men who were allegedly murdered upon their refusal to say 'Jai Shri Ram', stating,

The chargesheets were filed before Additional Chief Metropolitan Magistrate Vinod Kumar Gautam on June 29 for the alleged murder of nine people—Hamza, Aamin, Bhure Ali, Mursalin, Aas Mohd, Musharraf, Akil Ahmed, and Hashim Ali and his elder brother Aamir Khan. Investigation revealed that the accused bludgeoned nine Muslims to death in the Ganga Vihar–Bhagirathi Vihar area between the morning of February 25 and February 26 midnight. The armed men stopped whoever they came across, asked them their name, address, ID proof and told them to chant "Jai Shri Ram", said the police.

Anybody who refused to do as ordered, or who was discovered to be a Muslim, was then brutally assaulted and thrown into a drain in Bhagirathi Vihar. On the morning of 26 February, the author headed to the locality to speak to a few survivors and the family members of the departed. A well-intentioned policeman took the author to the edge of Bhagirathi Vihar, before departing with a piece of advice, 'I cannot assure you of safety beyond this point. I would not advise you to go further all alone. There are bodies still floating down the canal.'[8]

There was no other policeman in sight. I took his advice and retreated, only to come across the charred remains of scores of houses and shops. Bodies of men, probably brutally murdered, lay a few metres down in a drain. Along the road, on a burnt wall of a shop, a rioter had scribbled 'Jai Shri Ram' with the soot.

The success of the BJP in the 2019 General Elections emboldened not just the average goon or rioter on the street. Many of our parliamentarians used the religious slogan to heckle newly elected Opposition members during the oath-taking ceremony at the commencement of the new Lok Sabha session. At the receiving end, predictably, were All-India Ittejahadul Muslimeen chief Asaduddin Owaisi, increasingly being seen as the voice of Muslims in the country, Azam Khan, the motormouth MP from Rampur, and his party colleague and veteran Parliamentarian Shafiqur Rahman Barq, besides MPs of the Trinamool Congress, the Bengal-based party which had called the slogan a threat to Bangla culture.

Popular news portal, The Print observed, '[Jai Shri Ram] was used as a political slogan in Parliament at the arrival of Muslim MPs, mainly to heckle them… It is now a forceful assertion of Hindu supremacy in an India, which wants to say at every turn that it is now ruled by the BJP's self-proclaimed Hindu nationalist Narendra Modi.'[9]

Another portal, First Post, was even more upfront about it. It commented:

This is not the first time Jai Shri Ram was used as a rallying call to assert the idea of a muscular Hindu Rashtra. The chant has long been used to create a divisive politics of hate, starting with the violence in Ayodhya and the destruction of the Babri Masjid. In September 1990, LK Advani, the then BJP president, started the Ram Rath Yatra with the VHP and other Sangh cadres dressed as mythological figures, chanting Jai Shri Ram. The chant embodied the Sangh's construction of an imaginary Hindu nation through myth and propaganda.[10]

What Owaisi and the other heckled MPs had to face were taunts, sarcasm, and much more than just majoritarian bullying. It was an overt use of religious symbolism that legitimized hate—hate that was used as a prelude to communal violence, maybe even genocidal aggression. Laced with vile intent and spoken with disdain, it was heard on the floor of India's Parliament, the temple of democracy. Clearly, 'Jai Shri Ram' was no longer a salutation alone. It had become a symbol of conquest.

12.

Bilquis Bano: Remission and Felicitation of Convicts

IN TODAY'S INDIA, THE RULES of the political game are different for different people. The law too is applied in the same fashion, arbitrarily and discriminatorily. The identity of the criminal is often paramount when deciding matters of punishment, retribution or rehabilitation. A Muslim can rot in jail for years for a statement that would not bring anything more than a rap on the knuckles for a Hindu.

Take, for example, the classic case of a union minister asking the crowd to 'Shoot the traitors' and getting away with it as the judge felt the instigation to kill came with a smile![1] A Hindu leader can hope, and indeed be confident, of going scot-free after issuing calls for genocide, apartheid or at the very least, the social boycott of Muslims. In the rarest of rare cases, where the law is pursued with due diligence and the accused punished for their crime, as in the gangrape of Bilquis Bano, a teenage Muslim woman in Gujarat back in 2002, the perpetrators are given special amnesty because they are 'sanskari Brahmins' with a good value system! Or maybe because they had criminally assaulted a Muslim woman, and not a woman from the majority community. A Muslim woman's honour, like a Muslim man's life today, is often deemed of much less value than that of the members of the majority community.

These 'sanskari' Brahmins, 11 of them, had been convicted by the Supreme Court of India, no less, for the gangrape of Bilquis Bano, a woman blessed with a never-say-die attitude who fought all the odds and pitfalls of the system to finally get her assailants behind bars for a lifetime. In August 2022, as India completed 75 years of Independence, her rapists and the murderers of her three-year-old child were released simply because a panel, which included a BJP legislator, felt they deserved to be let out. The men released on 15 August 2022 were Jaswant Nai, Govind Nai, Shailesh Bhatt, Radhyesham Shah, Bipin Chandra Joshi, Kesarbhai Vohania, Pradeep Mordhiya, Bakabhai Vohania, Rajubhai Soni, Mitesh Bhatt and Ramesh Chandana. They were said to have been released as they had completed 14 years in prison and their behaviour during incarceration was 'good'. The crime of these men with 'good behaviour'—proven, not alleged—being the gangrape of the then five-month pregnant Bilquis and the murder of 14 members of her family. These included her mother, her sisters, her baby brothers, her aunts, her uncle, her cousins, a day-old infant and Bilquis's three-year-old daughter, whose head was smashed in front of her eyes.

Barely hours before the release of the criminals, Prime Minister Narendra Modi had, from the ramparts of the Red Fort, on India's 75th Independence Day talked about empowering women, giving them security, and every opportunity to be the best they could be. Either the distance between his words and actions was longer than the route the Ganga takes from the Himalayas to the Bay of Bengal, or his words were meant for the mere consumption of the fawning multitudes who seem to derive special joy with every utterance of the prime minister without subjecting it to the crucible of truth and sincerity.

The special amnesty for the 11 criminals could not have been possible without the permission of the Central Government headed by Modi as the case was investigated by the Central Bureau of Investigation. A BJP government was heading the state where the criminals were let loose. The Centre too had a BJP government. Within two weeks of the men being released, four petitions were filed before the Supreme Court against the remission of their sentences. The three activists who moved the top court were CPI(M) leader Subhashini Ali, journalist and filmmaker Revati Laul and Professor Roop Rekha Verma. The fourth petition was later filed by Trinamool Congress MP Mahua Moitra.

In October 2022, the Gujarat government told the Supreme Court that it decided to release the 11 convicts as they had 'completed 14 years and above in prison… Their behaviour was found to be good' and, significantly, the Centre had also 'conveyed concurrence/approval'. The Centre had conveyed approval—let that sink in. The Government of India stood with convicted rapists and murderers, men who had raped Indian women and murdered Indian children, and the government was fine with remitting their sentences. In fact, the Home Ministry's approval came on 11 July, within two weeks of the Gujarat government seeking its permission. As for the criminals' behaviour which 'was found to be good', well, the convicts were out of jail for over a thousand days on parole while serving a life sentence.

NDTV reported on 18 October 2022, 'One of them was out of jail for over 1,500 days before the convicts walked free this Independence Day. Rameshbhai Rupabhai Chandana enjoyed 1,198 days of parole leave and 378 days of furlough (short-term temporary release of convicts from jail), amounting to a total of 1,576 days outside the jail.'[2]

In an affidavit, the state government, responding to the petitions challenging the remission granted to convicts, stated, 'Superintendent of Police, CBI, Special Crime Branch, Mumbai' besides 'the Special Civil Judge (CBI), City Civil and Sessions Court, Greater Bombay' had in March 2021 opposed the early release of prisoners. Also, in a letter to the superintendent of Godhra sub-jail, the CBI official dubbed the crime as 'heinous, grave and serious…and [claimed that] no leniency should be given.'[3] The state chief minister preferred to remain silent on the issue in public. The prime minister did not say a word on the special amnesty to the convicts. No Mann ki Baat, no tweet, nothing. The actions of his party legislators and their affiliates had spoken enough.

If there was anything worse for Bilquis than the premature release of the culprits, it was the reception that awaited them outside the prison walls in Godhra. The men, all clothed in smart casuals, were welcomed with sweets. Women were on hand to greet them by applying tilaks on their foreheads. Young men sought their blessing by touching their feet. The criminals smiled. Then smiled some more, shook hands, offered salutations, even their blessings. A little later, they were said to have been seen at what was purportedly the local office of the Vishwa Hindu Parishad; an allegation that was subsequently denied by the VHP. The men sat in a neat row on plastic chairs this time, garlanded like heroes. Some of the garlands were of marigold, others of rose and jasmine. The flowers though failed to stem the stench of the crime that had been committed. And Bilquis Bano, indefatigable in the face of heavy odds for years, broke down. A tear escaped her eyes as she saw the visuals of the men who had killed her daughter, her mother and other family members, and brutalized her body, being hugged, embraced and showered with love by the nation.

Back in 2002, when the grisly tragedy took place, it was a question of survival for Gujarat's largest minority. In 2022, when these men were released, it seemed Bano's battle had been waged, won and lost. She stood alone, lonely and forlorn, the prime minister's Red Fort address ringing especially hollow. A few weeks later, in November 2022, the BJP gave a ticket to Payal Kulkarni, daughter of Manoj Kulkarni, to contest the Vidhan Sabha elections from Naroda. Manoj Kulkarni, it may be recalled, was sentenced to life imprisonment for his role in the Naroda Patiya massacre in 2002 in which 97 people were killed by a rioting mob. He was granted bail on grounds of ill health, but was seen canvassing for his daughter. The party fielded CK Raulji from Godhra, the same man who 'was a part of the Godhra Jail Advisory Committee that granted remission to life-term convicts in the case. He was at the centre of controversy when he referred to the released convicts as "Brahmins with good sanskar".'[4]

Of course, sundry voices of protest were raised in society, including Justice UD Salvi who in his capacity as the sessions court judge had awarded life terms to the 11 men. But the reaction in the larger society was muted in comparison to the outrage that had followed the ghastly gangrape of Nirbhaya on the roads of Delhi in December 2012. Within days of the crime, there had been huge public protests in Delhi as men and women descended on India Gate and Raisina Hill seeking justice for the unfortunate girl who was rechristened Nirbhaya or the Fearless. Several metro stations had to be closed to avoid protesters reaching the Rashtrapati Bhawan. Former Army Chief VK Singh was among them. There were protests in Bengaluru and Kolkata, too, as Indian society grappled with the heinous nature of the crime. When news spread of the victim succumbing to the injuries inflicted on her, Bhubaneshwar, Mumbai, Thiruvananthapuram, Chennai, Hyderabad and other cities also rose as one in protest. Many sought the resignation of the chief minister of Delhi, Sheila Dikshit, who feebly protested that while she sympathized with the victim, she could have done nothing to avert the crime as the police reported directly to the Centre. Such excuses mattered not a bit to the masses. Perception, not reality, was paramount. And in the next election to the state Assembly, Dikshit was booted out. Meanwhile, nothing less than sending the six accused in the case to the gallows would have satisfied the collective conscience. Four men were hanged to death in March 2020, with one escaping the noose as he was pronounced to be a juvenile at the time of committing the crime, and another man having died before the final sentence was delivered.

From the prime minister of India to the chairperson of the UPA to almost every Opposition leader, everyone spoke up for the honour of Nirbhaya and drew attention to the plight of women in the country in general. On 22 December 2012, a judicial committee headed by JS Verma, former Chief Justice of India, was appointed by the Central government to submit a report within 30 days to suggest amendments to criminal law that would help sternly deal with sexual assault cases. The Justice Verma Committee report was submitted within a month. It indicated that failures on the part of the government and police were the root cause behind crimes against women, and recommended setting the death penalty rather than life imprisonment as the maximum punishment for rape.

On the day the Verma Committee had its first sitting, 26 December 2012, a Commission of Inquiry headed by former Delhi High Court Judge Usha Mehra was set up to identify lapses, determine responsibility in relation to the Nirbhaya incident, and suggest measures to make Delhi and the NCR safer for women. Within a couple of months, in February 2013, the Criminal Law (Amendment) Ordinance, 2013, was promulgated. It provided for death penalty in cases of rape.

Yet, in August 2022, the rapists of Bilquis Bano were given special amnesty and released amidst much celebration as part of Azadi ka Amritutsav. As mainstream media questioned the release of the convicts but confined itself to using velvet gloves, it was left to *Saamna*, the Shiv Sena's newspaper, to question the remission and felicitation without mincing words. As reported by *The Indian Express*,

> Who is Bilkis Bano? Just because she is a Muslim that does not mean that atrocities against her, rape and murder of her child is pardonable. Had it been our mother or sister? We cry out loud when similar atrocities take place in neighbouring Pakistan and Bangladesh. Then where has our sensitivity gone in the case of Bilkis Bano? Neither the Prime Minister nor our Union Home Minister have spoken a word on this. What is the reason?[5]

However, in these very words of support for the victim, a clear line has been drawn: 'Had it been our mother or sister'! Bilquis, clearly, was the Other in today's India.

13

(A)Dharam Sansad: A Call for Genocide

No more delay. Be ready to kill, ready to die. Start preparations, do not delay. Like in Myanmar, politicians, government, army, police and Hindu citizens will have to, the police here, the politicians here, the army and every Hindu will have to start this 'cleansing campaign' to pick up weapons and we will have to conduct this cleanliness drive [safai abhiyan]. There is no solution apart from this. I say this upfront, before you get distracted elsewhere.

—Swami Prabodhanand Giri, President, Uttarakhand Hindu Raksha Sena

Nothing is possible without weapons. If you want to eliminate their population then kill them. Be ready to kill and be ready to go to jail. Even if 100 of us are ready to kill 20 lakhs of them [Muslims], then we will be victorious, and go to jail… Like [Nathuram] Godse, I am ready to be maligned, but I will pick up arms to defend my Hindutva from every demon who is a threat to my religion. I will raise swords, to save my Hindu dharma, and rip them with my tigress like nails.[1]

—Sadhvi Annapurna aka Pooja Shakun Pandey,
General Secretary, Hindu Mahasabha

When we needed help, the Hindu community did not help us. But if any youth worker is prepared to become the Hindu Prabhakaran, then before anyone else, I will give him Rs 1 crore… if anyone takes on the responsibility to become the Prabhakaran of the Hindus, I will give Rs 1 crore, and if he continues for one year, I will raise at least Rs 100 crore to give.[2]

—Yati Narsinghanand
Chief Organizer, Dharam Sansad, Haridwar

We take an oath and make a resolution that till our last breath, we shall fight, die for and if need be, kill, to make this country a Hindu rashtra…[3]

—Suresh Chavhanke at Delhi hate conclave
Editor-in-chief, Sudarshan TV

TOWARDS THE END OF 2021, I happened to meet a gentleman in Puri who ran a chain of hotels in Varanasi, Haridwar, Ujjain and Konark, besides Puri. Dwelling on the spiritual significance of Haridwar and Varanasi, he invited me to be his guest in both the cities. Even as I was contemplating taking up his offer, television screens started beaming pictures of the prime minister inaugurating the Kashi corridor amidst great frenzy and fanfare. There were excited announcements of the prime minister taking a dip in the Ganga here, priests garlanding him there. It was mid-December, and except for the niggling threat of Covid-19, the best time to travel across north India.

At the inauguration Modi thundered,

> The India of today is not just beautifying the Somnath temple, it is also laying thousands of kilometres of optical fiber in the sea. The India of today is not just rejuvenating the Baba Kedarnath temple, it is also preparing to send Indians to space on its own. The India of today is not just building Lord Ram's temple in Ayodhya, it is also opening medical colleges in every district. The India of today is not just making the Baba Vishwanath temple grand, it is also making pucca houses for hundreds of poor people.[4]

That was on 14 December 2021. For the next few days, the media could not have enough of Modi, how he took a dip in the Ganga, how majestic the new corridor of the Kashi Viswanath temple was, how the grand facelift to the temple complex was a wish fulfilment for millions of Hindus in India and abroad. My mind was made up. Kashi another day. Not so soon after the VIP visit and the possible tourists' trail in its wake. So Haridwar it had to be. Soon, I got busy trying to find a suitable date to visit the holy city. I had already visited the place a few times, but the chance to visit Haridwar in the winter was too good to resist. Just then messages started popping up on my Twitter account about a Dharam Sansad in Haridwar. Haridwar is among the seven holiest centres for Hindus, so a Dharam Sansad there was not surprising. The devil, as they say, lay in the details though. As a number of videos and tweets flooded my timeline, I was left shocked and speechless. It was anything but a religious congregation for spiritual uplift, or an exchange of ideas about faith. It certainly was not about spiritual accomplishment or listening to one's inner calling. For all purposes, it seemed like an Adharm (irreligious) Sansad. It was actually an unprecedented hate conclave, the kind not seen in the history of modern India. Speaker after speaker not only tore to shreds the pluralist fabric of the nation but had the temerity to ride roughshod over the law of the land, issue naked threats of genocide to Indian Muslims even as they urged Hindus to pick up weapons and transform into a new Bhindranwale or a new Prabhakaran.

The mainstream media was slow to react, leaving it to portals like Scroll.in and TheWire.in to plug the gap. Social media though did not hold back: There they were the Hindu extremists, clad in saffron, anything but sagely in their pronouncements in video after video issued between 17 and 19 December 2021. They sat on stage and competed with each other in an unprovoked show of militant Islamophobia. They hated Muslims. They were proud of it and wanted others to hate Muslims too. Organized by Yati Narsinghanand—the hate-spewing priest of Dasna temple who had back in 2016 banned the entry of Muslims to the temple, calling it 'Hindus' sacred place'—the conclave had participants that included the likes of Swami Anand Swaroop, Sadhvi Annapurna, Jitendra Narayan Tyagi (earlier known as Wasim Rizvi) and Ashwini Upadhyay, former spokesperson of Delhi BJP.

A few days after the hate conclave, A Faizur Rahman, a progressive Muslim intellectual, wrote in *The Indian Express*,

> If Narsinghanand allegedly instigated Hindus to take up arms against Indian Muslims, Sadhvi Annapurna, the general secretary of the Hindu Mahasabha, reportedly wanted them killed. She claimed that India was steadily moving towards becoming an

Islamic state, and for it to be converted into a 'Sanatan Vedic Hindu Rashtra' Hindu youth must throw away books and start wielding weapons. Another Hindutva leader, Swami Anand Swaroop, narrated how he had been extorting money from the Muslims of his locality for years. He also warned that resolutions passed against Muslims (which include decrees to socio-economically boycott them) at the Sansad had the authority of a holy writ ('dharam aadesh'). Therefore, governments will have to accept and implement them, failing which a war more gruesome than the 1857 uprising in India against the British would be waged.[5]

Of course, Narsinghanand invited the new-age Bhindranwales and Prabhakarans with the tempting incentive of a prize of Rs 1 crore!

Around the same time, a parallel hate conclave was going on in New Delhi. This time it was held in the precincts of an educational institute in south Delhi and organized under the aegis of the Hindu Yuva Vahini. In the presence of the Vahini's co-founder Rajeshwar Singh, a minister in the Adityanath Cabinet in Uttar Pradesh, the participants were led by Suresh Chavhanke, the controversial editor-in-chief of Sudarshan TV, in taking an oath stating that they were ready to kill and to die in the pursuit of a Hindu Rashtra. If one went by the calls at the two conclaves, it seemed a civil war was almost upon us, and the Hindu youth had to take up arms and slay Muslim men and women who were allegedly out to destroy their religion. The police in both Haridwar and New Delhi remained tight-lipped about the genocidal meets until prodded and then pushed by the courts. On 23 December, an FIR was filed naming Jitendra Narayan Tyagi. On 25 December, the names of Annapurna

Ma and Dharamdas Maharaj were added to the FIR. On 1 January 2022 the Uttarakhand police added the names of Narsinghanand and Sagar Sindhuraj Maharaj to the FIR. The offence in the FIR was initially limited to promoting enmity between groups (Section 153-A), an act punishable with upto three years of imprisonment or with fine or both. Subsequently, the police added the charge of outraging religious feelings 'with deliberate and malicious intention' (Section 295-A), which also has the punishment of up to three years of imprisonment or fine or both. A second case was also lodged against Narsinghanand in Haridwar on charges of insulting religious beliefs and making derogatory remarks about women. Nobody was arrested for weeks after the conclave concluded. Hours after the videos went viral, photographs surfaced in social media showing the state's chief minister reverentially touching the feet of one of the organizers of the Haridwar conclave. It was only on 16 January 2022 that Yati Narsinghanand was arrested, though not in connection with his alleged hate speech initially but for his derogatory remarks against women in a separate case; however, the police promised to include the hate speech details also in the remand application later. Earlier, Tyagi had been arrested on 13 January. This followed the Supreme Court's decision to inquire into the state government's steps taken to arrest the accused.

> The Supreme Court on Wednesday (Jan12, 2022) asked the Ministry of Home Affairs and the police chiefs of Delhi and Uttarakhand to respond to petitions that people accused of delivering hate speeches at a Dharm Sansad organised in Haridwar have not been arrested yet. A Bench led by Chief Justice N.V. Ramana issued notice even as petitioners contended that the declarations of communal hatred made by the speakers

at Haridwar and in Delhi were unlike anything seen or heard before. They had made 'open calls for the extermination of an entire religious community', senior advocates Kapil Sibal and Indira Jaising submitted.[6]

In their petition before the honourable Supreme Court, former High Court judge Anjana Prakash and veteran journalist Qurban Ali had contended that 'hate speeches consisted of open calls for genocide of Muslims in order to achieve ethnic cleansing. The speeches are not mere hate speeches but amount to an open call for murder of an entire community. The speeches thus pose a grave threat not just to the unity and integrity of our country but also endanger the lives of millions of Muslim citizens.'[7]

Delhi Police, meanwhile, failed to move against Chavhanke and others who delivered provocative speeches and took pledges in the capital. A couple of days before the arrest of Narsinghanand, Keshav Prasad Maurya, deputy chief minister of Uttar Pradesh, refused to condemn the provocative speeches, asking the media instead to show the speeches made by minority leaders.[8] In an interview with BBC Hindi he remained tightlipped on the reporter's question on why Prime Minister Narendra Modi and the chief minister of Uttar Pradesh remained silent after the statements inciting violence against Muslims were made from the Dharam Sansad in Haridwar. Instead, Maurya defended the right of the 'dharmacharyas' (religious leaders) to express their views from their own platform. Of course, the prime minister, the home minister of India and the chief ministers of Delhi, Uttarakhand and Uttar Pradesh stayed mum. Nobody felt the need to condemn the unparalleled threat issued to India's largest minority, or to quell the fears of fellow Indian citizens on the threat to the Constitution of India from the Hindu extremist elements who openly abused the police, the judiciary, the legislature and the media. Pertinently, on the arrest of Tyagi, Narsinghanand even threatened the police. Earlier, a speaker had even wished to assassinate former Prime Minister Manmohan Singh for a statement he is said to have made in favour of the minorities having the first right over the resources of the country. Hate was the reigning emotion driving the extremists, whom the Indian media continued to address as 'seers' or 'religious leaders' or 'dharma gurus'. For instance, following his arrest, Narsinghanand was addressed as a 'religious leader' by Zee News.[9] For all speeches promoting terror, nobody was dubbed a terrorist.

Despicable as the utterances of these hate-filled men were, they were neither speeches made in a social vacuum nor a spontaneous outburst. The groundwork for these congregations had been laid over the past few years with the threats and the hate speeches against the minorities getting progressively worse. While sundry Maharaj-es and Pinki Chaudhuri—the man who formed the Hindu Raksha Dal and claimed to be behind the attack on the Jawaharlal Nehru University students in January 2020 in which 39 students and academics were injured in the attack by around 50 masked men allegedly from the ABVP, the students' wing of the BJP—joined along the way, the lynchpin of the most recent conclaves was Yati Narsinghanand, a self-styled, saffron-clad man, who claimed to have converted Rizvi in 2020. The journey started with Narsinghanand forming a Hindu army, the Hindu Swabhimaan Sena, in late 2015. Back then, he had held 50 training camps in Dasna on the outskirts of Delhi, besides Meerut and Muzaffarnagar. The participants were given training in the use of lathis, swords and pistols, much like the speakers urged in the Haridwar meet. Some of the participants at these training camps were school-going children, still in the single-digit years of life. The philosophy being to, as *Times of India* was quoted by *Huff Post*, 'catch them young where after the first six months of training, children begin learning how to use guns.'[10] They were called child soldiers by Narsinghanand; again, much like the oath administered in Robertsgunj in December 2021, where school students were asked to repeat the pledge taken in Delhi by Chavhanke and others.[11] Back in 2016, Narsinghanand had urged the faithful to pick up arms as the ISIS was likely to 'occupy western UP by 2020'. He addressed two panchayats every month. 'At the panchayats, I ask my Hindu lions to be brave and make sure they keep weapons with them at all times,' he had told the media, adding, 'I am preparing my people for civil war.'[12] Narsinghanand had then gone on to bar the entry of Muslims in the local temple, putting up a signboard, 'This temple is a holy place of Hindus. Entry of Muslims is prohibited.'[13] The government had ignored his provocative and innately violent actions then. He was dubbed a fringe element by the media until he gained prominence in the public domain during the pandemic when his volunteers thrashed a Muslim boy who had entered the temple to drink water. A video of the Dasna temple caretaker Shringi Nandan Yadav allegedly beating the helpless boy went viral in March 2021.

Unrepentant, Narsinghanand launched into a diatribe against the Prophet in April 2021. Addressing the media at the Press Club in New Delhi, less than a kilometre from India's Parliament and barely a few yards from the New Delhi Jama Masjid on Red Cross Road, he abused the Prophet, calling the Islamic faith 'filthy' and much worse. Delhi Police filed an FIR under Indian Penal Code Sections 153-A and 295-A. Narsinghanand went back home safe and sound. There was no arrest, nothing. It seemed just like another day at work for him.

Despite the police report, Narsinghanand continued in his vile ways, even going on to release a book against the Prophet later in the year. Meanwhile, his accomplice Chaudhari upped the ante, participating in a meet where vengeful calls were raised against Muslims at Jantar Mantar on 8 August 2021. He surrendered to the police amidst a lot of fanfare, only to be released on bail a month later. Chaudhari too continued to incite violence against Muslims, moving to Loni in Ghaziabad, where he addressed a meeting of his followers from the premises of JD Public School. Issuing an open threat to All India Majlis-e-Ittehadul Muslimeen chief Asaduddin Owaisi, he remarked, 'As long as the warriors and volunteers of Hindu Raksha Dal work together as a unit and follow the path of Hindutva, they will behead you (Owaisi) and make my name.'[14] During the same address, he said, 'We face real danger from mosques and churches… If we face danger it is from the Communist ideology. It is from mosques and madrasas. It is from the churches. If we face danger it is from those who greet (each other) on Eid. If Islam is there, it is like fast poison. Christianity is like slow poison.'[15] Chaudhuri, who was out on bail, remained relentless in spreading Islamophobia. And the Indian state turned a Nelson's eye, a deaf ear, a pursed lip. As the *Telegraph* reported, 'BJP govt seals lips on calls to kill Muslims, establish Hindu Rashtra… The BJP dodged the daily's questions on the calls to "kill" Muslims and establish a Hindu Rashtra at a conclave of sadhus last week, while WhatsApp messages to government representatives drew a blank despite blue ticks suggesting they had been read.'[16]

The hate speeches and slogans constitute a crime not only in India but also under Article II of the United Nations' Genocide Convention, which includes in its definition of genocide any act that intends to destroy a religious group completely or partially or inflicts on it 'conditions of life calculated to bring about its physical destruction in whole or in part'.

As for the Dharam Sansad, it was a hate fest of professional communalists seeking to give themselves dignity by donning the saffron robes of a renunciate. The conclave's message aimed at the extermination of a section of Indians was summed up in the words of Swami Prabodhanand Giri, president, Hindu Raksha Sena. He equated Prime Minister Narendra Modi's Swachh Bharat Abhiyan with the need to get rid of Muslims, pledging to conduct a so-called cleaniliness drive. The imprint of the Final Solution was hard to miss.

14

Bulldozers for Muslims

A FEAR RAISES ITS HEAD every time there is unusual activity in a city. The activity could range from a Hanuman Jayanti or Ram Navami festival to a protest against a new law or action of the government. The revellers might be Hindus, the protesters of any community, but bulldozers usually visit Muslim quarters only. Lofty houses and shanties, showrooms and kiosks, mosques and mausoleums, nothing is safe from the destruction wreaked by the bulldozers. In today's India, the earth-mover has become a symbol of an aggressive state happy to use weapons of destruction on the properties of Muslims who raise their voices for justice and equality, such as when they organized the anti-CAA stir, demanded action against the BJP spokesperson Nupur Sharma for making derogatory remarks about the Prophet in a live television debate, or objected to Hindutva goons raising provocative slogans outside a mosque and Muslim houses.

The victims range from noted activist Mohammed Javed in Allahabad, whose multi-storeyed house was brought down in a matter of minutes because he had taken part in a protest seeking action against Sharma, to Wasim Sheikh of Khargone, who has no arms and somehow eked out a livelihood managing a kiosk, to an unfortunate man in Ujjain whose house was demolished because his son was guilty of spitting.

To a state keen on quashing all voices of dissent—and a dissenting Muslim is even worse—bulldozers are a Godsend. For the cheering masses, often found raising slogans of 'Jai Shri Ram' at a spectacle where bulldozers go to work destroying Muslim properties, sometimes recording it as an 'event' on the mobile, there is nothing illegal about bulldozers. The bulldozers see an 'enemy', the bulldozers smash the 'enemy'. Simple. A short and effective way of showing Muslims their place in today's India. As *The Guardian* quoted Javed's neighbour, 'This is the new pattern now. Bharatiya Janata Party (BJP) leaders provoke us, arrest us when we react and then bulldoze our homes.'[1]

Those who escape the bulldozer pay with their lives and property for the audacity of protesting.

Continued *The Guardian*,

The latest protests were a continuation of a fortnight of sporadic demonstrations by Muslims that began when the BJP spokesperson Nupur Sharma made derogatory comments about the prophet during a raucous television debate. The unrest left two dead in Ranchi, hundreds injured and several hundred under arrest. The chief minister of Uttar Pradesh, Yogi Adityanath, ordered officials to demolish the allegedly illegal buildings of Muslims accused of involvement in the protests. His media adviser, Mrityunjay Kumar, tweeted a photograph of a digger and said: 'Unruly elements, remember, every Friday is followed by a Saturday'.[2]

Like Javed's neighbour, the widely respected newspaper discerned a pattern to the provocations, violence and demolition.

> Over the past two years there has been a rise in violent rhetoric about Muslims by BJP officials and extremist Hindu groups, covering subjects including how they worship, what they eat, the hijab, and the status of mosques. Modi, the prime minister, and the top BJP leadership have remained silent about the provocations, while opposition parties, wary of antagonising the Hindu majority, have also chosen not to intervene.[3]

Here's how the well-rehearsed strategy works in the so-called Muslim-dominated areas: men wearing saffron scarves and bandanas, with vermilion on their foreheads and swords in their hands, stop outside a mosque as part of a Hanuman Jayanti or Ram Navami procession. It could be a march for the immersion of the idol of Durga too. There may or may not be police permission for it. The men atop tempos and open-top trucks park themselves outside the mosque, raise deliberately provocative slogans, such as 'Hindustan mein agar rehna hoga, Jai Shri Ram kehna hoga (If you want to live in India, say, Victory to Ram).' At other times, the threat is more direct with more than a hint of genocide in the air; take this slogan used often: 'Jab mulle kate jayenge, Jai Shri Ram chillayenge (When Muslims start getting killed, they will scream, Hail Lord Ram).' Accompanied by expletives, some sword brandishing and drum beating, it is a deadly cocktail, one that tests the patience of Muslim men, many of whom might be inside the mosque offering prayers just at that very moment. They keep quiet as much to keep a tenuous peace in place as out of fear of life and limb. They realize they are vastly outnumbered and possess no weapons to retaliate. Occasionally, a processionist or two tries to climb a minaret of the mosque and plant a saffron flag in a clear declaration of conquest over the Muslim place of worship. All along, policemen remain silent spectators, as seen in Delhi's Jahangirpuri and Khargone in Madhya Pradesh.

In this tension-filled atmosphere, all that is needed is for a man to throw a stone at the procession, or one of the processionists to hurl a stone inside the mosque, and all hell breaks loose. In the ensuing melee, the mob targets Muslim businesses and houses in the vicinity. Some attack the mosque. Meanwhile, the police disperse the crowd; only to come back after a few hours, or a day or two, this time armed with bulldozers. The bulldozers smash the property of Muslims, holding them responsible for hurling stones at a 'peaceful procession'. As Scroll.in wrote in September 2022,

> According to a senior home department official, 49 properties owned by Muslims were torn down by the administration that day (April 11, 2022). Amjad Khan and other members of the town's Muslim community insist that the demolitions were not prompted by municipal violations.
>
> On April 10, a day before the demolitions, a procession to celebrate Ram Navami, the birthday of Ram, made its way through Khargone… The rally, which featured young men dancing to loud music and waving saffron flags, halted in front of a mosque. Suddenly, stones were pelted. Hindus claim that Muslims started the violence, while Muslims claim it was Hindus. The next day, Madhya Pradesh Home Minister Narottam Mishra declared that the properties of those who hurled the projectiles 'would be turned into a pile of stones'. Khan's bakery was among them.[4]

No questions are asked about the vituperative slogans raised by the supposed devotees. No one asks about the permission sought, granted or denied, to flash naked swords in the procession, or about who permitted these men to pass through the Muslim mohallas or about their decision to park themselves outside mosques. It is an age-old ruse which has not gone out of frequency yet. Seasoned journalist Ajaz Ashraf put things in perspective. Writing about Hanuman Jayanti and Ram Navami processions, he said, 'Such processions are about establishing psychological domination of Hindus over Muslims in order to subjugate them.'[5]

Coming back to Nupur Sharma's remarks and Javed's protest against it while Sharma's safety continues to be guaranteed by the police, Javed was arrested, and his house demolished. Wrote Rekha Sharma, former judge, Delhi High Court, in *The Indian Express*,

> What happened on June 12 (2022) in Prayagraj can best be described as a violation of the Constitution and the law. That day, a two-storey house that stood in the Karala area of Prayagraj, and in which Mohammad Javed lived with his family, was bulldozed by the Prayagraj Municipal Authority. The house reduced to rubble on the ground that it was constructed on without obtaining necessary sanctions and clearances from the concerned authorities… Apparently, the demolition was carried out to teach Javed the lesson of a lifetime, who according to the UP police, was the mastermind behind the violence on June 10, that erupted after the Friday protests against the now-suspended BJP national spokesperson Nupur Sharma's remarks on Prophet Muhammad. The whole episode, it seems, was scripted to send a message not only to Javed but also to his community that anyone running foul of the state administration, whether by way

of a tweet on social media or by staging dharnas or by leading protest marches, will meet the same fate.⁶

Incidentally, Javed was taken into custody a day before the demolition. On the same day, the municipal authorities pasted a notice, addressed to Javed, on the gate of his house, stating that parts of the ground and the first storey was constructed without obtaining requisite permission from the authorities. The house, however, was owned not by Javed but his wife, Parveen Fatima, who received it as a gift from her father. It mattered little. The bulldozer swung into action anyway. Just as it had in Jahangirpuri in Delhi in April 2022.

That April, the bulldozer, reeking of untamed power and sordid masculinity, had reduced the houses of many a poor Muslim in the area to rubble for the crime of one or some of them throwing stones at a shobha yatra (parade of religious splendour). Men wielding swords, tridents and wooden sticks sang some devotional songs, raised some provocative slogans against Muslims and parked themselves outside a mosque even as they did so. *The Hindu* reported the loss of the local residents, 'Riot-hit Jahangirpuri was a scene of destruction, despair and helplessness…after an "anti-encroachment" drive by the North Delhi Municipal Corporation (NDMC) left the area's shops in ruins, and its residents, mostly Muslims, without their source of livelihood. Apart from the shops, the area's revered Jama Masjid's gate and boundary walls were also destroyed during the drive. As the bulldozers drove at around 10.15 am towards the area's C-Block, where most of the Muslim residents live, and began razing the makeshift kiosks and shops lining the road opposite Kushal Cinema, shopkeepers were left picking up whatever remained in the aftermath of the destruction. While some of the shops were partially damaged with the razing of their roofs and outer walls, most temporary structures were completely destroyed.'⁷

NDTV reported, 'According to the police, the clashes erupted when a Hanuman Jayanti procession that did not have permission took a route alongside a mosque. The "shobha yatra" was passing by the mosque, with religious music blaring, around the same time as the azaan or Muslim call to prayers. Two groups started arguing and eventually, bricks were thrown at the procession.'[8]

Next came the bulldozers for those who threw bricks. Reported ThePrint, 'Accompanied by hundreds of police personnel, officials of the North Delhi Municipal Corporation demolished shops, temporary structures and the external gate of a mosque in the riot-hit area of Jahangirpuri in north-west Delhi on Wednesday—continuing for some time even after the Supreme Court ordered status quo.'[9]

The demolition came after Delhi BJP Chief Adesh Gupta wrote to the north Delhi Mayor asking him to identify 'illegal encroachments' and constructions by those arrested after communal violence broke out in Jahangirpuri during a Hanuman Jayanti rally. 'Encroachment done by these rioters should be identified, and there should be bulldozers run over it', Gupta said in his letter.[10]

As the bulldozers wreaked havoc, India's popular Hindi news channels could barely conceal their joy. To see a Muslim being punished for an alleged crime was to see a robust majoritarian state in action. One anchor actually climbed onto a bulldozer herself to give a running commentary on the demolition of the property of Muslims and the gate of the mosque!

The widely respected *National Herald* observed, 'Days after communal clashes broke out in Jahangirpuri area in north-west Delhi on the occasion of Hanuman Jayanti, BJP-ruled North Delhi Municipal Corporation (NDMC) demolished the front gate and wall of a mosque located in C-Block even as a mandir located just 100 meters away from it in the same row escaped the wrath of bulldozers deployed to carry out the so-called anti-encroachment demolition drive. It led many to wonder why the mandir was not touched by the authorities who took no time to demolish alleged illegal constructions, which included commercial as well as residential structures belonging to both the communities.'[11]

A little later, when the BJP spokesman Sambit Patra appeared on TV, he was asked about the allegation that only Muslims were targeted by the demolition drive. He responded, 'If Ajhar [sic] and Abdul make bombs and throw stones at Shobha Yatras, why would Sharma ji and Gupta ji be arrested?' The anchor did not deem it necessary to point out that provocative slogans were raised during the yatra, and that there was the flashing of naked swords and knives, pistols and tridents. 'Instead, she reminded the viewers… "Yehi woh masjid hai jahan char din pehle Shobha Yatra par pathrav hua thha (This is the very mosque where stones were thrown at the Shobha Yatra four days back)."'[12]

Around the same time, on 10 April 2022, Khargone in Madhya Pradesh reported similar trouble. Here too Hindu groups had been given permission to assemble at Talab Chowk as part of a Ram Navami Shobha Yatra at 2 pm before proceeding to other areas. Instead, the processionists stayed at the place till about 5 pm, when it was time for Muslims to offer their early evening Asar (prayer). As music blared from the procession, stones were hurled. Hindus claimed they came from a lane behind the mosque. The Muslims claimed they came from the procession. Within an hour, rioting and arson had broken out in Khargone, properties of many an innocent Muslim and Hindu plundered or burnt down.

> On the morning of April 11 [the next day], Madhya Pradesh's home minister told reporters in the state capital: 'The houses of those pelting stones will be turned into a pile of stones'. By noon, while Khargone was still under curfew, bulldozers came

crashing down on the modest single-room home of Hasina Fakhroo built on government land using Pradhan Mantri Awas Yojana, or Prime Minister's housing scheme funds. The front of Javed Shaikh's chemist shop, housed in the compound of the Talab Chowk mosque, was shaved off. A tin-shed kiosk of a disabled man, Wasim Sheikh, was flattened. According to a document that a senior official of the state home department sent to reporters in Bhopal, 49 properties were demolished in Khargone that day. All were owned by Muslims.[13]

All part of everyday life in New India, where for a section of the society, no cruelty is too much to inflict on a Muslim person, property or place of worship. By the summer of 2023, bulldozers brooked no opposition. A Muslim's house could be demolished for merely spitting at the time of a Hindu celebration. As noted academic Ghazala Jamil wrote,

> Along with lynchings, Muslims in India's 'double-engine' states face the additional spectre of their houses being bulldozed on the flimsiest pretexts. The latest performance of this dark carnival occurred in Ujjain on 19 July, when the authorities in Bharatiya Janata Party-ruled Madhya Pradesh—no doubt with the tacit approval of the party government at the Centre—bulldozed the home of a family whose sons had been accused by Hindutva supporters of spitting on a Hindu procession. Officials claimed that the three-storeyed building was dilapidated. As if the tragedy of the demolition of a family's home was not enough, to assuage the sadism of the police and municipal authorities, in this instance, the destruction was conducted in an atmosphere of revelry. The demolition proceeded to the accompaniment of drummers and chants of 'Govinda, Govinda' playing over the electronic music... This fiesta of chaos orchestrated by

Madhya Pradesh government officials to escalate oppression and perpetuate an environment of fear and helplessness among the persecuted should terrify all Indian citizens.[14]

The New York Times summed it up as follows, 'In India, where a divisive brand of Hindu-first nationalism is surging, bulldozers have become symbols of oppression and a focus of the escalating religious tension that has resulted in the government-led destruction of private homes and businesses, most of them owned by members of the country's Muslim community.'[15]

A bulldozer, the symbol of ugly majoritarianism, soon went beyond the boundaries of India and was paraded on the roads of a New Jersey town in the US during an event to commemorate the Indian Independence Day, exposing the world to the dangerous toxicity of rampant Hindutva.

Clearly, bulldozers smashed more than just the property of Indian Muslims. With every wall and every ceiling they brought down, the image of a law-abiding society and polity collapsed too. The international media was quick to read the danger, often pointed to the risk to life and property of Muslims in a practically Hindu India. Much of our media though asked no uneasy questions and visuals of the all-conquering bulldozer were happily reproduced by many news channels. It seemed to cater to the hidden bigotry of vast multitudes. The road leveller had become a vehicle of majoritarian triumphalism. Greater was the tragedy. As Time magazine summed up in August, 2023 after the Nuh violence and demolition, 'The demolition drive in Nuh is just one example among many of how bulldozers have become a major extrajudicial tool wielded by politicians from the ruling Hindu nationalist Bharatiya Janata Party (BJP) to destroy homes, businesses, and places of worship of thousands of Muslims.'[16]

PART 4

Wrath on Houses of Worship

15

Targeting Mosques

A COUPLE OF METRES INSIDE the green-and-white-tiled gate of Maula Baksh Masjid in East Delhi's Ashok Nagar locality, a heap of pages lie on the mosque's marble floor. The heap consists of several torn pages, and many more are half-burnt and hidden, too delicate to be lifted by hand. Also there, in sinister provocation are two slippers, and one half of a worn-out plastic sandal. Less than 48 hours earlier, I gather from my visit at the site, the now torn and charred pages were part of neatly bound copies of the Quran placed respectfully on shelves inside the masjid. In one of the copies, whose top part has now been reduced to ashes, a verse from the Surah Hujurat translated from the Arabic original has managed to remain safe and clear: 'Allah sees all you do'.

Indeed, He does, as He doubtlessly did when rioters struck the 46-year-old mosque. It was Tuesday, 25 February 2020. Tension ruled the air, as the traumatized Muslim residents whose houses shared their wall with the mosque's western wall, recalled in a meeting with the author shortly afterwards.

The masjid's imam, young and gaunt with a ruffled beard, as the residents described him, had been hurrying back to lead the prayer after attending to some chores. The more seasoned muezzin, who sports a henna-dyed beard, was finishing his ablutions before azaan, the invitation for prayer. A little before the devout could be extended an invitation for the afternoon prayer, a mob had laid siege to the mosque, the residents say. The frightened muezzin had bolted the gate from the inside and ran for safety towards the top floor, which led to the rooftops of some Muslim neighbours who resided just behind the mosque. 'They came right to the roof my house,' said Qamaruddin, whose house was ransacked on the ground floor, the top floor being mercifully left untouched. The muezzin and his wife sought strength in the company of the faithful. 'They climbed over to the top floor where my tenants stay,' Qamaruddin told me.[1] The imam thought it wiser to stay away, it appears from the accounts. The mob, armed with batons and iron rods, pickaxes and tridents, had then tried to break the mosque gate open. 'I had bolted the main gate from inside in a desperate attempt to protect the mosque,' said the muezzin, adding, 'Some men shouting "Jai Shri Ram" hurled petrol bombs, plastic bottles and canisters of inflammable liquid from the road.'[2] Some had even hurled gas cylinders. The cylinders in the courtyard of the mosque had fallen, partly damaging the floor and burning the prayer mats spread out on the floor for namaazis (worshippers), as the author found on his second visit on 1 March 2020 (the first visit was on 29 February). 'Roused by the cries of "Jai Shri Ram", the mob pushed hard at the gate. It gave way. The mob was inside the mosque. Within seconds, the bookshelves full of copies of the Quran were burnt down,' recalled the muezzin who had been serving in the mosque for more than 15 years.[3] Added to the conflagration were expensive carpets from the inner sanctorum of the mosque and the prayer mat of the imam. 'It was a total mess,' chipped in Mohammed Rashid, adding, 'Somebody hurled another petrol bomb, reducing the ceiling fans to an ugly mash. There was fire everywhere. There was a lot of smoke. It was difficult to breath.'[4] The fans ended up bringing down with them a chandelier and a few tube lights as well. The Muslim neighbours had scurried away. Only a vegetable vendor remained. From morning to around 1 pm, the sinewy young man would sell his wares in the colony. A little before afternoon prayer, he would park his vehicle near the mosque and wait for worshippers to come shopping. On the fateful day, he was the one who called the police. Later, he recalled to the author, 'The attackers were mostly young men. They held batons and tridents.'[5]

'Some of them rushed upstairs. Soon, the only sound one heard in the mosque were chants of 'Jai Shri Ram', Rashid, who plies an autorickshaw for a living, told me.[6] He was away on duty when a phone call from a neighbour brought him rushing back. 'I had barely crossed the road to save myself when I heard a young man, in an apparent reference to the demolition of the Babri Masjid in Ayodhya in 1992, scream, "Har masjid Babri bana do! Ek dhakka aur do! Mulla ki masjid tod do!" (Reduce every mosque to Babri. Give one more push. Demolish Muslims' mosques.) Another climbed to the roof. Even as the crowd raised cries of "Jai Shri Ram", he climbed to the top of the minaret of Maula Baksh Masjid and planted a saffron flag.'[7] The planting of the flag[8] seemed to be a declaration of victory, a mark of conquest. The mullah's mosque had been conquered.

Nobody could go to the mosque for prayer that afternoon. The police kept away too. The mosque was reduced to an unholy rubble. The prayer mats turned to ashes, and the holy book was desecrated.

Allah sees all you do.

Meanwhile, all but one of the shops adjacent to the mosque were systematically set on fire. The sole shop to survive belonged to a Hindu who sold shoes. He had been renting the place from the mosque's management committee since 1990 to foster communal harmony. Clearly, that had not helped. The BBC reported about it, stating:

> There are some 200 homes and shops in riot-hit lanes of Khajuri Khas, a fifth of them owned by Muslims. However, it is virtually impossible to tell exactly which of the slim, serried structures that dot the untidy skyline are owned by Muslims, and which by their Hindu neighbours. The buildings even share common walls and continuous rooflines. Yet, last week, the mob targeted the Muslim houses and shops with chilling ease. Soot-laced, gutted Muslim homes with broken doors, melting electricity cables and mangled CCTV cameras stand next to unspoilt and neatly painted Hindu homes. Muslim-owned chicken, grocery, mobile phone and money transfer shops, a coaching centre, and a soda factory are scorched. Shops owned by Hindus are beginning to open their shutters.[9]

To the left of the gutted shops in Ashok Nagar were the equally gutted houses of Rashid, Khursheed, Qamaruddin and others. Rashid's house was burnt down, from floor to ceiling, and all the amenities of a usual middle-class house such as a fridge, television, gas stove and bed were stolen. A motorcycle with no petrol in it had been buckled to a hook in the wall to prevent theft. What could not be stolen had been set on fire, as the author saw on a visit on 1 February 2020.[10] Rashid helped photograph the place, hoping the media coverage of his ruined dwelling would help get him a decent compensation from the government.

At the adjacent house, where Khursheed lives, the marauders seemed to have been more patient. The goods for his footwear shop, as he recalled in tears, had just arrived. 'The cardboard boxes were stacked up to the ceiling at the house to be transported to the shop a couple of days later,' Khursheed said, adding, 'The goons chose and tried on the shoes at leisure, asking fellow marauders for their opinion on each pair. They chose what fit their feet, passed on to others what didn't.' It was daylight robbery in the capital of India conducted with the patience of a craftsman at work. So certain were they that the policemen would not come calling anytime soon. 'Once they had tried on and chosen what they wanted, they picked up and placed the stuff on the waiting vehicle outside. Only then did they set the house on fire,' Khursheed said.[11] The floor and the ceiling fell apart, and the brown tiles on the walls became sad, voiceless witnesses to the sorry spectacle.

The same fate awaited Qamaruddin and others. The cops had whisked away all of them late in the morning to the local police station to ensure their safety.

The Hindu reported on almost the same lines, stating:

> For the first time in over 40 years, Friday prayers were not held at Masjid Maula Baksh in north-east Delhi's Ashok Nagar. The mosque was vandalised and a saffron flag was hoisted on top of it during the violence on February 25. A video recorded on Tuesday showed three persons climbing atop the minaret and sticking a saffron flag. The video, a grim representation of the riots, went viral. Right behind the mosque, on a street, what reminded of a few houses were broken doors, burnt bikes and belongings. The houses belonged to the minority community while those of others remained untouched. It was learnt that the families got scared and left after the violence to safer places

and haven't returned permanently though they have visited to take stock of the situation.¹²

None of the men—Rashid, Khursheed, etc.—went to the mosque for days on end after the attack. Their immediate priority was to hunt for papers to apply for the meagre compensation announced by Delhi government in response to the violence. These were also the papers they would have had to show in case the preparation of the much-talked about countrywide National Register of Citizens came to pass.

Popular portal Scroll.in wrote about the attack on 25 February 2020:

> A mosque was set on fire in Ashok Nagar locality of North East Delhi… as clashes over the Citizenship Amendment Act continued for the third straight day, The Wire reported. A mob shouting 'Hai Shri Ram' and 'Hinduon ka hai Hindustan' (A Hindustan for Hindus) paraded around the burning mosque, and a Hanuman flag was placed on top of the building, according to the website. Miscreants also looted the shops within and also around the mosque's compound.¹³

The mosque stood bare and forsaken. The Muslims had been shown their place in New India.

Allah sees all you do.

Barely a couple of kilometres from Maula Baksh (God's Blessing) Masjid stands Allahwali Masjid (God's mosque) in Karawal Nagar. The names are similar and identifiable—pious Muslims remember Allah in everything. Asked about their well-being, Muslims are known to reply, 'Alhamdulillah' (All praise be to Allah). On seeing something beautiful or worthy, they exclaim, 'Masha Allah' (What

God has willed) or 'Subhan Allah' (Praise of Allah). So, on the subject of naming a mosque, the House of Allah, it is common to find titles with terms like 'Maula Baksh', 'Allah', even 'Mecca' and 'Medina', the two holy places the faithful visit for Hajj. Next in popularity when it comes to the christening of mosques are the names of the four caliphs, Abu Bakr, Umar, Usman and Ali, followed closely by Ayesha and Fatima, wife and daughter of the Prophet, respectively. Yet almost every town in north India, besides Kerala and Hyderabad, in the south has a mosque named after Bilal, the first man to say the azaan, the prayer call. The reaction of non-Muslims society to the call for prayer betrays their Islamophobia like little else. We had popular playback singer Sonu Nigam, once said to have the potential to step into the shoes of the legendary Mohammed Rafi, going public with the allegation that the azaan from his neighbourhood mosque in Mumbai disturbed his sleep. That was in 2017. Interestingly, the same Mumbai witnessed the remarkable, and extremely rare, support of Shiv Sena leader Pandurang Sakpal, who expressed his love for the prayer call, which he said he finds soothing, and announced an azaan recitation event. Yet, he had to backtrack in the light of pre-existing pressures from BJP leaders in the state,[14] now eager to fill up the ideological vacuum created after the Shiv Sena formed the government in Maharashtra in alliance with the more centrist INC and NCP in 2019. It prompted the governor of the state to wonder if the Shiv Sena, named after one of the components of the Hindu Trinity of Brahma, Vishnu and Siva, had turned secular. As the Maharashtra government postponed the opening of places of worship following the outbreak of Covid-19, he wrote,

> You have (been) a strong votary of Hindutva. You had publicly espoused your devotion for Lord Rama by visiting Ayodhya

after taking charge as the Chief Minister. You have visited the Rukmini Mandir in Pandharpur and performed the puja on the Asgahi Ekadashi. I wonder if you are receiving any divine premonition…to keep postponing the reopening of place of worship time and again, or have you suddenly turned 'secular' yourselves, the term you hated.[15]

The governor was referring to reopening of places of worship when the Covid-19 pandemic raged in Maharashtra, with the state reporting the highest number of positive cases regularly. For a few minutes, lost on him was the import of the Preamble of the Constitution of India, which identifies the country as a sovereign, socialist, secular, democratic republic.

In Delhi, the state ruled by the Aam Aadmi Party, Arvind Kejriwal never came out in the open to support the anti-CAA protests. Instead, he taunted the Central government's perceived inability to clear the Shaheen Bagh protest site, saying, 'We would have cleared the area within two hours.'[16] He was, however, quick to remember the Hindu God Hanuman in his victory speech. In February 2020, many a mosque in north-east Delhi was rendered physically incapable of calling the faithful to prayer, their often-hallowed names helping them not a bit. As it turned out, the fates of Maula Baksh, Allahwali, Chand, Mina, Fatima, Madina, Jannati and other mosques were intertwined. One by one, 19 mosques came under serious and deliberate assault.

Incidentally, popular portal The Quint reported in June 2020 that the police's official figures reveal that '8 mosques, 2 temples, 2 Madrasas & 1 Dargah were damaged during Delhi riots.'[17] This data given by the police, the portal said, was in response to two separate queries filed by Delhi-based RTI activist Yusuf Naqi. 'However, this is different from the figure given by the Delhi Waqf

Board, according to which 19 mosques had been damaged during the riots.'[18]

Each mosque was a symbol of what the Right-wing, homegrown terrorists hate, an embodiment of the Others' faith. No one was sure if they drew their inspiration from the 1992 demolition of the Babri Masjid alone, though at many places one heard the oft-repeated slogan, 'Har masjid Babri bana do, ek dhakka aur do, mulla ki masjid tod do (Make every mosque into a Babri; give it one more shove, break the mosque).' Sadly, terrorists certainly had other examples to emulate.

Such examples abounded: When Vinayak Damodar Savarkar was a 12-year-old, he led a bunch of schoolboys to pelt stones at the village mosque. Having damaged the mosque's walls and broken its tiles and windows, the boys returned triumphant. That was back in the 1890s. In 2020, the modern-day attackers were a bit older, much stronger and certainly more hateful. On 25 February, around 11 am, they attacked the Allahwali Masjid with hammers, pickaxes and tridents. They used gas cylinder bombs and petrol bombs to set the mosque aflame. Before attacking the mosque, they evoked terror by attacking Muslim houses in the neighbourhood, sending the community scurrying out of the colony. The Ashok Nagar template was to be repeated more than a dozen and a half times.

The houses thus vacated were looted and set on fire; a non-Muslim house in the neighbourhood of a Muslim resident was left unaffected. The Wire report on the incident reads, 'Of the four Muslim houses in the neighbourhood of the mosque, three were burnt. The last one shared a wall with a Hindu family. The Hindu family asked the mob to spare that house, for fear that their own house would also be damaged and the mob agreed.'[19]

With not a Muslim around to defend the mosque, the terrorists had free run. They broke open the gate of the mosque and installed an idol of the Hindu Goddess Durga. The idol was soon garlanded with marigold flowers.[20] *The Indian Express* reported a little later after a police complaint had bene filed against the accused, 'The FIR was registered in Karawal Nagar police station based on a complaint that stated that the Allah Wali Masjid at Shahid Bhagat Singh Colony was allegedly set on fire during the riots. It was also alleged that a sculpture had also been put on a slab outside the door of the mosque.'[21]

Meanwhile, the mosque was set ablaze with a series of petrol and cylinder bombs—its flooring caved in, a part of the ceiling fell apart and the walls' plaster was ripped out. Not a single prayer mat was left undamaged, and many copies of the Quran were burnt. The electricity wires were snapped, the water pipes twisted out of shape. The plastic prayer caps were mostly burnt and destroyed beyond recognition. They lay in a heap near the gate where the idol of Durga was installed.

Not satisfied with their handiwork, some members of the belligerent mob climbed to upper floors of the four-storeyed mosque. As they entered each new floor, the cries of 'Jai Shri Ram' grew louder, until finally, a few men reached the rooftop of the mosque. There stood two proud minarets, symbols of Islamic architecture, seemingly unaware of the macabre violence downstairs. Not for long, though. Soon, a man climbed atop one minaret, and threw down the loudspeaker tied to it for broadcasting the message of azaan far and near. It was replaced by a Hanuman flag, a kind of saffron jack which has gained in popularity over the past half a decade or so. As the flag flew from the mosque, cries of 'Har, Har Mahadev' and 'Jai Shri Ram' rent the air. India seemed to be walking back in time to the medieval era with a role reversal. The Muslim houses of worship were now the vanquished, the Hindutva practitioners the victors. Amidst this change in fortunes, lost was a simple fact: India, as we know now, did not exist then. At that time, the faith of the emperor was often synonymous with the faith of the state. The India of today is still a secular republic with no state religion.

At the Allahwali Masjid, nobody was invited to the afternoon prayer. The mosque's audio system having been ripped apart, there was no muezzin to proclaim the greatness of Allah nor beseech the faithful with the words, 'Come for prayer, come for success.' The faithful, sullen, angry and fearful had all departed from the Shaheed Bhagat Singh Colony in Karawal Nagar, preferring to save their lives over saving the house of worship. The mosque had fallen into the hands of attackers. The idol of Durga remained at the mosque, freshly garlanded every morning. Some locals bowed in obeisance as they went about their chores. The media stayed quiet. Deliberately quiet.

For the next six days, the idol stayed at the mosque and the Hanuman flag flew proud as the symbol of the new conqueror. There was no change of heart on the part of majoritarian communalists. A Muslim organization with its roots in the freedom struggle and ideological affinity in the pluralist ethos of India, Jamiat Ulama-i-Hind, had to step in to restore sanity. On 1 March 2020, an FIR was filed against the attackers for desecrating the mosque and disturbing communal harmony. Then, in the presence of police officials and those from the Special Cell, the Hanuman flag was taken down by a local resident, Vikas, a young practitioner of the Hindu faith who believed in pluralism. The idol of Durga was respectfully wrapped in a cloth and removed from the place. After that started the repair and reconstruction of parts of the mosque. For days on end, no azaan was heard, no prayer offered. Until finally, around Eid ul-Fitr, the faithful started trickling in.

The attacks on Maula Baksh mosque and Allahwali Masjid are just two of the symptoms of the disease of hate and unprovoked violence. As reported by *Frontline*,

> Almost every part of North East Delhi that was ravaged by targeted violence reported its own Babri Masjid. Every other kilometre or so, at least one mosque was either completely burnt down to the accompaniment of 'Jai Shri Ram' slogans or damaged by trishul- and iron rod-wielding attackers. Announcing the triumph of belligerent Hindutva, saffron flags were planted atop the main minarets of mosques. Copies of the Quran were desecrated; in some cases, entire shelves of the holy book were burnt. Often, the attackers reminded the faithful: 'Har masjid Babri banegi [Every mosque will be reduced to Babri Masjid].' At all places, the pleas of imams and muezzins went unheeded, as did their desperate calls to the police. The imams either fled or were badly mauled. In one case, acid was thrown at a cleric in Shiv Vihar. Delhi Police personnel stood accused of inaction or, worse, colluded with the attackers.[22]

The story was the same everywhere else. Much like the Allahwali and Maula Baksh mosques, the Fatima Masjid in Khajuri Khas Extension reported an attack that left scars that would take longer to heal than the mosque to be repaired.

The place of worship was the site of unbridled aggression and is located in the colony where the house of Mohammed Anees, a Border Security Force jawan, was gutted by the mob. Here too, the mob, in what seemed to be a well-calibrated plan, attacked the mosque on 25 February after the Fajr (dawn) prayers but well before the Zuhr (afternoon) prayers. Shortly after the faithful had returned home having offered Fajr prayers, young men wearing saffron scarves and sporting tilak on their foreheads gathered in the lane early in the day and raised slogans of 'Desh ke gaddaro ko, goli maaro saalo ko (Shoot the traitors)'; this was the slogan given by a BJP leader in the run up to the Delhi Assembly elections, which preceded these attacks on mosques by a couple of weeks. Here, too, the Muslim families were shaken. Unlike other places, they did not leave their colony, but took refuge inside the mosque, confident that it would not be touched in case of violence: There had been communal riots in many towns and cities in the past, but mosques—with the glaring exception of Gujarat in 2002—were more likely to be spared than burnt. After all, many pious Hindus have been known to bow in front of a mosque when they pass by one on the road. Many have even given land for mosques. That was in more accommodating times. Not in New India. The faithful were safe only for a few minutes. *Frontline* reported,

> The young men dispersed but were back outside the mosque a few hours later. This time they were wearing helmets or had covered their faces with black cloth. Some had even worn shields in anticipation of retaliatory violence. This helped them because as soon as the men tried to break open the mosque's front door, there was stone pelting by the Muslims inside. Soon, the door was broken down by the attackers, who went on to demolish everything they could lay their hands on, from benches and carpets to fans and lights and, finally, the shelves that stored copies of the Quran. They used batons, sticks, axes, swords, even hockey sticks.[23]

Members of the Muslim community retreated in the face of the onslaught. Meanwhile, another group climbed on to the roof of the mosque, jumping over from the terraces of neighbourhood houses. They hoisted a saffron flag atop the minaret of the mosque to declare their victory. As Anjali Mody, a seasoned journalist, summarised for Scroll.in, 'Some mosques look like they were fire bombed through windows that were prised open after their glass panes were broken. Others were clearly set alight by people who rampaged through them tearing up books, breaking furniture, wrenching off taps, battering anything they could not break, before setting everything on fire. In situations where the imam or muezzin were unable to flee in time, they were set upon by the mob with rods and batons.'[24]

'Soon after, cylinder bombs and petrol bombs brought everything down… Fatima Masjid was covered in soot, its ceiling all black, the verses of the Quran on its walls illegible. Desperate calls to the police for help went unanswered. The mosque went into mourning,' *Frontline* concluded.[25]

Veteran journalist Ajaz Ashraf talked of Fatima Masjid in his account of destruction of mosques in Delhi. He wrote in Newsclick, 'The attackers began by pelting stones and then switched to hurling petrol bombs. Muslims residents said they fled to the terraces of their houses, hoping for police assistance, which arrived many hours later.'[26] The neighbours, he wrote, helped the attackers.

Secular India has since not been able to get out of the state of ceaseless sorrow, unabated sighs and tears. They hurt. And hurt even more with the realization that the prime minister of the country, after winning the Lok Sabha elections in 2019, had taunted the polity, saying, 'In this election not even a single political party could dare to mislead the country by wearing the mask of secularism.'[27] Unfortunately, he was right.

Dastardly were the attacks on these places of worship that had come up over the last 30 years or so in north-east Delhi. Much of the region was developed in the wake of the Congress leader Sanjay Gandhi's efforts in the Emergency days to decongest Old Delhi by forcefully relocating people to Nand Nagri, Ghonda, Seelampur, etc.

Many of the displaced from Old Delhi were Muslims. They were made to leave their homes and bundled into a truck, with families, taking with them their meagre belongings. Many had walked miles with their bedding on their backs, suitcases on their heads. They had to begin their life again from scratch, migrants in a city now not much more familiar than a stranger. They worked hard, mostly honestly, with some finding quick ways to rehabilitate themselves and make progress. Shops came up inside lanes and by-lanes, the faithful collected money for mosques. Even as their houses were often single storeyed with unplastered walls, they collected enough to give their much-loved mosques marble flooring, a dome and a couple of minarets.

Not much of this was spared in the targeted attacks in 2020. However, the worst attacks were on a couple of dargahs in the locality. For ages, dargahs (tomb of a Muslim saint), khanqahs (places for gathering of sufis) and mazaars (a shrine) have been symbols of pluralist India, places where people across religions congregate. Orthodox Muslims have even frowned upon some of the practices at dargahs, like lighting incense, offering a garland of flowers at the tomb of the saint, or in many cases, a chador (a sheet to pay respect). Secular India could not care less for their sentiments. Men and, importantly, women gathered at these sites, which were soon raised to the status of a place of worship. Keeping bearded maulanas with skullcaps company were women in saris and sindoor. There were women in burqas, just as there were new generation men in jeans and T-shirts, their religion not identifiable by their clothes. Every evening they would gather at the dargahs in north-east Delhi, the one near Bhajanpura chowk just off Chand Bagh being a particular favourite.

In the 2020 violence, though, the dargah was not spared. A fact-finding committee appointed by the Delhi Minorities Commission found Dargah Baba Shaikh to have been attacked just as violence had been inflicted upon other mosques. In fact, the dargah was among one of the first to be attacked, if one goes by the account of a witness on the day.[28] Its boundary wall was broken, but an attempt to set it on fire met with only partial success as the dargah is largely an open-air space. It also saw the one of the first few attacks on a Muslim man, my witness. This was merely the prelude to the violence that subsequently claimed the lives of 53 people, 38 of them Muslim. The victim-witness I spoke to was Mohammed Zubair, a wiry 37-year-old small-time businessman who was returning after attending a religious congregation of the Tablighi Jamaat in Qasabpura, less than a dozen kilometres away.[29]

While speaking to me a couple of weeks later, Zubair had his arm in a sling, his knees were bandaged, his back was still blue and hurting after repeated beatings with tyres, batons, belts and rods, these being the injuries inflicted by the mob that waylaid him near the dargah. He had a beard and wore a skullcap with a kurta-salwar, clothes that helped the assailants identify his religion.

The Guardian reported:

He lay in a bloodied ball on the floor, but the baton blows kept on coming. As the 30 strangers beat him without stopping, Mohammad Zubair closed his eyes, brought his forehead to the ground and prayed. 'The blows kept raining on my head, hands and back,' said Zubair. 'I did not ask them to stop beating me. I became silent, tried to hold my breath and stiffen my body.' As he spoke, tears rolled down his face. 'First I asked, "Why are you attacking me? What wrong have I done?" But they did not listen to my words and went on hitting me from all sides. They were shouting maro saale mulle ko [kill the bastard Muslim] and jai Sri Ram [a Hindu nationalist slogan]. There were many other men who stood by who did not come to save me.' The photo of Zubair being ruthlessly beaten in broad daylight in the streets of Delhi by a mob of young Hindu men was one of the most shocking images of the brutal religious riots that engulfed Delhi.[30]

'It was Monday. I was returning home in Chand Bagh after attending prayers at the Tablighi Jamaat congregation in Qasabpura. When I reached Panchwa Pushta, I heard there was some communal tension in the area. I tried to reach home via Bhajanpura market thinking it is a crowded market, so it will be fine. But I found the entire market closed,' he told this author.[31] He added, 'There was a crowd which had gathered. People looked at me, but nobody said anything. At that time, I could not make out whether they were Muslims or Hindus. I walked to the subway to go across the road towards Chand Bagh. As I was entering the subway, a man standing there advised me not to take the subway as it could be dangerous. He had a tilak on his forehead. I took him to be a religious man and believed him. So, I resumed walking straight towards the mazaar. After walking barely a few metres I saw a stone-pelting mob. The mazaar had been burnt. One of the stone-pelters saw me and rushed towards me... A man hit me with a sword. Another man hit me with a stump. Some wore helmets, some used masks. They raised cries of "Jai Shri Ram". They shouted, "Mulla ko maro...bolo Jai Shri Ram". Nobody came forward to help me or protect me. The men kept hitting me. I fell unconscious from the blows.'[32]

A complete stranger to the attackers, who, in all likelihood, were strangers to each other too, Zubair had this to say on being asked why he was attacked: 'I really have no clue. All I can say is that they did not attack me but my Muslim identity. I was wearing a skullcap and a salwar–kameez at that time. With my cap, dress and beard, they realized I was a Muslim.'[33]

He would have been consigned to the ranks of anonymous victims of violence, the faceless multitudes reduced to mere statistics, but for a photograph by Reuters' award-winning photographer Danish Sididqui. The photo became a symbol of the north-east Delhi violence, much like Qutbuddin Ansari's photograph came to represent the tragedy in 2002 Gujarat, where he was seen pleading for mercy with folded hands and fear written across his face. Incidentally, Siddiqui, wrote The Caravan, had taken the picture from roughly a metre away, and his gas mask was spattered with Zubair's blood. 'I'm trained for a hostile environment,' he said.[34] A disinformation campaign to discredit Siddiqui's photograph of Zubair had been launched almost instantaneously by the Right-wing social-media ecosystem. On 23 July 2021, the writer and self-confessed BJP supporter Madhu Kishwar tweeted to her nearly 2 million followers, referring to Siddiqui as a 'jihadi'.[35] Irrespective of Kishwar's bile, Siddiqui's picture of Zubair captured his angst, his humiliation, and the present danger to life. It showed Zubair crouched on the road, bleeding from his forehead, hand and shoulder with about a dozen men raining blows on him. One had him under his foot. That he survived was no less than a miracle.

As Zubair lost consciousness, the attackers believed he was almost dead. They decided to dispose of his body. 'I was not fully conscious, but I have a faint recollection of men holding me by the hands and feet. They shouted, "Throw him on the other side of the grill." They dumped me on the other side. I do not know for how long I stayed there. Next I heard somebody saying, "Let's take him to the hospital, he is badly injured. He could die",' Zubair recalled.[36]

Against all odds, Zubair survived. India survived. Yet another minor miracle in an everyday series of fresh attacks on the soul of India, the identity of a community.

Allah sees all you do.

16

Felled Like a Pack of Cards

ON 30 SEPTEMBER 2020, WHEN the CBI's special court acquitted all 32 accused of conspiring to demolish the Babri Masjid in Ayodhya, there was a sigh of relief and resignation in the Muslim community. After 28 years of painstaking investigation, written across 2,300 pages, the verdict made it clear to all countrymen and women that there was no conspiracy at all. The medieval mosque must have demolished itself or perhaps caved in on being confronted with the power of faith of the men and women who had gathered around it with tridents, hammers, iron rods and axes, and such other weapons on 6 December 1992. We had all seen the visuals on television. We had seen the entire Rath Yatra, the hate it fuelled and the riots that followed. We had also seen Anand Patwardhan's trenchant film, *Ram ke Naam*. We had read newspapers and seen the photographs of dozens of men, many in saffron scarves, who had climbed atop the mosque's dome. Then there was the painful but memorable dialogue we had all heard, 'Ek dhakka aur do', attributed to Uma Bharti, who was then considered a firebrand leader. Turns out, by today's standards, she was almost a peacenik.

Or, we were gullible. The court acquitted all the accused, including top BJP leaders LK Advani and Murli Manohar Joshi, in the case, rubbishing the FIR accusing them and 42 others. The court held that there was no 'conclusive proof' against them. The verdict was completely against the findings of the Liberhan Commission report. The Liberhan Commission inquiry, led by retired High Court judge MS Liberhan, had been set up on 16 December 1992 by the Government of India to investigate the destruction of the mosque. The commission indicted several top BJP leaders, including the then chief minister of Uttar Pradesh, Kalyan Singh, Joshi and Advani, holding them 'intellectually and ideologically responsible' for the destruction of the mosque. Yet, the CBI special court thought otherwise. Immediately after the judgment, LK Advani waxed eloquent, 'I wholeheartedly welcome the judgement by the special court in the Babri Masjid demolition case. The judgement vindicates my personal and BJP's belief and commitment toward the Ram Janmabhoomi movement.'[1]

Yet, the Muslims did not protest. Not even a whimper was heard from them. It was the saddest moment, probably sadder than even the demolition itself, as the country's largest minority resigned itself to its fate, convinced not much was to be won in the Babri Masjid legal imbroglio—not even punishment for the man who started the Rath Yatra or Murli Manohar Joshi, the man who instead rose to become the human resource development minister of the country a few years later in the Atal Behari Vajpayee Cabinet. The feeling was akin to being orphaned all over again. Like having come back home after burying one's parent only to be told that the doctor you thought guilty of negligence was innocent after all. It did not matter then. The dead were already buried. And they do not come back even in New India. Of course, Babri Masjid demolished itself. We are convinced.

The Supreme Court judgment in November 2019 merely reinforced the sentiment. The mind went back to the measured words of seasoned journalist Sajeda Momin. Writing in The Federal, she recalled, 'Soon after the demolition of the Babri Masjid on December 6, 1992 Mahant Avaidyanath, one of the accused in the criminal conspiracy to destroy the mosque, when asked about the events of that fateful day had replied sarcastically "the *dhancha* (disputed structure) fell down by itself". Those of us who had been eyewitness to the crime that changed the course of Indian politics a few weeks earlier, dismissed the off-hand comment as an attempt at humour and pressed him further to which he replied the destruction was an "outpouring of emotions by the *kar sevaks*" who had gathered in lakhs in the tiny temple town of Ayodhya. However, 28 years later, the "joke" has been turned into a reality!'[2] Was the mosque even ever standing in the first place? Not there in any case. That exact spot was where Lord Ram was born. Oh, never mind that Tulsidas, the great saint of the 16th century renowned for his devotion to Rama, who lived near the spot, never mentioned Ramjanmabhoomi in any of his writings, or in his words of wisdom. But why are we nitpicking? Weren't we told by the special court that it held the 1992 demolition 'an egregious violation of the rule of law' that was not pre-planned, and the accused persons were 'trying to stop the mob and not incite them'? If nobody demolished the mosque, maybe we were all experiencing a collective hallucination that the mosque was there in the first place!

The mosque was an ugly pothole blocking the relentless march of Hindutva. Out of sheer shame, or maybe self-abnegation, the mosque collapsed on its own.

Its sorry fate, though, emboldened the attackers who were drunk on the power of sheer numbers. When the Babri Masjid was demolished wall by wall, dome by dome, niche by niche, Uttar Pradesh was under the watchful eye of Kalyan Singh, not renowned for being a fan of the pluralist ethos of the country. Soon after taking over as the chief minister of the state in 1991, he is said to have gone to Ayodhya to take a pledge to construct a Ram temple at the very site of the Babri Masjid. A little earlier, he had pledged to uphold the Constitution of India and discharge his duties without fear or favour during his swearing-in ceremony as the chief minister. Long after the demolition of the mosque, the Supreme Court of India gave Singh a day-long jail sentence for contempt of court as he had given an affidavit to the court assuring it that no damage would be done to the Babri Masjid before the Kar Seva (service by religious volunteers for building the Ram temple at Ayodhya) that was being planned. Singh could not have been more pleased. He had, after all, earlier stated, 'I am ready to go to jail not once but hundreds of times for the Ram temple. I own to up the responsibility for whatever happened.'[3]

The little tap on the knuckles sent a message down the line. Many more were ready to go to jail, not once but many times over, as long as a mosque, and not just the one built by Babur's General Mir Baqi, was demolished. Of course, it helped that the jail sentence was not likely to be long or rigorous. A little under 10 years after Singh's loud proclamations, a tragedy visited Gujarat. The state of the Mahatma was then ruled by Narendra Modi, who was not a member of the state Legislative Assembly. In February–March 2002, the state saw some of the worst communal violence. The mayhem claimed, according to official figures, the lives of around a thousand people. The unofficial figures were three times over. Besides mortal beings and their dwellings, unofficial sources suggested, hundreds of Muslim places of worship, mosques and dargahs were damaged, the former used almost exclusively by Muslim men, the latter by men and women of all faiths. That did not matter. Both were identified as symbols of the largest minority, who formed a little under 10 per cent of Gujarat's population. They had to be done away with as the 90 per cent felt threatened. Or maybe they felt emboldened. Nobody even whispered the word 'Islamophobia' then. The violence was called a 'communal clash'—an expression that denotes a local element of passing fury rather than a considered and coordinated attack on a community.

Much of the Indian media refrained from going into the details of attacks on mosques and madrasas, though some did write about a dargah that was first bulldozed, then levelled overnight. Few tears were shed for the 300-year-old shrine of Vali Gujarati. It was left to *The Guardian* to state things with the honesty that was needed. It wrote,

> Two hundred and thirty unique Islamic monuments, including an exquisite 400-year-old mosque, were destroyed or vandalised during the recent anti-Muslim riots in the Indian State of Gujarat, according to a local survey. Experts say the damage is so extensive that it rivals the better publicised destruction of the Bamiyan Buddhas in Afghanistan or the wrecking of Tibet's monasteries by the Red Guards. Several monuments have been reduced to rubble in the course of the riot, in which 2,000 people, mainly Muslims, have died. In other disturbances, Hindu gangs have smashed delicate mosque screens, thrown bricks at Persian inscriptions, and set fire to old Korans.[4]

Even after *The Guardian* drew a parallel between the deliberate wreckage of culture and heritage in Gujarat with the destruction of the Bamiyan Buddhas, no Indian political party sought even a reconstruction of the places of worship, forget mourning for the dead. The prayer houses were demolished, levelled, forgotten.

The Gujarat model of 2002 reached Delhi some 17 years later. A mosque in Dwarka, the colony near the international airport that came up almost despite itself around two decades ago, was repeatedly attacked. Another mosque in the city, in Bijwasan, also came under repeated assault, first in 2019, then during the pandemic in 2020. The same pandemic which drove people indoors during the lockdown from 24 March to mid-May 2020 also failed to prevent another attack by a 200-strong mob on a mosque in Delhi's Alipur locality. The men ransacked this mosque, partially burnt its walls and broke its roof. The incident took place barely a few kilometres from the residence of the Delhi chief minister, and a few more from the police headquarters. No questions were asked. The next morning, it was business as usual. Delhi was at peace with frequent attacks on Muslim places of worship.

The Wire reported,

> In a notice issued on the Commissioner of Delhi police today, the chairman of the panel, Zafar-ul Islam Khan stated that the Commission has received a report and a video which says that at around 8 pm on April 3, around 200 people attacked a mosque in Mukhmelpur village under the Alipur police station in North West Delhi while there were two or three persons inside. The notice said the mob attacked the mosque, ransacked it, burnt it partially and demolished some of its parts, including the roof. It further said that it was unbelievable that this could happen in the national capital. "The issue cannot be patched up artificially by arranging a compromise where a religious place has been ransacked and partially burnt and demolished. If no proper legal action is taken, this lawlessness will become common," the Commission cautioned.[5]

A few days later, the fortnightly *Frontline* reported,

> Twenty-four such attacks have taken place on Delhi's Muslim houses of worship this year, spreading fear among the minority community. Some of them are too afraid to even register a formal complaint with the police, preferring to settle for negotiations under duress with the vandals. Take, for instance, the Dwarka mosque, located near Shahjahanabad Apartments in Sector 11, which has been repeatedly targeted. When miscreants attacked the mosque in February, the police defused the situation and brought about an amicable solution with local Hindu residents expressing regret. In fact, many members of the majority community went out of their way to instil confidence among Muslims by leaving messages of communal amity at the mosque's gateway. The mosque authorities installed a CCTV (closed-circuit television) in the front portion of the building to prevent further violence. Prayer services continued.[6]

Not for very long though. At the height of the pandemic, with markets still not fully open and shoppers still too fearful to step out, a repeat attack took place on 14 June, with Hindutva vigilante groups allegedly throwing stones at the mosque in the wee hours of the morning. Fortunately, no one was injured as the only person present at that time was the imam. He alerted local residents. A police complaint was filed when it was discovered that this time the attackers did not use the front portion of the mosque where the CCTV was installed, but instead threw stones from the road running parallel to the mosque. The media in Delhi underplayed the attack. Asad Ashraf of Karvaan India was among the few to write of the attack, stating, 'Four months after the last attack on the Mosque at sector 11 Dwarka in the heart of India's capital New Delhi, Hindutva vigilantes allegedly targeted the same mosque on the night of June 14, 2020, yet again and pelted stones from across the road running parallel to the mosque. However, there was no casualty reported (sic).'[7]

A few days later, the Jama Masjid Bijaswan in south-west Delhi was targeted. An attempt was made to place curbs on prayers, with 'outsiders' not being allowed by local goons to offer Friday prayers at the mosque. In the words of two writers from news portal India Tomorrow, 'They are also not allowing any Muslim from outside the village to offer daily five times prayers or even Friday prayers. There are about 300 Muslims from outside living in rented houses in the village but they are not allowed to pray in the mosque on account of them being outsiders to the village.'[8]

Nobody defined who an outsider was. A Delhiite from another part of the city? An Indian from the neighbouring state of Haryana? Or a foreigner? A desperate and uneasy truce was arrived at and forgotten was the basic azaan, the invitation sent to one and all to come for prayers and success. Talking of the azaan, it was this prayer call that the attackers had objected to first; next, it was the worshippers. Finally, the imam, who was not allowed entry. In the end, the mosque was forcibly locked. The local Muslims were browbeaten. Nobody was named in the FIR filed after the stone pelting incident, nobody sought judicial recourse.

Reported *The Hindu*,

> Two persons were arrested after they locked a local mosque and prevented the Imam from entering the place of worship in south west Delhi's Bijwasan village, said a senior police officer on Sunday… A local said that there are only a few houses of Muslims in the area, dominated by Hindus. In the past, an anti-social had tried to disrupt peace by targeting the only mosque in the village by restricting outsiders to visit the mosque for

Friday prayers. A few locals had earlier threatened and abused the Imam and asked him to vacate the area. A complaint was made to the police.⁹

The Bijwasan Masjid's azaan silenced itself. Like the Babri Masjid had collapsed on its own. Like the Vali Gujarati shrine caved in on its own. The Bijwasan Masjid silenced itself into submission.

In India, the Muslim places of worship are no longer targeted. They just disappear on their own. The one that did not in East Champaran, and came in the way of the victory celebrations of a newly elected BJP legislator Pawan Kumar Jaiswal in November 2020, was dealt with. Three worshippers suffered injuries as the victory procession stopped at the mosque to raise cries of 'Jai Shri Ram', a slogan increasingly in danger of being reduced to a vehicle of hate rather than being the greeting of much warmth it once was. Stones were hurled inside the mosque which, fortunately, did not suffer serious damage. The sunset prayers were then on within the mosque.

The news portal Muslim Mirror quoted a local journalist, Anzar Ahmed Sadique, 'They started creating much disturbance [with louder music and dance] outside the mosque.'¹⁰ When one of the devotees asked them to move ahead as people in the mosque were being disturbed by the loud music, the rioters resorted to pelting stones at the shrine.

The inherent tenet of justice, the protection of the weak from the powerful, was once again turned on its head. Some small-time workers were questioned by the police, the big fish being allowed to swim away. An uneasy truce was arrived at yet again, a truce that preferred peace over justice.

Elsewhere, not far from south Delhi, in the summer of 2023, when two other mosques were set ablaze in Gurugram and Sohna in Haryana. Reporting on the killing of the nineteen-year-old imam and the Gurugram mosque being torched, NDTV said:

> A mob attacked a mosque in Gurugram, killed one person, and injured several others just past midnight, police have said. The mosque, Anjuman Jama Masjid in Sector 57, was also set on fire. Fire control trucks were rushed to the spot and brought the fire under control. Union Minister and Gurugram MP Rao Inderjit Singh confirmed to NDTV that there was an attack on a mosque in Gurugram in which two people including the imam were shot.

The mosque in neighbouring Sohna was also charred by Hindutva proponents around the same time, despite an assurance of peace earlier. In early August 2023, The Quint reported,

> A mosque was vandalised in Haryana's Sohna on Tuesday, 1 August, a day after violence erupted in different parts of the state, starting from Nuh. The mosque, Shahi Jama Masjid, was attacked at around 2 pm on Tuesday, just hours after a peace march was held by the police and district authorities in the area. The caretaker of the mosque, Shamim Ahmed, said that a mob of around 200 men, with their faces covered, barged in during the afternoon and began destroying 'whatever came in their path.' 'We were about 50 people—including children who study here. We were hidden in the inner rooms of the mosque. It must have appeared to them that the mosque is empty, or they wouldn't have spared us. We would have died today,' Ahmed told The Quint… The mosque's prayer hall was vandalised, with the windows broken and glass shards spread all over. The van of

one of the mosque committee members, washroom, fans and other items too were damaged.

Sohna, Gurugram, Alipur, Bijwasan… The attacks on mosques were constant, and usually unprovoked. Just the fact that a mosque stood there, and people prayed in it, was sufficient to arouse hatred. The FIRs were filed against unknown persons, essentially giving a clean chit to all the assailants. Just like the Babri Masjid, these mosques also probably vandalized themselves. As mosques continued to be burnt down with increasing frequency post-2020, it not only amounted to a denial of the right to worship for Muslims, but also the failure of the state to guarantee their right to life and property as Indian citizens.

It takes us back to the words of MS Golwalkar, guru to millions, who, clearly inspired by Mussolini and Hitler, once said,

> Ever since that evil day, when Moslems first landed in Hindustan, right up to the present moment the Hindu Nation has been gallantly fighting on to take on these despoilers… The Race Spirit has been awakening… In Hindustan, the land of the Hindus, lives and should live the Hindu Nation… All others are either traitors and enemies to the Nation, or, to take a charitable view, idiots. The foreign races in Hindustan… may stay in the country, wholly subordinated to the Hindu Nation, claiming nothing, deserving no privileges, far less any preferential treatment—not even citizens' rights.[11]

The Muslims are to stay 'wholly subordinated to the Hindu Nation…claiming nothing…not even citizens' rights'.

17

Namaz, the Art of the Impossible

ONE EVENING IN MID-OCTOBER 2022 in village Bhora Kalan in Gurugram, a mob of over 200 attacked a small mosque where six Muslim men were offering Isha, the last prayers of the day. The attackers locked up the worshippers, who were forced to call the local police for help. The police's arrival did help, and the crowd thinned out. A truce was brokered by the police, and the vastly outnumbered Muslim community (the village has only around 200–250 Muslims and 30,000 Hindus) agreed not to press charges. They gave it in writing. The Hindu community agreed to maintain peace, too, though no assurance was given in writing.

Instead Yajinder Sharma, a resident, is reported to have said while campaigning door to door, 'There was no need for a mosque in the village… We won't let them build one. It is just a hall that they have converted from within.'[1]

About a year earlier, in the supposedly cosmopolitan part of Gurgaon (now Gurugram), for weeks on end, aggressive displays of Hindutva foot soldiers and mid-rankers were seen every Friday as Muslims gathered to offer weekly prayers in what was otherwise a car park. As Muslim men, caps on their heads, prayer mats tucked under their arms and heads bowed, walked towards the prayer site, they were almost invariably accosted by belligerent Hindu men wearing saffron scarves and tilaks on their foreheads. Amidst loud cries of 'Jai Shri Ram', Muslim men were told to go home. One Friday was particularly bad. The opponents of namaz had used every trick in the book to disrupt the prayers, including playing loud music at the time of namaz and reciting shlokas on a microphone, but had failed to stop the namaz, for conducting which the local administration had already given permission. The administration had granted permission to use the car park, in addition to 108 other sites, for Friday prayers as there is an acute shortage of mosques in the township. With a population of over 1.5 million Muslims, Gurugram has only 13 mosques. For years, the weekly prayer went off peacefully. That is, until some Hindutva leaders complained in 2018 against namaz being held on public land.

Normally, such a complaint would have been brushed aside as Indian public spaces provide scenes of great religiosity on a regular basis. Many Hindu festivals, including Holi, Vinayak Chaturthi and Dussehra, are celebrated in public parks, large barren stretches of land, even on roads. Gurdwaras, too, overflow with devotees on the birthdays of the Sikh gurus. On Fridays, similarly, mosques usually have more worshippers than they can accommodate in the premises. Muslim devotees are thus seen offering namaz outside the mosque, on pavements, parks and roads too. Some mosques obtain permission from the local authorities to use additional space for prayer for an hour or so every week. Many don't. Beyond stray cases of grumbling, not many complained about this in the years gone by. Indians have habitually made space for religion, whatever the hue—saffron, green, white or blue. A few in Gurugram didn't this time around.

One Friday morning, a few hours before the Muslim prayer, they spread cow-dung cakes at the site, rendering it unfit to be used for namaz in the afternoon. The belligerent opponents of namaz were not more than a handful. Unfortunately, they decided the discourse, with their leader Dinesh Thakur going to the extent of calling Friday prayers a part of 'land jihad'. Under pressure, the Gurugram administration whittled down the number of sites permitted for namaz to 37.

The Guardian wrote

> Every Friday for months, members of Hindu vigilante groups alongside local residents have been gathering, occasionally armed with axes and wooden rods, at the sites of namaz to try to stop them happening. Slogans including 'shoot the traitors' have been shouted and Hindu prayers and songs read out to try to drown out Qur'an readings. Cow dung has been placed at the sites and police have regularly had to hold back the mob so namaz could continue.[2]

One Friday, as the paper reported, Thakur rushed towards Shehzad Khan, the imam who was there to lead the prayer, and confronted him, getting within inches of his face shouting 'no namaz here', until he was dragged away by five police officers. As the Muslims filed silently into the area for namaz, a line of armed police held back the Hindu nationalist mob. Seven were detained by the police.

As *The Guardian* reported, "'Conducting namaz in the open is land jihad,' Thakur said before being arrested. "It's an international conspiracy. They do namaz outside, then they build a shrine, then they build a mosque and then inside the mosque they are harbouring terrorists and weapons and they are a threat to the nation. I will not stop my fight until this becomes illegal.'"[3]

Thakur got plenty of help in his 'fight'. He was detained or arrested more than once but always released soon afterwards. No Friday was he arrested/detained before he could reach the site of namaz. The same was true for his followers.

The popular portal Newslaundry reported on cow dung cakes being spread, on the occasion of Govardhan puja in November 2021, at the site of Muslim prayer.

'Hindu ke gadaro ko, goli maaro saalo ko.' (Shoot the enemies of Hindus.)

'Sector 12 toh sirf jhanki hai, pura Gurugram abhi baaki hai.' (Sector 12 is just the beginning, the whole of Gurugram is left.)

These are some of the slogans raised on November 5 at Gurugram's Sector 12A, where a Hindu right-wing group organised a Govardhan puja to protest against namaz being offered at a ground in the area.

The puja – or protest – was attended by the likes of Amit Hindu, who is associated with the Bajrang Dal and the Rashtriya Swayamsevak Sangh; Dinesh Bharti from the Bharat Mata Vahini; and BJP leader Kapil Mishra, who is well-known for his incendiary speech shortly before the Delhi riots last year.

Over the last two months, Hindu right-wing groups and locals have fanned communal tension in Gurugram, objecting to Muslims conducting their Friday prayers in the open… Seven days later, no action was taken by either the police or the district administration against those who raised the slogans… On November 12, namaz did not take place at the Sector 12A ground at all.[4]

The Muslims were quietly nudged out of yet another prayer space. New India made space for a puja in the park, failing to defend namaz at the same site.

There is a well-rehearsed pattern to it. First a mosque is attacked. Then Muslims praying in the open are attacked, booked and arrested. Finally, a handful of Muslims praying together at home are accused of disturbing public peace and communal harmony. The idea is not to maintain peace and order, the plan is to make offering namaz impossible, anywhere, everywhere.

A template was followed: After mosques were burnt down or damaged came the next stage of violence, the next phase of harassment. That stage was crossed when a handful of Muslims silently saying their prayers—perhaps on the pavement or in a corner outside a metro station or a secluded part of a railway platform or on board a moving train—were booked by the same police that turned a blind eye to processions of the majority community where members fearlessly carried around naked swords and tridents.

The subsequent stage was reached soon after. Within months of the first complaints of Muslims being filmed, warned or arrested for praying in a park or by the roadside, we had the sorry spectacle of a Muslim professor being sent on leave for praying on the lawns of his college; of a Muslim woman being warned for praying in a hospital room for the well-being of her ailing family member admitted there; and of some villagers in Moradabad complaining about a handful of men who had gathered in the house of a community member to say their prayers.

NDTV reported,

> For a 'mass gathering to offer namaz' at a house 'without prior permission', a police case has been registered against 26

Muslims at Dulhepur village in Uttar Pradesh's Moradabad district. The village does not have a mosque, and some residents have objected to gatherings for namaz, even if inside homes. Police cited 'objections from neighbours' and booked the namazis under Indian Penal Code's Section 505-2—technically speaking, for mischievous statements in a gathering performing religious worship. 'By reading the namaz in a gathering, these people are spreading hatred and enmity among people,' says the FIR registered on a complaint by local resident Chandra Pal Singh on August 24 (2022). Sixteen of the people have been named, while 10 others remain unidentified, all reported to be locals.[5]

Following a social media uproar, the local police cancelled the case a couple of days later. Meanwhile, the woman seen praying in a hospital in Prayagraj was warned for offering namaz. Imagine being warned for praying in private!

'Superintendent of Tej Bahadur Sapru Hospital Dr MK Akhauri said that Sabiha had come on Thursday to meet a patient admitted to the dengue ward, and suddenly in the afternoon, she started offering namaz there itself. Someone made a video of her, and posted it on social media, he said, adding, the hospital administration reached there, and warned the woman not to do it,' a Press Trust of India report in *The Indian Express* reads.[6]

From trying to demolish a mosque to disrupting a Muslim prayer in a public space, or defiling a sacred Muslim space, such as by urinating there, the attempt has always been to invisibilize Muslims, harass them and intimidate them into submission. If in the case of mosques, the objection was to the azaan, to namaz—whether that involves someone praying in peace and quiet by the roadside or a man quietly offering his prayer sitting on his seat in a train—there could be no such complaint of disturbance to pedestrians or those around. Just the visual of a Muslim woman or man prostrating in prayer was enough to outrage the sensibilities of the Right-wing crowd, as was the case with the professor of Shri Varshney college in Aligarh who was found praying all alone in a corner of the campus park in May 2022. Following protests by the BJP Yuva Morcha, the principal of the college constituted an inquiry committee. Before it could submit its findings, the academic was sent on a month's leave. The principal assured that 'further action will be taken only after the report is received'.[7]

With every prayer session came accusatory cries of 'land jihad', 'economic jihad', even allegations of conversion! No excuse remained untapped in the relentless bid to throw a marginalized community completely off the public square, mind and vision. The incidents were never about upholding law and order, public safety or the smooth flow of passengers or traffic. They were simply to send a message to a minority community that graded citizenship was now a lived reality in the country. All are equal but some are less equal than others in New India. Clinching evidence for this came when a group of men in Moradabad's Lajpat Nagar locality were fined Rs 5 lakh each for offering Taraweeh (special congregational prayers on Ramzan) in a private warehouse in March 2023. Earlier, the Bajrang Dal State President Rohan Saxena, along with a group of men, had barged into the godown of one Zakir Hussain and stopped the Taraweeh. In a video that went viral on the internet, Saxena said Hussain had started a 'new tradition' by holding prayer meetings at his home and that he would not allow it. He warned that if the police failed to file an FIR, the Bajrang Dal would hold an agitation. The police obliged by sending notices to the Muslims. And the larger Muslim community was sent a message.

18

Following the Babri Template

BACK IN 1990, IT WAS not easy being a Muslim in Uttar Pradesh. The satellite township of Noida on the outskirts of Delhi was still very young. Law and order were not exactly its best claim to fame. An unspoken tension hung in the air as the local units of the Vishwa Hindu Parishad and Bajrang Dal went door to door pasting stickers seeking to instill pride in being a Hindu. 'Garv se kaho main Hindu hun (Say that you're Hindu with pride)' read a little sticker found pasted on doors and even cash counters of local grocery shops and chemists. The idea behind the stickers seemed to not be so much the revival of pride in Hinduism but sending a message to non-Hindus. Frankly, it was unsettling. Days were relatively peaceful, but evenings arrived with a sense of foreboding. It was after sundown that young men, seemingly back from colleges and day-time jobs, wore saffron bandanas, picked up tridents and maybe a sword or two to take out what was then described as a peaceful procession for the construction of a Ram Lalla temple in Ayodhya.

As a young man, I often stood in the balcony area of my house to look at these men, taking care to switch off the lights so that the processionists could not see me. It was less out of curiosity, more a measure to overcome any cowardice in my heart. It was a hard reality I had to confront. Every evening I heard slogans, 'Ayodhya toh jhanki hai, Kashi–Mathura baki hai' (Ayodhya is a trailer, Kashi-Mathura is yet to see the same fate) and 'Bachcha bachcha Ram ka, Ramjanmabhoomi ke kaam ka... Jis Hindu ka khoon na khaula, khoon nahin woh pani hai, Ram ke kaam na aayi woh bekar jawaani hai' (Every child belongs to Ram, every child is for Ramjanmabhoomi's cause; whichever Hindu's blood does not boil, that is not blood but water, for a youth not spent in Ram's service is a youth wasted). Of course, there was that one which equated cemeteries and Pakistan, giving the Muslims two options, die and be buried, or migrate. The firebrand brigade screamed with tridents and swords in hand, 'Musalman ke do hi sthhan, Qabrastan ya Pakistan' (Only two places for a Muslim, graveyard or Pakistan). Left, right or behind, wherever I looked, mine was the only Muslim family.

On the evening of 6 December 1992 after the Babri Masjid had been reduced to rubble, some volunteers in Noida sought to distribute sweets, calling it prasad. After giving a little portion, they would invariably tell the recipient, 'Sab Ram ji ki kripa hai. Aage Mathura–Kashi hai. Hans ke li hai Ayodhya, ladh ke lenge Kashi–Mathura' (All Ram's grace. Mathura–Kashi lie ahead. We have laughingly taken Ayodhya, we shall take Kashi–Mathura after a battle). They were soon eased out of the middle-class residential colonies by the police. But they left an indelible impression on all. The fight, which started with the 1949 placement of idols inside the Babri Masjid compound and resulted in the demolition of the mosque almost 43 years later, was not about to end. Rather, it will not be allowed to end anytime soon. For on the wishlist of the Hindutva brigade was not only building a temple for Ram—

Ayodhya already had scores of temples, many of which claimed to be the actual birthplace of Lord Ram—but using religion as a political currency. After Ram, it will be Shiva, then Krishna, then… the listless is endless.

Barely a few months after the Supreme Court's judgment on Ayodhya, on 9 November 2019, a little-known sadhu outfit sprung up to seek the abrogation of a section of the Places of Worship (Special Provisions) Act 1991. The Act, cleared at the height of the Ayodhya campaign, seeks to preserve the status of each place of worship as it existed on 15 August 1947. The Act was passed to send a message to the larger society and polity that the state was duty bound to protect each place of worship as it existed at the time of our Independence. Incidentally, the Supreme Court's verdict on the Babri Masjid issue itself stated that 'law cannot be used as a device to reach back in time and provide a legal remedy to every person who disagrees with the course which history has taken'.[1]

The words failed to dissuade a group of Hindu priests from doing exactly that: use the law to reach back in time to seek a remedy for any perceived wrongs of history. Seven months after the Supreme Court's Babri Masjid verdict, the Lucknow-based Vishwa Bhadra Pujari Purohit Mahasangh filed a petition in the Supreme Court through Advocate Vishnu Jain in June, seeking directions to declare Section 4 of the 1991 Act as ultra vires. The petitioners insisted that the remarks made in the Ayodhya verdict were mere observations without any judicial force as the Places of Worship Act was not under challenge in that case. 'The impugned Act has barred the right and remedy against encroachment made on religious property of Hindus exercising might of power by followers of another faith,' the petition contended.[2]

The little-known Hindu body alleged that the Act prevents Hindus from seeking redress for their grievances in civil courts and from invoking the jurisdiction of High Courts under Article 226 of the Constitution. It further claimed that the majority community was discriminated against because it was not able to have the religious character of endowments, temples and mutts restored, as these were encroached upon before 15 August 1947. 'The Parliament by making an impugned provision has without resolution of dispute, through process of court, abated the suit and proceedings, which is per se unconstitutional and beyond its law-making power,' the petition stated.[3]

Soon after the petition was filed, the Jamiat Ulama-i-Hind decided to challenge it in the apex court. It filed a plea that the court should not entertain the petition. Advocate-on-record Ejaz Maqbool filed the plea on behalf of the Jamiat's president, Arshad Madani. The plea, as reported by *Frontline*, stated: 'At the outset this application is being filed to oppose the present writ petition, so that this court is pleased to not issue notice in the present petition. It is submitted that even issuance of notice in the present matter will create fear in the minds of the Muslim community regarding their places of worship, especially in the aftermath of the Ayodhya dispute, and will destroy the secular fabric of the nation.'[4]

The Jamiat plea said that the Mahasangh petition assumed that Section 4 of the Places of Worship Act, 1991, 'validates the alleged illegal and barbarous action of invaders who had converted the Hindu places of worship by restricting rights of Hindus'.[5] It pointed out that the petition sought to indirectly target places of worship that were at present of a Muslim character. The Muslim body also pointed out that the Places of Worship Act applied to all places of worship and was not limited to any one community.

A Muslim, too, could not demand restoration of a mosque if it had been turned into a temple, as was the case in many instances in Punjab and Haryana where many mosques had fallen into the hands of local Hindu and Sikh communities after the large-scale migration of Muslims to Pakistan in 1947.

The Jamiat added that the Places of Worship (Special Provisions) Act was enacted to fulfill two purposes. First, to prohibit the conversion of any place of worship and in doing so speak to the future by mandating that the character of a place of public worship shall not be altered. Second, the law seeks to impose a positive obligation to maintain the religious character of every place of worship as it existed on 15 August 1947. The Jamiat plea said that the court recognized these purposes in its recent judgment in *M. Siddiq* v. *Suresh Das*, popularly known as the Babri Masjid–Ram Janmabhoomi verdict, which noted that the Places of Worship (Special Provisions) Act, 1991, protected and secured the fundamental values of the Constitution.

'Ultimately this court concluded that the Places of Worship (Special Provisions) Act, 1991, imposes a non-derogable obligation towards enforcing our commitment to secularism under the Indian Constitution. It was further observed that it was legislative instrument designed to protect the secular features of the Indian polity, which is one of the basic features of the Constitution,' the Jamiat petition stated.[6]

The Jamiat, which was a party in the Babri Masjid case, too, approaching the court had a ring of déjà vu to it. Then too the case had started with a little-known Hindu saint's plea. The RSS had stayed away though only technically, preferring to lend all support from outside. This time too, the RSS chief Mohan Bhagwat refused to give a categorical answer about the possible involvement of the RSS in the plea for the restoration of Hindu places of worship. Commenting on this silence, The Quint said, 'Interestingly, Bhagwat was asked twice by reporters if the RSS had plans to move forward with building temples at Kashi and Mathura, two towns also considered holy for Hindus. Bhagwat, however, offered no response at all. Since the destruction of the Babri Masjid in 1992, a parallel demand among right-wing groups' claims over the Gyanvapi mosque in Varanasi (Kashi) and the Shahi Idgah in Mathura have gained currency.'[7]

'The Sangh does not work for andolan or movements, it works for manushya nirmaan or fostering humanity,' Bhagwat said.[8]

Shortly after the Hindu pontiffs' petition, the Jamiat chief Arshad Madani could see the emerging picture of the days to come. He told *Frontline*,

> After the Babri Masjid verdict, sectarian powers have felt emboldened. But they cannot be allowed to play with the intrinsic pluralist ethos of the nation. We have approached the Supreme Court to protect historic mosques, many of which could be on the wish list of bigoted elements. Already, there have been media reports of fresh activity in the vicinity of the Gyanvapi mosque in Varanasi with land around the mosque being levelled and smaller temples demolished to pave the way for a grand Kasi Viswanath temple. If not stopped today, these elements will not stop at anything. They have in the past laid claim to the Taj Mahal too.[9]

He was right. Even before he expressed the apprehension, Baba Balak Das of Varanasi's Patalpuri Math had asked the Muslim community to hand over the site at Kashi and Mathura to Hindus of their own volition. 'In the interest of long-lasting peace and communal harmony, Muslims should amicably hand over these sites to us,' he is reported to have said.[10]

With the construction of the proposed Ram temple to begin soon at Ram Janmabhoomi in Ayodhya, fringe Hindutva outfits have started flexing their muscles with slogans of 'liberating' the Kashi Vishwanath temple from the 'clutches' of the Gyanvapi mosque in Varanasi. New organizations have sprung up in Varanasi claiming ownership of the movement. Two such organizations, the Akhil Bharatiya Sant Samiti and the Shri Kashi Vishwanath Mukti Andolan, have announced immediate programmes to commence a mass movement.[11]

According to journalist Tripathi's report,

> Liberating the Ram Janmabhoomi temple was the first phase of our movement, and it is now complete. The second phase will involve the freeing of the Kashi Vishwanath temple from the stranglehold of the Gyanvapi mosque. The third phase will focus on the liberation of the Krishna Janmabhoomi temple in Mathura. These are the only three temples the Hindu samaj wants. Now that the Ram temple project is over [that is, the Supreme Court verdict that the disputed site in Ayodhya should be given for the construction of a Ram temple], we will start work on the second phase,' said Baba Balak Das, the national spokesman of the Akhil Bharatiya Sant Samiti. The samiti he claims to represent is an umbrella organisation of 18.5 lakh sants from all over India.[12]

The fringe outfits decided to hold a grand puja for Shringaar Gauri and Mukti Andolan; taking a leaf out of the Ramjanmabhoomi campaign which began with cries of 'Jai Shri Ram', they launched a Har-Har Mahadev campaign, exhorting the Hindus to blow the conch, beat ghanta-ghariyal (a ritual bell) and chant Har-Har Mahadev for complete possession of the Kasi Viswanath temple–Gyanvapi Masjid complex. In May 2022, claims were made that the Gyanvapi Masjid had a Shivling in the pond on the premises, which was used for the performance of ablutions before daily namaz. NDTV reported,

> After a sensational claim by Hindu petitioners that a Shivling had been found in a pond at the Gyanvapi Masjid complex in Uttar Pradesh's Varanasi, a court ordered it sealed. The Shivling (symbol of Lord Shiva) was said to be found this morning, on the last day of the court-mandated filming of the mosque complex following a petition seeking access to pray at a shrine behind the mosque. Water was drained from the pond and a Shivling was found, claimed Subhash Nandan Chaturvedi, the lawyer representing a group of Hindu women who have sought year-long access to pray at the shrine.[13]

Even as the faithful's sentiments are beginning to be whipped up over the Gyanvapi Masjid–Kashi Viswanath temple controversy, what was not allowed to enter into public discourse was the actual history of the place, the beliefs and politics of the Mughal emperor Aurangzeb, the age-old villain for Right-wing propaganda. The fact that Aurangzeb issued a farman in 1659, soon after ascending the throne, wherein he pulled up Mughal officials who were accused of harassing the Brahmins of Varanasi was almost totally ignored. With a touching faith in the goodwill of the Brahmins, Aurangzeb asked his officials to let the Brahmins live in peace so they could pray for the continuance of his Empire.

As Audrey Truschke commented in the Quartz,

> Writing in February of 1659 Aurangzeb said he had learned that 'several people have, out of spite and rancour, harassed the Hindu residents of Benares and nearby places, including a group of Brahmins who are in charge of ancient temples there.'

The king then ordered his officials: 'You must see that nobody unlawfully disturbs the Brahmins or other Hindus of that region, so that they might remain in their traditional place and pray for the continuance of the Empire.' The ending of the 1659 Benares farman became a common refrain in the many imperial commands penned by Aurangzeb that protected temples and their caretakers: they should be left alone so that Brahmins could pray for the longevity of the Mughal state.

As a matter of fact, in Varanasi, in 1687, Aurangzeb gave a piece of land near the ghat to a certain Ramjivan Gosain to build residential dwellings for Brahmins and holy faqirs.

As for the Kashi temple, noted scholar Catherine Asher wrote in *Architecture of Mughal India*, 'The destruction of Raja Man Singh's famous Vishvanath temple in Benares was largely to punish Hindus, especially those related to the temple's patron, who were suspected of supporting the Maratha Shivaji.'[14]

The Kashi Viswanath project, inaugurated by prime minister Narendra Modi towards the end of 2021, aims at a grand new Kashi Viswanath temple and has striking similarities with the acquisition and demolition of properties around the Babri Masjid that were carried out in Ayodhya between October 1991 and December 1992 by the BJP government led by Kalyan Singh in Uttar Pradesh. The state government had then acquired 2.77 acres of land in Ayodhya adjoining the Babri Masjid and the Ram Chabutra (Ram's platform) used for Hindu worship in October 1991. This area had many temples, places of religious worship and other structures. The reason stated by the government for the acquisition then was the 'beautification and modernisation' of the temple town of Ayodhya and some of its structures. But Sangh Parivar outfits, led by the Vishwa Hindu Parishad and the Bajrang Dal made it clear that the acquisition was in fact for the construction of a grand temple—much like what happened a little under 30 years later in Varanasi with the clearing of the area around the Viswanath temple, including the razing of some age-old small temples. Back in 1991, government agencies had demolished scores of structures around the Babri Masjid and the Ram Chabutra, including temples like Sumitra Bhawan and Sakshi Gopal Mandir. The priests of these temples, Mahant Raj Mangal Das and Mahant Ram Kripal Das, raised objections to the demolition spree and approached the High Court and the Supreme Court. The limited demolition exercise culminated in the final razing of the Babri Masjid in December 1992.

The *Frontline* reported, 'Nearly 26 years later, yet another BJP administration is invoking the "beautification and modernisation" mantra to unleash yet another round of frenzied acquisition and demolition. According to informal estimates, as of the second week of November 2018, as many as 168 structures, including about 95 residential buildings, have been taken over. Demolition of these buildings is at various stages of completion. The number of temples and places of worship that have been demolished would be approximately 55, say social activists associated with the Joint Action Committee and the Sajja Sanskriti Manch, which has been monitoring the demolitions.'[15]

The Muslim community leaders, meanwhile, expressed fear that they were looking at a possible Babri Masjid Part II. More so because there were unconfirmed reports of azaan not being allowed at the Gyanvapi Masjid. Even as the governments at the Centre and state kept a rehearsed silence, social media was agog with lists of numerous mosques that were built allegedly by destroying Hindu places of worship. 'If the present petition is entertained, it will open floodgates of litigation against countless mosques in the country and the religious divide from which the country is recovering in the aftermath of the Ayodhya dispute will only be widened,' Arshad Madani, president, Jamiatul Ulama-i-Hind, told the author.

The petition though was entertained with a Varanasi fast-track court ruling in the Gyanvapi case on 17 November 2022, that an application filed by the Hindu plaintiffs seeking to bar Muslims from entering the Gyanvapi mosque premises was maintainable, thereby rejecting the application of the Anjuman Intezamia Masjid Committee. The application sought the possession of the Gyanvapi premises on behalf of the deity Lord Visheshwar Virajman. It also sought the unfettered right for Hindus to perform worship activities there and sought a prohibitory injunction against the masjid panel and any of its members or agents from interfering in these activities. The application sought that the structure currently standing at the site be 'removed'. This ruling came even as the Supreme Court extended interim orders directing that no Muslims be prevented from offering prayers at the Gyanvapi mosque and that the site of dispute be protected until further orders. 'Suit filed by Hindus in Gyanvapi case maintainable, says Varanasi court... Court says religious character of site as on Aug 15, 1947 "doubtful", suit not barred by Places of Worship Act,' *The Hindu* reported in November 2022.[16] The Varanasi court order followed the one on 26 April 2022, when a videographic survey of the Gyanvapi complex was ordered. On 6 May, the inspection began amidst heavy security, and on 16 May, the court was informed by the Hindu side that a shivling was found inside a pond in the mosque complex. On the same day, the court directed the District Magistrate to seal the place where the said shivling had been recovered. This order came a day before the Supreme Court was set to hear the Masjid Committee's plea challenging the Allahabad High Court order, which had dismissed their appeal against this survey. What began as a single petition by five Hindu women in 2021 seeking access to pray inside the precincts of the Gyanvapi Masjid, which they alleged was built on the ruins of a Shiva temple, had risen to 15 separate petitions by November 2022, with the members of the majority community virtually seeking a replay of the Babri Masjid verdict. By July 2023, a team from the Archaeological Survey of India had started a 'scientific survey' of the mosque even as the mosque management committee filed a petition in the Supreme Court against the Varanasi district court's order allowing the inspection. The survey—which began at 7 am—extended to all areas except the sealed wuzukhana (place for ablutions before namaz), where a structure that Hindu litigants claimed to be a Shivling was allegedly found during an earlier survey in 2022. The mosque management committee boycotted the survey. The Allahabad High Court stayed the survey till 3 August 2023.

It did not dissuade the state's chief minister, Yogi Adityanath from asking Muslims to give up their right over the mosque. Like LK Advani started calling Babri Masjid, Babri Dhancha (structure) around 1989, Adityanath too did not call Gyanvapi Masjid a mosque. Speaking to NDTV at the time when the mosque's survey had been stopped by the court, and hours before two mosques were torched in neighbouring Haryana, he said,

> If we call it a mosque, there will be a dispute. I feel whoever has been blessed with sight by God, that person should see. What is a trishul (trident) doing inside a mosque. We did not put it there. There is a jyotirlinga, dev pratimas (idols)…
>
> The walls are screaming and saying something. I feel there should be a proposal from the Muslim society that there has been a historical mistake and we need a solution.[17]

In a piece analyzing how 'a Hindu march turned riotous', which underscored 'how the partisan stances of India's top Hindu leaders have given license to chaotic elements in the country,' *The New York Times* said,

> Both Mr. Modi and Mr. Adityanath, and indeed the whole nationalist movement led by Mr. Modi, are widely understood to stand on the same side of any conflict that pits India's Hindus — who make up almost 80 percent of the country's population of 1.4 billion — against its Muslims, who make up its largest minority, at roughly 14 percent...

In the summer of 2022-23, we could as well have been in the cold winter of 1989-90.

Meanwhile, in Mathura, where local residents had initially foiled attempts to start a movement for the restoration of Krishnajanmabhoomi in place of the Eidgah Masjid, there were 12 lawsuits in various courts seeking to prove it was the birthplace of Shri Krishna. The reek of the Babri Masjid stir was too pungent to ignore.

Madani's words were almost a reiteration of what Muslim leaders had said at the time of the Ayodhya controversy back in the late 1980s and early 1990s. When some far-Right Hindu leaders and even some members of the Muslim community asked Muslims to surrender their claim over the mosque in Ayodhya to promote communal harmony, the leaders had expressed apprehension that this could embolden the Hindutva forces further. Much like what Madani said after the Mathura petition was filed by a Hindu body.

Madani's words came true shortly after. Within six months of the Mathura petition being filed, another petition was filed in Delhi seeking the restoration of an alleged temple in the Qutb Minar complex! A civil suit was filed before Delhi's Saket Court alleging that the Quwwat-Ul-Islam Masjid situated within the Qutb Minar complex in Mehrauli was built in a temple complex. The plea, filed on behalf of Jain deity Tirthankar Lord Rishabh Dev and Hindu deity Lord Vishnu (through their next friends, much like a petition on behalf of Ram Lalla in the Ayodhya case), sought restoration of the alleged temple complex, which supposedly consisted of as many as 27 temples.

The *National Herald* reported,

> The plea alleged that 27 Hindu and Jain temples were dismantled, desecrated and damaged under the command of Mughal emperor Qutub-Din-Aibak, who raised some construction at the same very place of temples naming it as, "Quwwat-Ul-Islam Mosque". It is submitted that the Mughal ruler failed to completely demolish the existing temples and only partial demolition was carried out and after reusing the material of the temples, the said mosque was erected.[18]

According to a *Herald* report,

> The petitioners urged the court to decree the suit in nature of declaration, declaring that deity Tirthankar Lord Rishabh Dev and deity Lord Vishnu, along with Lord Ganesh, Lord Shiva, Goddess Gauri, God Sun, Lord Hanuman including presiding deities of 27 temples, have right to be restored and worshiped with rites & rituals, performance of regular pooja within the temple complex situated in the area of Qutb Complex in Mehrauli.

The petitioners in the *Tirthankar Lord Rishab Dev v. the Union of India and others* obviously knew very little history. Qutb ud-Din Aibak came more than 300 years before the Mughals. Once a slave of Mohammed Ghori, he founded the Mamluk or Slave Dynasty in 1206, and is considered the first sultan of the Delhi Sultanate. But such is the Hindu Right's preoccupation with the Mughals that everything Muslim is considered the work of the Mughals!

As in the Mathura case, a countersuit was filed stating that the said Quwwat-ul-Islam Masjid complex is a protected monument, declared as such under the Ancient Monuments Preservation Act of 1904. Incidentally, the Quwwat-ul-Islam Masjid—whose construction began in 1193 and was twice expanded, first under Iltutmish, then Alauddin Khilji—is considered the oldest extant mosque of north India. Its stature in the Sultanate days conferred on it the title of Jama Masjid. In December 2021, a Delhi court rejected the suit seeking the restoration of Hindu and Jain deities, stating, 'Wrongs may have been committed in the past, but such wrongs cannot be the basis for disturbing peace of our present and future.'[19]

Babri, Mathura Eidgah, Gyanvapi, Quwwat-ul-Islam… The list grows longer and longer. Always at the receiving end is the present-day Muslim community, being asked to atone for alleged wrongs committed 800 or more years ago. The government stays quiet. The petitions continue to be filed, their frequency increasing by the month. The minority community continues to live in fear. It is dark and lonely to be a Muslim in the age of Islamophobia.

19

'Jai Shri Ram', Again

ON 6 DECEMBER 1992, THE day the Babri Masjid was brought down by kar sevaks in Ayodhya, 'the atmosphere tense but under control' in the town, as Doordarshan was in the habit of describing any township that had registered a case of communal violence. In Noida too—where I lived and where the kar sevaks in the days gone by had announced their violent intention well in advance—things were 'tense but under control'. The evening was cold, dark and somewhat scary. Not many people ventured out. A handful of men were celebrating the 'success' in Ayodhya and distributing sweets from a local shop as a prasad but were quickly dispersed by the local police. Yet, tension hung in the air. There were rumours of the boundary wall of a mosque being attacked; it turned out that the mosque had no boundary wall, merely a barbed wire for a fence.

For hours that day, there were regular updates from Ayodhya about how the kar sevaks had brought down the 16th century mosque with their shovels and pickaxes, tridents and rods; how LK Advani, Murli Manohar Joshi and Uma Bharti were present there;[1]

a 'jubilant' Bharti hugging a 'beaming' Joshi; how by evening the state government had been dismissed by the Centre; and how the idol of Ram Lalla had been installed under a plastic sheet at the site.

In Noida, there was a premonition that the worst was yet to come. Except mine, there was not a single Muslim family in the vicinity. The day had passed—regrettable, shameful but gone; the night seemed loaded with fear. It was then that a Hindu family in the neighbourhood, displaced from Pakistan in 1947, a family which had seen the lady of the house deliver a baby aboard the running train on which the family left Peshawar for the safer climes of Delhi, came to our rescue. The same lady, by then into her mid-60s, sought to comfort us and even offered to sleep at our house with her son, then in his mid-40s, to keep us company. We put up a brave front, more to hide our fears than from any real fortitude. This lady, who had seen death, devastation and displacement from close quarters, understood. She calmly took my mother away to her place, and a few minutes later came back to our family, 'I am your mother tonight. I will not leave you alone. Your Ammi will sleep at our place. Do not worry about her. I will sleep at your place. If anyone knocks at the door, I will open it.'

She repeated the exercise over the next few days, instilling in us confidence that, God forbid, if things went from bad to worse, we had some support, maybe even an anchor.

Cut to 5 August 2020. I am once again in the same satellite town. Once again, I am still a minority; this time, though, there are a handful of other Muslim families in the vicinity. Once again, the media is relaying constant news from Ayodhya. With the advancements in technology over the past 30 years, now images are being beamed live by hundreds of channels. From early in the morning, the exultant anchors seem to be waiting breathlessly for the moment when the prime minister of India, Narendra Modi, would lay the foundation of a grand temple dedicated to Ram at the very site where the Babri Masjid once stood. The television's remote control is rendered superfluous. The faces of excited anchors and correspondents change, their tone and content remain the same.

The news channels display unabashed exuberance at the bhumi pujan as if the Ram temple was part of their long-held agenda, and not merely of the BJP. The Congress party, realizing it had lost out badly to the BJP despite its critical contribution to the Ayodhya saga, belatedly jumps on to the Hindutva bandwagon. The party, it needs to be recalled, was in power when the mosque was demolished; the party was in power when the locks of the mosque were opened; the party was in power when the idol was installed in the mosque. Surely, the Congress had done all the hard yards and deserved its moment in the Ayodhya sun. Except, it was put in the shade by the BJP, which now clearly was acting as the sole spokesperson of the pro-temple crowd. Where the Congress whimpered, the BJP roared.

It is not only the Hindi news channels but even the English ones that have happily hopped on to the temple bandwagon. 'India is emotional as decades of wait has ended,' NDTV reported Prime Minister Modi saying from Ayodhya. 'Crores won't believe that they have seen this day in our lifetime... Today, Ram Janmabhoomi has been liberated.'[2]

Sitting in Noida or Nalanda, there is no escaping the Ayodhya celebrations and epithets such as 'historic', 'freedom after 500 years' and 'moment of national pride', which are heard through the day on the small screen. It strikes no one that Muslims form part of the nation too.

Sample this: The India Today channel, whose print avatar had in 1992 described the Babri Masjid demolition as the day 'when India was shamed',[3] now calls the foundation stone-laying ceremony of the temple 'nothing short of Diwali in Ayodhya'.[4] This speaks as much about the vicissitudes of politics as of the channel's zeal to play to the lowest common denominator. The channel's correspondent is then seen digging up a report on how the event is being celebrated across the world. 'Temples across the United States have announced special events to celebrate the foundation laying ceremony of the historic Ram temple in Ayodhya,' he says.[5] Turns out India Today's print magazine carries a similar report. The channel's correspondent, meanwhile, goes on to talk of 3D portraits of the temple and giant billboards beaming them at the iconic Times Square on 5 August. It seems the ceremony concerns the whole world and not just the BJP followers. Then there is a report, which calls the ceremony 'a momentous occasion'. 'Shame' is a thing of the past.

Amidst the euphoria, forgotten is the Supreme Court's judgment from 2019, which said that the masjid's desecration in 1949 and its demolition in 1992 were in violation of the law. 'Muslims have been wrongly deprived of a mosque which had been constructed well over 450 years ago,' the apex court noted when speaking about the 1992 demolition of the mosque. The demolition 'was an egregious violation of the law', it said.[6] The court, invoking Article 142 of the Constitution, to 'ensure that a wrong committed must be remedied' had gone on to allot five acres of land to the Muslim party to build a mosque elsewhere. It matters not a bit to the jubilant media.

Nobody questions the significance of 5 August as the day for the bhumi pujan. Is it part of the same chest-thumping exercise that followed the simultaneous division of Jammu and Kashmir and the abrogation of Article 370 in 2019? Or was the bhumi pujan the most important thing as India faced the Covid-19 challenge? Nobody asks. Not in the Hindi media. Not in the English media. The lines between the two do not just blur; they almost disappear.

But on 5 August, the fig leaf of media's sense of fair play was blown away in the Hindutva avalanche. As *Frontline* observed a little later,

> The media, a huge part of it anyway, were happy to slip into the role of cheerleaders rather than being an ever-alert watchdog. The viewers had the mortification of watching an anchor like Navika Kumar on Times Now singing; 'Sri Ramchandra Kripalu' live on TV a few minutes before the actual pooja in Ayodhya as if the show was a celebration and not a mere report of the ceremony. No questions asked. No answers expected. Life was all about living in the moment, soaking it in. Dispassionate journalism could wait another day.[7]

Or another age.

Coming back to electronic media, India TV came up with 'non-stop superfast news on Ayodhya'. The anchors and correspondents were suitably breathless. In another show, the anchor reminded the viewers of the role played by Modi as the shepherd of Advani's rath yatra. 'It was a result of 29 years of patience,' the reporter says, clearly itching for the then upcoming moment. Twenty-nine years of whose patience? Which community's? He did not deem it necessary to explain himself; life was all about majoritarian sentiments. Later, RSS leader Arun Kumar called the struggle for Ram temple, 'a positive and a constructive movement to bring a change in the society'.[8] Widely respected academic Christophe Jaffrelot wrote a year later:

> The prime minister himself acted as the grand priest of the Bhoomi Pujan. This event was paradoxical, not only because the shilanyas had taken place in 1989 but also because, in contrast to

Modi's call to unity, the date of the ceremony, August 5, 2020, marked the first anniversary of the abolition of Article 370, which reflected a specific conception of unity... As soon as it became clear that Narendra Modi would attend the Bhoomi Pujan, hundreds of secularists signed—in vain—an open letter, stating, 'The Prime Minister going to Ayodhya to lay the foundation of the temple undermines our secular framework, and clearly endorses the majoritarian agenda... It implies the negation of the Constitutional values.'[9]

It could be seen as the officialization of the status of the majority community's faith as the basis of the new republic. Predictably, the BJP leader Ram Madhav said that it was synonymous with the aspirations of the country, not one specific community. 'Every nation has its sacred spaces and every religion its sacred places... The restoration of the temple at Ayodhya must be seen in the context of this sacredness of a value system that is at the core of this country.'[10] The marriage of the majority community with the country was complete, the exclusion of the largest minority not spoken about, but certain, nonetheless.

Back in Noida where I live, things are starkly, and sadly, different from 1992. Back in the day, the Hindutva votaries had raised provocative slogans off and on for a couple of years. They had gone door to door to invite people to join kar sevaks in Ayodhya. At that time, the remarkable Hindu family from Peshawar had stood with us like brothers caught in a storm. Not so in 2020. There is not a single family from the majority community in my neighbourhood which spared a thought for a Muslim amidst them. Nobody came to my home to put his arm around my shoulder, nobody to even say, 'It happens.' Instead, at every other house fluttered a saffron flag; some had the ubiquitous 'Om' on it; most had a picture of

Hanuman painted on. Most flags flew from balconies or windows. The entrance of the colony was arched with crosswires of saffron strings; at each end were tied saffron flags. The main gate itself had a banner announcing the victory in Ayodhya. The signage with the colony's name is covered in a calendar art replica of the Ram temple. In the evening, the residents gathered at the unauthorized temple constructed in the parking space in the colony. They distributed sweets, raised slogans of 'Jai Shri Ram' and followed it up by bursting crackers and beating drums. Then followed some more slogans of 'Jai Shri Ram', as men delirious with joy decided to scream their lungs out. It was not a day to hold back. No pretense was needed. It was a moment of unabashed glory, marking maybe even the celebration of the arrival of the Hindu Rashtra in spirit, if not yet in letter. Nobody seemed to remember Covid-19. Nobody had a mask on, no need was felt for social distancing. The exultant men and cheering women decided to hold a victory march, much like sportsmen do a victory lap of a stadium. Inside the stadium, the victors turn a blind eye to the losers, who usually quietly shuffle out. That is mere sports. Here, I closed the doors of my house, asked my kids and wife to stay indoors and switched off the lights. I hang out on the balcony amidst my carefully cultivated greenery. Defiant, silent but brooding. How far have we come since 1992!

20

All Things Muslims

IN EARLY 2023, *The New York Times* was researching a story about what it meant to be a Muslim in Modi's India, and it got in touch with me. The underlying assumption that they seemed to be working with that the Muslim community in India was a under siege—a community which had its mores, its language, food and clothing, its religion, indeed, its reason for existence itself questioned. It was also a community whose better-off members were now increasingly mulling over the idea of migration; this despite the fact that all of them or their elders had turned down the chance to shift to the Islamic Republic of Pakistan in 1947, confident as they were of being able to lead a dignified life in India based on principles of freedom of religion and equality. For many Muslims today, the confidence of their elders, in retrospect, seems misplaced. The prospect of hijrat (migration) loomed large all over again. Many began by sending their children abroad, ostensibly for higher studies, but with the tacit understanding that they would settle there in an atmosphere of peace and security. And may be, over a period of time, reach a position that allows them to help their younger siblings and retired parents migrate and stay with them. Some couples with younger children started looking for opportunities to move abroad. Not many were willing to surrender their Indian citizenship, but most were looking to get away from the atmosphere of all-pervasive hate and little security for their businesses, places of worship or residences. The economy was on a downswing. The unnerving reports of frequent attacks on mosques or bulldozers visiting Muslim businesses or houses shook their confidence. Social media too was full of hate and bigotry. The daily barrage of abuse and exclusion impacted the minds of many from the community. A study by the Islamic Council of Victoria, the apex Muslim body in the Australian state of Victoria, found 'a strong correlation between spikes in hate and newsworthy events related to Islam, particularly protests, terrorist attacks and eruptions of violence in the Muslim world'.[1] The report, quoted by Sabrang India, found that over 55 per cent of Islamophobic content originates in India. As a result, after the 2019 General Elections, more and more foreign placement agents started getting calls from Muslim families looking to shift, bag, baggage and barrel. Those looking to migrate included film and television actors, RJs, journalists, advocates, book publishers and businessmen. Though the conversation within the community was largely hush-hush, it was loud enough for the imam at Jamaat-e-Islami Hind's mosque in Delhi to try to dissuade them from shifting abroad with words of solace to the faithful. 'This is our land. Our ancestors fought the British. We cannot leave the country just because a handful of people have taken the law in their own hands. Throughout Islamic history, there have been many cases of much worse circumstances,' the imam reminded the congregation, which included this author, in his Eid-ul-Fitr address in the summer of 2022.

The sermon probably dissuaded a few. Others had more at stake. They were willing to shell out a few lakhs to migrate. Such migration was, relatively speaking, almost entirely peaceful, even luxurious. Yet, it brought a tear or two to the eyes of the community elders, many of whom had seen or experienced displacement themselves at the time of Independence. Those inclined towards religion were often heard talking of hijrat (migration) to console themselves. In Islamic history, there was a time when Muslims in Arabia during the Prophet's time were persecuted for their beliefs. There were companions of the Prophet who were laid bare-back on scorching sand and dragged across it for hours. There were others whose hands and feet were tied, while being denied a sip of water during the peak of summer. The Prophet went grey with anxiety. Many a surah of the Quran was revealed during the challenging time. To escape the extreme torture and make a fresh start, the Prophet and his companions finally migrated to Medina—an event that came to be referred to as hijrat. Some even went to Ethiopia, then called Abyssinia.

Back in India, the Partition in 1947 split millions of families on both sides of the border. Even as millions of Muslims undertook the life-threatening trip to the newly formed state of Pakistan, millions of Hindus and Sikhs fled in trains and buses to India, their travel every bit as risky. In 2023, *The New York Times* reporters tried to find out if Muslims were hopping on to an airplane to Canada, the US or maybe the UK to save their life, limb and maybe their livelihood (businesses). The exact number of migrants will only come to light in the years to come, but the report did reveal that the beginning of the Great Indian Muslim migration was confirmed by experts in New Delhi, Mumbai, Jaipur and Chandigarh. The migration experts confirmed what was till then a quiet fear: more and more

Muslims were looking for greener pastures abroad, their migration forced largely by the lack of security back home. Often, they read news of lynching or attacks on mosques or on girls wearing hijabs. None of this did much to restore their confidence. There were Indians of other faiths too who were migrating, I was told, almost to soften the blow, but the percentage of Muslims was higher, much higher than it had been in the past. Some tried to draw parallels with the migration in the 1960s and 1970s when people went to Saudi Arabia, the UAE, the US and Canada. The comparison was futile as everybody knew that back then the migration was a result of the search for more remunerative employment, with the men often leaving behind their wives, children and parents in India.

This current displacement was far from voluntary. It stemmed not from a wish to expand business or seek better education and improve the career prospects of youngsters but from an existential threat, a threat to life and limb, a threat to the freedom to choose one's food and dress, prayers and places of worship, and a threat to one's very being. Noted sociologist Imtiaz Ahmed, not one to mince his words, understood that each attack on Muslims, whether lynchings on allegations of cow slaughter, disrobing girls wearing hijabs or threatening the faithful praying inside a mosque, was part of a larger design to intimidate the community and scare it into silence. It was a design to put the fear of death and destruction in the minds of millions by ruining the lives and livelihood of a few hundred. A religious minority running into millions, and by itself the second largest Muslim population in the world, could not be wished away or subjected to a Rohingya-type extermination or displacement. What could not be annihilated had to be browbeaten, controlled, maybe even invisibilized. Hence the attacks on Muslim food, apparel, language, places of worship. Sociologist Ahmed wrote,

The grand design has finally unfolded itself. If Muslims cannot be annihilated physically (they are too many) annihilate them culturally so that they can be converted to the Hindu fold. Preventing Muslim girls from wearing hijab, preventing Muslims to perform their prayer, projecting madrasas as the den of terrorism so that they are shut down and Muslim children do not get religious education, claiming all mosques to be temples, and insisting that Muslims do not eat beef even in states where there is no beef ban and become vegetarians, etc., are all part of this design.[2]

Ahmed's words shared with his followers on Facebook in September 2022 were in response to several incidents occurring around that time. A few weeks before Ahmed expressed his fear of cultural annihilation, Adityanath, chief minister of Uttar Pradesh, had ordered a survey of non-recognized madrasas in the state. On the face of it, it seemed a perfectly innocent step meant to provide better education to students, better pay to teachers and usher in greater transparency in the whole affair. After all, madrasa students are often first-generation learners, and the madrasas provide them with elementary education in addition to teaching them how to read and memorize the Quran. But the Muslim community suspected that the chief minister's true intentions, unfortunately, were not so innocent. They asked: Why had a similar concern not been shown towards gurukuls or the Saraswati Shishu Mandir Vidyalayas run by the RSS? Didn't the survey amount to a limited, even discriminatory, NRC?

Well, the government did not say it in so many words, but behind the survey were oft-repeated—but never substantiated—claims of madrasas being dens of terrorism. Often one hears Right-wing leaders making irresponsible utterances about madrasas. Instead of lauding their role in providing complimentary education to the poorest of the poor left out of the formal schooling system, madrasas have often been targeted as if they were repositories of weapons and training grounds of terrorism. As most madrasas in the country are attached to mosques, many mosques in Hyderabad, Mumbai, Bengaluru and Delhi felt compelled to start 'Visit My Mosque' events post-2016 in a bid to dispel wrong notions about these places of learning and houses of worship. Under the programme, non-Muslim men and women were invited to visit a mosque, see the prayer facility, use the literature available and even observe prayer sessions.

Despite all these well-meaning efforts, the reality is that the powers that be were trying to create an irrational fear of these institutions of learning in the minds of the common Indian. The fear-inducing mechanisms ranged from the Adityanath government asking madrasas to hoist the tricolour on Independence Day to issuing instructions to them to start their day with a rendition of the national anthem. Again, as the government did not issue similar instructions to other religious institutions, it naturally left a lingering feeling in the mind of the common man that maybe, just maybe, madrasas had not been celebrating our Independence Day or that their pupils did not sing the national anthem. Irresponsible and discriminatory, the government's actions first singled out a community for no fault of its own. Then marginalized its institutions with calls for surveys, sowing suspicion that the madrasas could be hiding something, that they may not be just centres of learning. This was much like in the case of the beef ban.

In the case of meat consumption, the alleged crime of cow slaughter was never proved, yet many paid with their lives. In the case of madrasas, nobody can ever get a speck of proof of anti-national activities—we have had the likes of Raja Rammohun Roy and Dr Rajendra Prasad who have studied in madrasas. Yet, the damage was done.

Speaking at an event organized by the RSS in the summer of 2022, the Assam Chief Minister Himanta Biswa Sarma called for madrasas to 'cease to exist'.[3] 'The word "madrasa" should disappear. Teach the Quran at home, but children should be taught science and math in school', Sarma said. His words spoke eloquently of his own ignorance. Little did he realize that the word 'madrasa' itself stood for 'school', derived as it is from the root word 'dars' or lesson/lecture. Meanwhile, Adityanath, his Uttar Pradesh counterpart, stopped grants to new madrasas in the state and asked the existing ones to sing the national anthem every day.

The state government had earlier allocated Rs 479 crores under the Madrasa Modernisation Scheme in the 2021–22 Budget. There are around 16,000 registered madrasas in the state, out of which only 558 are aided by the government. Five days before stopping grants to new madrasas around mid-May 2022, the Uttar Pradesh government had come up with its own version of the Norman Tebbit test (a provocative test of loyalty devised by a Conservative British politician in 1990) by making the singing of the national anthem 'mandatory for all students and teachers in madrasas' across the state.[4] The state Madrasa Education Board passed an order applicable to all recognized, aided and non-aided madrasas to this effect. With similar orders not being passed for government, public or private schools, the underlying message seemed to question the patriotism of madrasa students and teachers.

Whether the madrasa survey, the calls for singing the national anthem in Uttar Pradesh or the pledge to wipe out madrasas altogether in Assam, the idea was to defame the institutions and the community that runs them.

As the sociologist cited above said, 'If you cannot annihilate them, invisibilize them.'[5] No mosques, no madrasas, no hijab, no students learning about Islam, and the community loses it mooring, its learning. Hijrat beckons.

PART 5

Matters of Love, the Jamaat and the Hijab

21

The Tablighi Jamaat as a Metaphor for Muslims

FOR MONTHS, NO, ALMOST FOUR years, the Corona virus travelled across cities, countries and continents with barely any rest. From the largely atheist China to the largely Christian Europe and the US to the completely Muslim Saudi Arabia, the virus did not discriminate based on faith, or even the absence of faith. If the early reports from Wuhan were disturbing, those coming first from Italy and Iran, and then the US, were equally unsettling. There were many videos shared online of people being left to die as countries, many of which were running short of ventilators and had to choose between the sick and sicker. Highways and bylanes, airports and railway stations, interstate bus terminuses and local bus stations were all locked down. Capitalism—with its promotion of greed masquerading as profit—communism, socialism and all isms, were brought to their knees by a virus which could not be seen but whose impact cost millions and millions of human lives.

It had a name but no religion, and for an Indian, no caste, that age-old method of implementing social apartheid. All that changed on 30 March 2020 almost five months after the virus' global travel. Corona did have a religion, or so we were told by some of our hate-spewing, Islamophobic television channels as well as many newspapers, now locked in a battle for survival and happy to follow the TV channels' hate-filled ways. Suddenly, terms like 'Corona Jihad' and 'Corona ki Jamaat' entered the vocabulary of the middle class. Considering many in this social segment often prefer to lace everyday conversation with slurs, it naturally translated into hatred for India's largest minority and unabashed bigotry. We had the electronic media talking energetically of a Muslim man who had disrobed himself in front of a lady nurse. Turns out, the aforesaid video was of a mentally impaired man in a mosque in Karachi. The man, in all probability, had never set foot in India but the incident was used to paint a section of our population as a superspreader of the dreaded virus.

That, however, was not even a blip for our media. It marched ahead, breathlessly, relentlessly and recklessly. We were told men from a particular community had asked for biryani during quarantine, the popular dish now having found a clear religion. The men, on being denied the biryani, had reportedly urinated in water bottles, which they then flung at health workers. To buttress the contention, file photos of men in beards standing behind iron bars were passed off as of those in detention. And they were not done yet. Many gated housing societies with middle-class residents having disposable incomes and dispensed-with scientific temperaments happily shared and forwarded videos of bearded men in kurta-pyjamas breathing, no, sneezing loudly in a congregation to spread the virus. Another one showed a few men, who were again believed to be from the same community, licking used spoons with relish before passing them on. Yet another showed a man spitting on fruits. It was maddening. It was frightening. It was shameless, and seemingly, endless. Nobody knew when, and if, corona would be defeated, but thanks to the Islamophobic sections of our media, large as they are, everybody thought they knew which community was responsible for the virus spreading. A year later, the apex court came down heavily on such coverage, stating, 'The problem is, everything in this country is shown with a communal angle by a section of the media. That is the problem. The country is going to get a bad name ultimately.'[1]

Back in 2020 nobody bothered to verify the authenticity of the videos in circulation. After due investigation, they were found to be either completely false or unrelated to the pandemic. For instance, the one which showed men licking spoons was actually from a Bohra community function—an exercise the men regularly undertake to prevent food wastage. And the one showing men sitting in a group and sneezing loudly was actually a sufi video of loud inhalation and exhalation with nothing, absolutely nothing, to do with either Covid-19 or the Tablighi Jamaat, whose members had been accused of spreading the disease through this method! The truth did come out, but by then a lot of damage to the community, and the nation, had been done.

A large section of society seldom cross-checks a news report or video. And frequently buys into blatant lies as long as they corroborate what it would like to hear. In fact, the well-being of many people is derived from this consumption. So, they happily consume context-less videos with much relish and circulate them, almost like teenagers share pictures of their crushes. But what of the doctors or our political representatives? Surely, they were bound by their professional oaths. They are, but, unfortunately, albeit entirely predictably, were no different than the layman. Thanks to a sting operation, we came to know about Dr Aarti Lalchandani, principal of Ganesh Shankar Vidyaarthi Medical College in Kanpur, who made no effort to cloak her malignant views about the Tablighi Jamaat and, almost incredibly, accused the Yogi Adityanath government of Uttar Pradesh of appeasing Muslims!

'I should not say that but they are terrorists. We are giving them VIP treatment, food and water, everything; we are exhausting our resources on them, making our doctors sick. We are paying their bills every day. We are using a hundred kits due to them. The chief minister is indulging in appeasement by getting them treated. They should be put in jail,' Dr Lalchandani said in an almost five-minute long video that went viral in April 2020.[2] Interestingly, a few days earlier, she had appeared on India TV to talk of the Tablighi Jamaat and how she was treating its members who had tested positive, claiming, 'The administration has provided us security. Police inspector wore a PPE kit to go inside to control these people. And these people are spitting everywhere. They are leaving their contagion everywhere…They spit on their hands and rub (their saliva) on the walls, sinks, stairs. So, we have to sanitize the premises two-three times a day.'[3]

No one needed to guess who 'these people' were. The visuals said it all. This not-so-subtle ostracization was being preached on prime time television, helped along by the anchor, who almost seemed hand in glove with the doctor! Lalchandani was not the sole doctor to hold the organization, and through it the entire community, responsible for the spread of Covid-19. The Valentis Cancer hospital in Meerut openly discriminated between patients based on their religion and residential address, the latter reflecting and reinforcing the practice of ghettoization, which has been long used to isolate many sections of our society. The hospital put out an advertisement in the Hindi daily *Dainik Jagran* in April 2020 stating,

'Several Muslim patients are not following the guidelines (like using a mask, maintaining hygiene) and they are also misbehaving with hospital staff. For the security of hospital's staff and patients, the hospital administration requests all new Muslim patients that they and one designated caretaker get tested for Covid-19 and visit the hospital only if their reports are negative.' The hospital did not deem it necessary to tell us how many Muslim patients had misbehaved with the staff, and what was their proportion to other communities. No such condition was imposed on other religious communities. The fact that the action was a violation of the National Human Rights Commission's charter of patient's rights did not matter to the hospital. The advertisement was a casual, even callous, remark thrown in the public domain for obvious reasons. It was Islamophobia, plain and clear.

The Meerut case did force the district chief medical officer to seek an apology from the hospital, but it clouded things to such an extent that when news about Bharatpur's Zenana hospital, where a full-term pregnant Muslim woman was denied admission allegedly because of her religion, was shared, many from the Muslim community were quick to believe it. Later, an inquiry by the state government concluded there was no discrimination on the basis of religion. The clarification came a bit late in the day. Many sections of the community now suffered from a trust deficit, plain and simple. And the actions of many Right-wing elements did nothing to foster a culture of trust and brotherhood. After repeated Tablighi Jamaat insinuations and several statements by the likes of Dr Lalchandani coming to light, anything seemed believable. Such was the lot of India's largest minority.

It did not help that in Himachal Pradesh, foul allegations continued to dog the community. Being a follower of Islam became the reason for a man's death in Himachal Pradesh shortly after a section of the media began to link Covid-19 with Muslims in March 2020. The man had attended a Tablighi Jamaat congregation in Delhi. As reports came in of some volunteers from the event testing positive, he got himself tested. He came out negative. Ideally, this should have meant that he could now thank his stars and carry on with his life. His circumstances were less than ideal, though. His neighbours in his village believed neither the tests nor the man. Their constant barbs forced the man to take his own life.[4]

His death went in vain. Neither the media nor the political leaders learned a lesson. In Uttar Pradesh, we had the ruling party's leaders shunning Muslim vendors on camera or asking people to boycott Muslim shopkeepers. Suresh Tiwari, BJP MLA from Deoria, for instance, was seen asking the public not to buy vegetables from Muslims. 'Keep one thing in mind. I am telling everyone openly, no one should purchase vegetables from mians, Muslims,' he said in a video. When the media approached him, a defiant Tiwari asked, 'Did I say anything wrong?'[5] Fellow party legislator Brij Bhushan Rajput was also seen in another video threatening a vendor, asking him to go away after discovering he was a Muslim. In the video shot by Rajput's neighbours, he was first seen asking the vendor his name. When the man replied with 'Raj Kumar', Rajput asked a minor boy accompanying him to confirm his name. He was told the man was actually called Azizur Rahman, following which Rajput banished him from the colony, telling him, 'Dikh mat jaana yahan mohalle mein (Make sure you're not seen in this locality again).'[6] The vendor was ostracized because of his religion, which is something he had anticipated and thus had given a Hindu name before. For both Tiwari and Rajput, being a Muslim was reason enough to be subjected to social exclusion and humiliation.

In parts of Delhi and Madhya Pradesh, vendors were asked to show their Aadhar cards to gain entry into residential colonies.[7] A

Muslim name promptly translated into denial of entry. It was a clear attack on the livelihood of poor Muslims. No politician of any hue, not even from the Opposition ranks, said a word of protest. And, of course, it did not end the harassment, with many in Haryana, Uttar Pradesh and Delhi beginning to object to azaan being pronounced from mosques during the lockdown!

It all started with the 2020 March-end police raid on Markaz, the headquarters of the Tablighi Jamaat in New Delhi. The largest Muslim organization stood accused of violating the norms of social distancing outlined by Prime Minister Narendra Modi when he announced a nationwide lockdown on 24 March through a televised address. With his speech, everything came to a halt—offices, markets, colleges, schools, railway stations, public and private transport, everything. Further, he advised people to stay where they were. Many of us, privileged ones, stayed in the safety and comfort of our homes with our near and dear ones. Our fans and air-conditioners were in order, there were extra groceries in the kitchen, and our LCD TVs beamed us images from across the world. Covid-19 was a television spectacle. Tens of thousands of fellow Indians, meanwhile, had no roof over their heads, and no bread to eat after a day or two. They set out with their often aged and ailing parents, malnourished babies and gaunt selves for their hometowns and villages, presenting the saddest spectacle since Partition. The villages offered no guarantee of livelihood, just the warmth of familiarity, and possibly slow death among loved ones. Then there were the devout stranded in their respective places of worship. Some 400 Hindus were stranded in Jammu on their way back from Vaishnodevi. And 200 Sikhs were left in a gurdwara at Majnu ka Tila in Delhi. But in the case of the media coverage on the Tablighi Jamaat, 3,000 men were reported to be 'hiding' in Markaz, according to our ever-ignorant but seldom-shy-of-

Islamophobia media. The choice of the word 'hiding', of course, pre-supposed the deliberate commission of a wrongful act. A fairly large section pronounced the Tablighi Jamaat guilty of hosting a congregation defying all norms of social distancing. Some channels were more adventurous; they saw in the international conference of worshippers a global conspiracy. Others called them terrorists out to wage a 'Corona Jihad' against India. Some anchors, having shed their secular pretence since 2014, saw in the moment an 'Islamic insurrection' and 'Islamic terrorism'. This was the moment to deflect attention from the abject failure of the government in devising a clear strategy to combat the pandemic. The government had gone from imposing a whimsical lockdown to being responsible for a burgeoning humanitarian crisis. Clearly, it was much easier, and more viable, to blame a Muslim body for the spread of Covid-19 than to focus on the manifest proof of arbitrariness of a lockdown that had resulted in tens of thousands of men and women, ill-clothed, hungry, thirsty and alienated, walking for hundreds of kilometres along the highways. Some had walked all the way from Ludhiana in Punjab to Bhagalpur in Bihar via Haryana, Delhi and Uttar Pradesh! The king could do no wrong. And the courtiers could ill-afford to talk of any wrong. The media was a happy cheerleader of the government. Modi's then minister for minorities affairs, Mukhtar Abbas Naqvi, went one step further than the rest, stating, 'Tablighi Jamaat is a Talibani crime, not negligence.'[8]

Lost amidst this din was an important fact: The Tablighi Jamaat held its international conference between 13 and 15 March much before the lockdown, which was imposed on the midnight of 24 March, and well before the Delhi Government had fixed a limit on the number of people who could gather at a place of worship. There was absolutely nothing illegal about the religious meet. The foreigners who attended had valid visas; so one could assume that they had been tested for the virus at the international airport, which was their port of entry. And on the first day of their congregation, 13 March, the Union Health Ministry had declared that coronavirus was not a health emergency as there were only 81 cases in the country at the time!

But facts are an easy casualty in a quick search for bad boys. With a Right-wing government at the Centre and in many of the states, the media's hunt for a villain—that one person or community responsible for the spread of the dreaded disease, the one organization not allowing the government to function even during the lockdown—led to an inevitable, easy conclusion. The age-old Tablighi Jamaat, with its Markaz in Delhi, was held entirely responsible for the spread of Covid-19 in India, not just Delhi. Fake news and false reports ran parallel to fake videos on social media until it was drummed into everybody's mind that the largest Muslim organization had been irresponsible, maybe even deliberately so, and furthered the spread of the disease. The 'BJP leaders, including Yogi Adityanath…blamed the Tablighis through May, and TV anchors, including Arnab Goswami on Republic TV and Rahul Kanwal on India Today TV, went berserk. This hysteria resulted in hundreds of arrests'.[9] Nobody talked of the Namaste Trump event in Gujarat anymore. The delay in imposing lockdown to enable the toppling of the Congress government in Madhya Pradesh was also forgotten. It was just the Tablighi Jamaat, and by extension, the entire Muslim community that was painted as the villain.

The Tablighi Jamaat members were hauled up from every state or town that reported the presence of men with fist-long beards and pyjamas ending above the ankles. The Delhi Government helmed by Arvind Kejriwal of the Aam Aadmi Party had for almost two weeks, in its daily dispatch on Covid-19 patients in the city, a special section on the Markaz Masjid. This segmentation also went a long way in telling the media, and through it the common man, that the Markaz had played an important role in the spread of the disease. The religion-based division continued till 11 April, when the Delhi Minorities' Commission protested, wrote to the Delhi Health Department,

> Your bulletins of coronavirus victims are showing a separate column 'Markaz Masjid'. Such a thoughtless classification is feeding into the Islamophobia agenda of lap media and Hindutva forces and has been easily turned into a handle to attack Muslims across the country. As a result, Muslims are being attacked in various areas, calls are being made for their social boycott.[10]

Hundreds of volunteers of the Tablighi Jamaat event were sent to quarantine centres, from where many did not emerge for months.[11] Others were arrested and charged with various provisions of the IPC, such as the Epidemic Diseases Act, the Foreigners Act and the Disaster Management Act. The Nizamuddin Markaz was sealed and the Tablighi Jamaat chief, Maulana Muhammad Saad, was charged with culpable homicide. Also arrested were foreign nationals from Malaysia, Djibouti, Ghana, Kuwait, Thailand, Indonesia and the US. Weeks later, their respective governments raised the subject on the sidelines of official parleys. The arrests threatened to derail foreign relations. The Wire commented,

> On April 28, Indonesian President Joko Widodo spoke to Indian Prime Minister Narendra Modi. The official Indian read-out mentions that Widodo thanked the Indian side for pharmaceutical supplies, but also adds that the leaders 'discussed issues related to their citizens present in each other's countries'.

While the Indian press release did not spell it out, Indonesian foreign minister Retno Marsudi told the media that President Widodo had raised the issue of the Tablighi Jamaat (known as Jamaah Tabligh in Indonesia) with his Indian interlocutor. In total, 1,129 Indonesian Tablighi members were abroad when borders started to shut down, over 60% in India. Stranded Indonesians nationals started to return from May on Vande Bharat flights in a slow trickle. However, it took another two months—in early July—for the first Indonesian Tablighi members to board a flight.[12]

The men were then released in batches. Meanwhile, Indian citizens knocked on the doors of various High Courts for relief. Quashing the FIRs filed against 29 foreigners and six Indians, the Aurangabad Bench of the Bombay High Court put things in perspective, stating, 'A political government tries to find a scapegoat when there is pandemic or calamity, and the circumstances show there is a probability that these foreigners were chosen to make them scapegoats.'[13]

The words of the court must have acted as a balm to the embattled organization, and indeed the community itself. The well-respected daily *The Hindu* reported,

> The Aurangabad bench of the Bombay High Court…said, 'the Maharashtra police acted mechanically.' A division bench of Justice TV Nalawade and Justice MG Sewlikar said, 'It appears that the State Government acted under political compulsion and police also did not dare to exercise powers given to them under provisions of procedural laws and substantive laws. The court was hearing a plea filed by 29 foreign nationals who were booked under sections of Indian Penal Code, Epidemic

Diseases Act, Maharashtra Police Act, Disaster Management Act and Foreigner's Act for allegedly violating their Tourist Visa conditions by attending the congregation. The 58 page judgment said, 'The allegations are very vague in nature and from these allegations inference is not possible at any stage that they were spreading Islam religion and there was intention of conversion. The Government cannot give different treatment to citizens of different religions of different countries.'[14]

In response to three separate petitions filed on behalf of foreign nationals from Indonesia, the Ivory Coast, Djibouti, Ghana, Benin and Tanzania, the division bench of Justices T Nalawade and MG Sewlikar ordered the quashing of the FIRs against 35 accused persons. Justice Nalawade observed that because of these FIRs, Muslims who participated in the protests against the Citizenship Amendment Act (2019) and the National Register of Citizens were given a 'warning' that 'action in any form and for anything can be taken against Muslims'.[15] 'It was indicated that even for keeping contact with Muslims of other countries action will be taken against them. Thus, there is a smell of malice to the action taken against these foreigners and Muslim for their alleged activities.'[16] His fellow judge, Justice Sewlikar did not agree with him though. He stated that the decision to file FIRs en masse against the men who had gathered at a religious congregation was taken to give an indirect warning to Indian Muslims who had participated in the protests against the CAA in huge numbers.[17]

In its 58-page order, the court held:

There were protests by taking processions, holding dharna at many places in India at least from prior to January 2020. Most of the persons who participated in protest were Muslims. It is their contention that Citizenship Amendment Act, 2019 is discriminatory against the Muslims. They believe that Indian citizenship will not be granted to Muslim refugees and migrants. They were protesting against National Registration of Citizenship (NRC). There were protests on large scale not only in Delhi, but in most States in India. It can be said that due to the present action taken fear was created in the minds of those Muslims. This action indirectly gave warning to Indian Muslims that action in any form and for anything can be taken against Muslims.[18]

The court rubbished charges that Tablighi volunteers were seeking to convert non-Muslims to their faith. It was not quite a surprise for those who know the body from close quarters. Founded in 1927 in Mewat by Maulana Mohammad Ilyas, the Tablighi Jamaat works only among Muslims, aiming to promote the ideals of Islam among them. Its aim is self-rejuvenation within the fold of Islam. The volunteers undertake 40-day and four-month-long self-financed outstation trips for spiritual uplift. It has no outreach programmes for people of other faiths. Accordingly, the court held: 'The material on the record shows that Tablighi Jamaat is not a separate sect of Muslims but it is only a movement for reformation of religion. In any case, even from the record it cannot be inferred that the foreigners were spreading Islam by converting persons of other religion to Islam. The record shows that the foreigners were not talking Indian languages like Hindi or Urdu and they were talking languages like Arabian, French, etc (*sic*).'

The court ruling came in 2020 August. Another order came in December 2020 when a Delhi court freed all 36 foreigners facing trial for allegedly flouting Covid-19 deadlines. The court not only pulled up Delhi Police for its shoddy investigation, but also acknowledged the plea of some of the accused that they were not present in Markaz and had been arbitrarily picked up 'from different places so as to maliciously prosecute them under directions from the Ministry of Home Affairs'. The court went on to add, 'It is beyond comprehension of the court, as to how IO (Inspector Satish) could have identified 952 foreign nationals out of 2,343 persons who, as per the SHO, were found flouting the guidelines, without any Test Identification Parade, but on the basis of list provided by the Ministry of Home Affairs.'[19]

The 36 men were the last of the accused from abroad to go on trial in the Tablighi Jamaat case. According to court records, 952 foreigners were accused of breaking Covid-19 regulations. Naturally, most did not want to stay in India and stand trial, but 8 had been discharged in August, and another 36 in December.

By then, however, hundreds had spent many weeks incarcerated and the entire community had been pronounced responsible for the spread of the dreaded disease. The attempts to link up anything related to the by now under-siege Muslim community with Covid-19 were not limited to fake news and the use of videos taken out of the original context. A popular news channel's anchor came up with a prime time show titled *Madrasa Hotspot*. Armed with preconceived notions, he rattled on about how madrasas in Delhi had housed 'hidden' students during the lockdown: how in a cramped room, a dozen students were staying with no social distancing and hardly any masks. It did not strike him that like the Tablighi Jamaat volunteers, the madrasa students too were stranded due to the sudden imposition of the nationwide lockdown. Most students in the madrasa were first-generation learners and hailed from extremely poor families in Bihar, Jharkhand and eastern Uttar Pradesh. The news anchor's privileged background prevented him from realizing that even under normal circumstances, the madrasas depended on community funding, their students having no resources to pay their academic fees, buy books or pay for dormitories or even their travel to and from home. Under the lockdown, the students and the madrasa management were both helpless; the students' poor parents could not come fetch them as there were no trains. The madrasas did not have enough resources to feed and clothe the poor students. Yet, rising to the occasion, they had given them shelter and two meals a day till the lockdown was lifted and their parents could somehow manage to come pick them up.

None of these fine details mattered to the anchor. Huddled in a limited space, the students were conspiring to spread the coronavirus, he claimed. He had probably never set foot in a madrasa in his life.

Despicable as the programme was, it was merely a cog in the wheel of Islamophobia. It told us that whether it was the pandemic, or any other time, it was not easy to be a Muslim in New India. Whether one was seeking lessons in spiritual rejuvenation, which the Tablighi Jamaat lays stress on, or the elementary the education madrasas provide, was immaterial. Being a Muslim was cause enough to be vilified.

22

Kumbh Mela, the Actual Superspreader

ON 21 MARCH 2021, THERE was a hoarding at Rajiv Chowk Metro station in New Delhi inviting people to the Kumbh Mela, the most cherished Hindu pilgrimage which takes place once in every 12 years in Haridwar. It was 'clean' and 'safe', it assured the travellers at the station, which registers a daily footfall of 5,00,000 passengers. India registered 46,951 positive Covid-19 cases on the day, a worrisome figure even if one goes by the notoriously underreported official count.

The same day there were full-page newspaper advertisements in major Hindi and English dailies inviting the unsuspecting faithful to the biggest human gathering on earth. In an obvious bid to lend legitimacy to the event, and maybe, appease the Hindutva votaries, the advertisements came reinforced with an image of Prime Minister Narendra Modi. Tirath Singh Rawat, the chief minister of Uttarakhand, the state that hosted the Mela, assured the pilgrims and seers, 'faith in God will overcome the fear of the virus', just in case anybody had apprehensions about such a large gathering turning into a superspreader.[1] Not everybody had forgotten the travails of the summer of 2020 when Covid-19 forced people indoors with a prolonged lockdown beginning on the midnight of 24 March. And many needed a bit of nudging. Rawat insisted, 'There should be no rok-tok (impediments) and the mela should be "open for all".'

Rawat himself, The Wire reported, 'has been an active participant in the organisation of the festival – and in images taken at the site, he can be seen with his mask around his neck rather than on his face. "Nobody will be stopped in the name of Covid-19," he had famously said.'[2]

The Mela had provisions for three days of Shahi Snan (royal bath) on 12, 14 and 27 April, each day being of special significance for the devotees. Over the next month or so, nearly nine million people descended on Kumbh, many doubtlessly won over by the assurance of Chief Minister Rawat, others taking up the invitation of the prime minister, with the belief that it was 'clean' and 'safe'. Bare-chested men, and much better covered women, sadhus clad merely in a loincloth and Naga sadhus with nothing but ashes on their bodies, all gathered on the banks of Ganga for the holy dip. When these pilgrims and priests called their near and dear ones from their mobiles in Haridwar, they invariably heard a recorded announcement before the call was connected. The voice they heard told them how essential it was to keep a distance of two yards from each other and wear a mask, 'Do gaz doori, mask hai zaroori'. The same voice was heard across India's telephone networks. It was the very easily recognizable voice of India's best-known film star Amitabh Bachchan; the message could scarcely have been more pertinent. Yet, the moment the people put their phones down, they seemed to forget the message and huddle together as if Covid-19 had already been relegated to the pages of history. Shoulder to shoulder, breathing down each other's neck, they all took a holy dip and emerged from the river with water dripping from their often-unwieldy locks and flowing down their often-translucent garments. India held its collective breath. Faith and the pandemic seemed to mock each other.

Three weeks of pilgrimage, and India overtook Brazil as the second worst-hit nation in the world. *The Guardian* reported, 'On 12 April, as India registered another 1,69,000 new Covid-19 cases to overtake Brazil to become the second-worst hit country, three million people gathered on the shores of the Ganges.'[3] There were more than a million estimated daily visitors to the Mela: Rawat's message of faith in God overcoming the fear of the virus was clearly taken to heart by vast multitudes. Even as reports started trickling in of Covid-19 sweeping across the country, the pilgrimage continued unimpeded. The trickle of the infected and ailing soon turned into a torrent as casualties hit an unprecedented and unimaginable high. The cremation grounds across north India ran short of space, with the poor falling desperately short of cash as they struggled to pay for last rites; expenses reportedly rose to Rs 30,000 per head, and the poor were forced to immerse their dead in the Ganga or give them a hurried sand burial on the banks. A priest in Varanasi, the constituency represented by the prime minister in Parliament, revealed that 686 bodies were cremated at one ghat on a single day. More ghats were opened. In cities, there were visuals of dead bodies in a queue as they awaited entry into the cremation grounds, which were now reeling out of control due to unforeseen traffic.

A day after the second Shahi Snan, India's new Covid-19 infections stood at 2,17,353. Significantly, only some of the pilgrims had begun the long journey back to their homes. Many were infected and unaware of it; others were infected, and insisted, it was not Covid. Tens of thousands returned home having neither been tested nor gone through a precautionary period of quarantine. Back home, they mingled with their near and dear ones, unwittingly passing on the infection to areas where the health infrastructure was at best elementary. The government was clearly keen not to allow the pilgrimage to be seen as a superspreader. In Madhya Pradesh, where more than 100 positive cases were detected in 700-odd Kumbh Mela returnees, four officials in different districts of the state confirmed that their 'seniors called them off for political reasons'. They were apparently told to concentrate on the Covid situation in general rather than paying special attention to the pilgrims. In the neighbouring Rajasthan, governed by the Indian National Congress, the officials were told 'to concentrate on the general Covid situation, and not focus on surveys and tracing of Kumbh returnees'.[4] *The Guardian* reported a 1,800 per cent increase in Covid cases during the Mela in Uttarakhand, adding in the same report, 'Police overseeing the event said that were they to enforce social distancing, "a stampede-like situation may arise".'[5] By 15 April, more than 2,000 festival-goers had already tested positive for Covid-19.

Modi was to wait another couple of days—by when the number of fresh infections stood at 2,61,394—to backtrack and ask the priests and seers for the Mela to be symbolic from thereon. 'Today I had a telephonic conversation with Acharya Mahamandaleshwar Poojya Swamy Avdheshanand Giri Ji. I asked about the health of all the Sants. I thanked the Sant Samaj for their full cooperation with the administration. It is my request to keep Kumbh symbolic from now on as two Shahi Snans have already taken place. This will strengthen the fight against the pandemic,' Modi tweeted on 17 April 2021.[6]

The same day, he had addressed tens of thousands of people at an election rally at Asansol in Bengal. Making no effort to control his emotion at seeing the crowd—many did not wear a mask, most others wore it around their necks—he said, 'Where I look, I see people, nothing else.' Caravan reported,

> Modi…surveyed the crowd, before telling them that he wanted to express a shikayat – a complaint. 'I have come here twice before, before the Lok Sabha elections, to ask for your vote… But, at those times not even one-fourth of the crowd I see here was in attendance.' He added, 'Aaj aapne aisa dam dikhaya hai, aisi takat dikhayi hai. Main jahan dekhta hun wahan mujhe log dikhte hain, baki kuchh dikhta nahin' – Today you have shown such courage, such force. Wherever I look, I see people, nothing else. After that, the crowd erupted into chants of 'Modi, Modi'.[7]

The newspapers reported this enthusiastically. The irony of the prime minister hailing a huge crowd at the time of the pandemic was lost on almost everybody.

'Have never seen such huge crowds at a rally, PM Modi said in Asansol,' NDTV reported.[8]

A majority of voters in Asansol, Uttar, where Modi beamed at the size of the crowd, ultimately voted for Trinamool Congress.

The spectre of the Tablighi Jamaat loomed large. Almost a year earlier, the nation was shaken out of its slumber. Even as 146 new Covid cases were reported, the focus was clearly on the Jamaat, the organization which counts among its members millions of unlettered Muslims and many others who can only read the Quran. In 2020 when the Jamaat was held solely responsible by a section of the media for spreading Covid cases in the country, the Delhi government too had come up as mentioned earlier, with a section on Tabligh victims called 'Markaz Masjid cases' in its daily dispatches on Covid.⁹ This time around, with the Kumbh, like much of the media, the Delhi Government too chose to stay quiet. It seemed that no Hindu resident of Delhi went to attend the Mela where millions had descended, but the entire Muslim world had congregated in Nizamuddin, where 3,000 Muslim worshippers gathered! Two modes of worship, two yardsticks.

23

The Politics of Love Jihad and Ghar Wapasi

IN NEW INDIA, AT LEAST in the states ruled by the BJP, it seems that it is a crime for a Muslim man to fall in love with a Hindu woman. If the man, or indeed the couple, insists on getting social approval for their relationship through marriage, it may result in imprisonment of up to five years for the man.

It is the Muslim man who is accused of trickery, deceit, even conspiracy, while the Hindu woman, it is implied, has no control over her mind or body; she is gullible. In this argument, the Hindu woman is regarded by many proponents of love jihad laws to not have the right to marry a man of her choice; she is considered a mere baby-producing machine, who is now under the control of a Muslim man who can use her to augment the numbers of his community. Through this devious design, one day, Muslims, who currently form a little over 14 per cent of India's population, are seen to be likely to overrun the number of Hindus, who now make up approximately 80 per cent of India's population!

This is the far-fetched premise of Love Jihad that was pursued relentlessly by Hindutva votaries even at the time of the pandemic. In 2020–2, far more energy and fantasy was expended on it than in finding the means to control the rising number of Covid-19 cases in the country, which had the second highest number of cases on the planet for months.

But Covid is for doctors to deal with. For social engineers, and saffron politicians, it is Love Jihad that is more important. Adityanath, the Uttar Pradesh chief minister, pledged to bring in 'an effective law' against conversion.[1] Shortly afterwards, we had a legislator in Uttar Pradesh urging his followers not to exercise restraint or wait for the law agencies to do their work when-ever they come across any case of a Muslim man and a Hindu woman in love. Instead, they were urged to pick up a stick or a shoe to mete out instant justice by tackling the man who dared to fall in love with a woman from the majority community. In a social media interaction with his voters, Sangeet Som, a firebrand BJP leader from western Uttar Pradesh, thundered, 'You must teach the love jihadis a lesson. Danda uthhao ya joota [pick up a stick or a shoe], but teach these love jihadis a lesson. It is up to the Hindus to protect their sisters and daughters.'[2] The same Som had defended the men accused of lynching Mohammed Akhlaq in 2015. Since then, he assiduously built his reputation on bricks of fake news cemented with false history. He once credited Mughal emperor Aurangzeb with building the Taj Mahal. As reported by Business Standard, 'Som has questioned Taj Mahal's place in history, distorting historical facts to say that it was built by an emperor who had imprisoned his father and targeted Hindus.'[3] So unaccustomed is he to ways of love!

Som got his cue from the state Chief Minister Yogi Adityanath. Preferring, as usual, to dish out street lingo, Adityanath had vowed in an election meeting on 31 October 2020, ahead of a by-election in Uttar Pradesh, to bring in a law to curb love jihad. 'I warn those who conceal identity and play with our sisters' respect, if you don't mend your ways, your Ram Naam Satya [Hindu funeral procession chant] journey will begin,' he warned.[4] Interestingly, back in 2014 a video emerged of 2009 in all likelihood where he had said, 'We have decided that we will convert 100 girls of their religion if they convert one Hindu girl.'[5]

A few days after issuing a death threat to anyone interested in an inter-religious marriage, he decided to frame an ordinance against love jihad. Called the Unlawful Religious Conversion (Prohibition) Ordinance 2020, it prohibited religious conversions not only through false representation, coercive measures, (undue) influence, oppressive measures, incentives, or fraudulent tactics but also through marriage. In other words, the ordinance, which was approved by the governor, prohibited conversion for marriage, except with the prior permission of the state. A person desirous of conversion before marriage had to apply to the district magistrate, who was to ask the police to find the real intention behind the wish. If the conversion was attributable to any monetary gratification or a better lifestyle, action was to be initiated against the person who 'caused' the conversion! It made no distinction between coercive conversion and conversions of free will. Clearly, in the view of many Hindutva practitioners, women had no free will! And for the foot soldiers of the self-declared Hindutva army, women need to be protected all the time, from the cradle to the crematorium. Just like Manu had recommended in the Manusmriti, a woman always had to be under the protection of a man. As a child, she was supposed to be protected by her father. As an adult woman, by her husband. An older woman had to be defended by her son! The same old suffocating patriarchal ways. The so-called love jihad, wherein a girl dares not only to fall in love but to do so with the evil 'Other', threatens to puncture this narrative!

Remarkably, the ordinance came within hours of the Allahabad High Court upholding the right of an adult to take a decision with respect to marriage without the interference of his family or the state. The bench of Justice Pankaj Naqvi and Justice Vivek Agarwal stated, 'We fail to understand that if the law permits two persons even of the same sex to live together peacefully, then neither any individual nor a family nor even the state can have an objection to the relationship of two major individuals who out of their own free will are living together.'[6] The bench was hearing the case of the petitioner Salamat Ansari and Priyanka Kharwar, who along with two others moved the court seeking the quashing of the FIR lodged by the father of Kharwar. They argued that the couple had attained the age of majority and hence were competent to contract marriage. Their nikah (Muslim marital contract) was solemnized in August 2019, with Priyanka embracing Islam. And the couple had been living peacefully since. In the landmark ruling, the court further said, 'We do not see Priyanka Kharwar and Salamat as Hindu and Muslim, rather as two grown-up individuals who out of their own free will and choice are living together peacefully and happily over a year. The Courts and the Constitutional Courts, in particular, are enjoined to uphold life and liberty of an individual guaranteed under Article 21 of the Constitution of India.'[7]

Meanwhile, other BJP-ruled states joined the fray to put in place laws against 'love jihad'. The Madhya Pradesh Government announced its plans to introduce the Madhya Pradesh Religious Freedom Bill, 2020, to prohibit marriage on the basis of forced religious conversions. The bill is aimed at making forced religious conversions and 'love-jihad' a non-bailable offence, wherein the main accused and his/her associates in crime will be awarded rigorous punishment of up to five years. The co-accused will be treated as the main accused and will be awarded the same punishment. However, these provisions will become applicable only when the complaint of such a nature is made by the person/persons 'converted by fraud, allurement or force' or their parents or siblings. That these new laws were framed to merely paint men from the minority community in a certain light and deny them their fundamental right became clear within a couple of weeks of the ordinance being passed in Uttar Pradesh. Two cases were reported within 24 hours. In one case, the man was jailed, and in the other, the woman got an escort for security.

Reported *The Indian Express* a few days later,

> Uttar Pradesh police have recorded five cases so far in the nine days since the state's anti-conversion law, which imposes stringent conditions on inter-faith marriages, came into force. But two of these cases, lodged within 24 hours of each other, present a sharp contrast—and show how police have wielded the new law selectively. In Bareiily, police did not entertain the complaint of a father that his daughter had married a Hindu man after conversion. Police said they went by the woman's testimony that she got married in September before the law came into force. But in Moradabad, police arrested and jailed a Muslim man under the anti-conversion law despite his wife Pinki saying that they got married in July. The man's brother was also arrested and jailed.[8]

Different strokes for different folks.

Later, towards the end of the year, in mid-December, Pinki left the shelter home where she was housed by the state police to go back to the house of her parents-in-law, having told a magistrate that she was 22, an adult, and had married Rashid in July 2020, of her own free will, and much before the Uttar Pradesh Prohibition of Unlawful Conversion of Religion Ordinance 2020 came into effect. Even as the police sought to check the details of her nikah and conversion, her husband spent many weeks in jail before being granted bail.

Interestingly, the concept of 'love jihad' is all-new, completely recent, much like the laws framed to curb it. Till 2014, hardly anybody had heard of the term. If it was mentioned, it was done so in passing. Never, even at the height of the Babri Masjid–Ramjanmabhoomi campaign, did senior BJP leaders, including LK Advani who gave currency to the concept of Hindutva as a way of life, mention it. If at all it was aired, it was in barely audible whispers. Noted historian Bipan Chandra in his work *Communalism: A Primer* wrote: 'Hindu communalism remained weak before 1947, and in fact, till 1984, possessing no real mass support. Hindu communalism did get aroused on the issue of the cutting of a peepal tree or the killing of a cow, or the selling of beef, or a Hindu girl marrying a Muslim boy… But these would remain local issues and would not sustain a prolonged communal divide.'[9]

It all changed following Narendra Modi's landmark victory in 2014. A victory that came riding on the plank of development only to switch to a polarizing one. Within weeks of Modi's assumption of power, and a little before the by-elections to 11 Uttar Pradesh Assembly seats, a love jihad campaign was launched that not only marked out Muslims as the evil 'other' but sought to unite Hindu society beyond the divisions of caste and class. Hindus were asked to be vigilant, and men, in particular, were asked to defend the honour of their women, to protect them from abduction and rape. Also, to protect them from marrying Muslim men or converting to Islam. *Frontline* commented:

> From 2014 onwards, love jihad was presented as a critical danger to the existence of the age-old Hindu society through a series of street corner meetings in western Uttar Pradesh, handbills, and posters stuck at vantage points in small towns of Uttar Pradesh, Bihar and Madhya Pradesh. Love was no longer a personal affair. The community, society, political parties and even the state could now step into an inter-community relationship.[10]

Noted historian Charu Gupta breaks the concept down as follows:

> This violent movement against love had multiple layers; it simultaneously attempted to invoke Hindu male prowess, promote images of an 'evil' and 'licentious' Muslim male, fabricate fears of declining Hindu numbers, construct a homogeneous Hindu identity and Hindu nation over a sharply caste- and class-divided society and reinstate familial patriarchies. At the same time, it also exposed grave anxieties and fears over women's independent and individual expressions of love, desire and intimacy.[11]

Soon after we started hearing of the twin terms 'love jihad' and 'ghar wapasi', each fed off the other. While attempts were made to prevent inter-religious marriages by insinuating that they were actually instances of love jihad, ghar wapasi was simultaneously made out to be an attempt to increase the numerical strength of Hindus. The Right-wing leaders saw love jihad or the conversion of a Hindu girl for marriage as a symbol of weakness in the larger Hindu society; and the campaign to convert Muslims (besides Christians and tribals) to Hinduism was not only a means to stem the tide of loss through love jihad but it was also aimed at restoring the masculine qualities of Hindu men. All this was a by-play of an overweening patriarchal society where, on the one hand, the protection of a woman's honour was the duty of men, and, on the other, bringing women and even men of other faiths within the umbrella of Hinduism was akin to victory in war. Unsurprisingly, at a congregation of Hindu ascetics in Bihar, Yogi Adityanath coined the slogan 'Sastra ke saath Shastra' (Weapons with scriptures).

The erroneous belief of the concept of 'ghar wapasi' all along is the idea that all Muslims of India were Hindus at one time. Back in December 2014, speaking at a Virat Hindu Sammelan in Kolkata, the RSS sarsanghchalak Mohan Bhagwat justified ghar wapasi, stating, 'We will bring back our brothers who have lost their way' like 'belongings stolen by a thief'.[12] He also called India a 'Hindu Rashtra'. 'Bhule bhatke jo bhai gaye hain, unko wapas layenge. Woh log apne aap nahin gaye, unko loot kar, lalach de kar le kar gaye… Abhi chor pakda gaya hai. Mera maal chor ke paas hai. Aur yeh duniya jaanti hai. Main apna maal wapas loonga, yeh kaunsi badi baat hai (We will bring back our brothers who have lost their way. They did not go on their own. They were robbed, tempted into leaving… Now the thief has been caught and the world knows my belongings are with the thief. I will naturally retrieve my belongings, so why is this such a big issue?).' Almost eight years later, in November, 2022, he repeated the claim, stating, 'Everyone living in India is "Hindu"… We have been telling since 1925 (when the RSS was founded) that everyone living in India is a Hindu. Those who consider India as their matrubhoomi (motherland) and want to live with culture of unity in diversity and make efforts in this direction, irrespective of whatever religion, culture, language and food habit and ideology they follow, are Hindus.'[13]

In other words, the Muslims of India were Hindus at one time, and they had strayed. Now was the time to facilitate their return. All that was needed to bring them home was a purification ceremony. Much like Dayanand Saraswati's Shuddhi campaign at the turn of the 20th century, not too dissimilar to Dilip Singh Judeo's efforts at the time of Vajpayee's prime ministership in the late 1990s. Towards the end of 2014, we saw a sorry spectacle in Agra where the Hindu Jagran Samiti claimed to have converted 50 Muslim families.[14] The newspapers splashed photos of men in skullcaps with tilaks on their foreheads taking part in a fire ceremony. Though the allegations of pecuniary benefits were denied, the families reverted to Islam soon after. No charges were pressed against the Samiti. Around the same time, the Dharma Jagran Manch stated that on 23 December 2014—the anniversary of the martyrdom of Swami Shraddhanand, who had been the leader of the Shuddhi movement in the late 19th–early 20th century—it would convert Muslims to Hinduism in at least 50 locations in west Uttar Pradesh. Of course, no pre-emptive action was taken against the Manch. 'The Dharam Jagran Samiti (DJS)—an offshoot of the Rashtriya Swayamsevak Sangh (RSS) and the Bajrang Dal—only recently announced that it aims to meet a target of converting one lakh Muslims and Christians into Hinduism every year.[15] Earlier this month in Agra, the DJS reportedly converted some 200-odd Muslims to Hinduism. The event came to light after the supposed converts, many of whom are among the most impoverished sections of the society, alleged that they had been misled into believing that they would be offered Below Poverty Line cards by consenting to the conversion.'[16]

In fact, a little more than a year later, Modi himself talked of 'adopting' Muslims in his address at the BJP National Council meeting in Kozhikode in 2016. Recalling the words of the Jan Sangh ideologue Deen Dayal Upadhyaya, Modi stated, 'Fifty years ago, Pandit Upadhyay said, "Do not reward/appease Muslims, do not shun them but purify them." Do not treat Muslims like vote ki mandi ka maal [vote bank]. Unhe apna samjho [Regard them as your own].'[17] His words came after criticism from some quarters over his sustained silence on the mob lynching of Muslim men. Modi did keep his word, though. Far from treating the community as vote ki mandi, he did not seek the Muslim vote at all! He gave the community no tickets to contest elections; he hardly sought their votes to form the government.

The foot soldiers of Hindutva, meanwhile, prevented Muslim men from marrying consenting Hindu girls. By the end of 2022, the allegations of love jihad were fused with those of land jihad and economic jihad. Maharashtra became the new rallying point for public demonstrations of hate against Muslims who fell in love with Hindu women. *The Indian Express* reported in March 2023,

> Starting November last year, at least 50 'Hindu Jan Aakrosh Morcha' rallies have been held across Maharashtra, in almost all of the state's 36 districts. Each of these events has followed a set pattern: a brief march through the heart of the city, amid a sea of saffron flags and caps, followed by a short rally, where speakers on a makeshift dais attack minorities, invoke 'love jihad', 'land jihad', 'forced conversions', and call for the economic boycott of the Muslim community.
>
> For the record, the BJP distances itself from these rallies, saying they are by the Sakal Hindu Samaj, an umbrella body of

Hindutva and Sangh organisations, but almost all of these events have had the presence of party leaders, including the local BJP MLA and MP.[18]

Interestingly, no such allegations of love jihad were levelled when a Hindu man married a Muslim girl! Love, you see, comes with blinkers! Meanwhile another bunch set about converting poor Muslims in Delhi, Haryana and other places. The highly respected daily *The Hindu* reported in April 2020, 'Around 35 people belonging to six Muslim families have converted to Hinduism in Haryana's Jind district this past week. The families claimed they were contemplating about converting for the past several months since their names, customs and rituals were akin to Hindus.'[19]

One of the-se converts pointed out the similarities in the lifestyle of Muslims and Hindus in the region. Another, Ramesh Kumar, a resident of Danoda Kalan village and belonging to the Doom caste, told *The Hindu* over phone that they had been staying in the village surrounded by Hindus for more than four generations, and their names and rituals were like them. 'My father is Ved Prakash. My brothers are Vikas and Sunil. We always had Hindu names. We have same customs as Hindus and celebrate Holi, Diwali and other Hindu festivals. I bought a home in January this year and held havan. Even three of the six houses of our families have temples,' he is reported to have said.

Two weeks later, *The Times of India* reported on the conversion of 40 Muslim families in the Hisar district of the state. 'About 250 members of 40 Muslim families from Budhmira village in Haryana's Hisar district embraced Hinduism on Friday and performed the last rites of [an] 80-year-old woman according to Hindu customs.'[20] Meanwhile, in Delhi's Bawana neighbourhood, 12 Muslim families did likewise, leading to allegations of coercion and economic boycott of the minorities if they did not join the majoritarian faith.

The conversion or ghar wapasi of Muslim families took place in and around the region where Maulana Mohammad Ilyas had worked nearly a century ago to prevent the conversion of local Muslims under Dayanand Saraswati's Shuddhi campaign. A passage in *Inside the Tablighi Jamaat* reads:

> Sometime in the 1890s, Swami Dayanand Saraswati started an energetic campaign to win over poor Muslims, many of whom had converted to Islam from Hinduism, but still retained half-Hindu names and followed many of the rituals of their earlier religion. Names like 'Bheema Sheikh' or 'Rahul Khan' were even more common in the first half of the 20th Century, speaking eloquently to the mixing of the two faiths in different generations of the same family or community. These Muslims, particularly, in eastern Rajasthan, Awadh and present-day Haryana, knew little about Islam. Largely poor farmers with small land holdings, or landless farmers who worked on the fields of zamindars, they were usually illiterate too. This combination of illiteracy and poverty made it easy for Dayanand Saraswati's Shuddhi campaign to take off in these areas in the first decade of the new century.[21]

Maulana Ilyas got the message of Islam to these poor people from the region. There is a popular anecdote about how he won over the locals with his piety. Those days Muslims from the region would go to Delhi in search of work. Many would find employment at construction sites in the city and return home after having saved enough from their daily wages. It so happened that once Maulana

Ilyas met a few construction workers in Delhi and brought them to his mosque, which is now known as Markaz or the headquarters of the Tablighi Jamaat. When they were asked about their daily earnings, the men thought they were being recruited for some fresh construction project in the vicinity. To their disbelief, they were told to stay there and learn a few verses of the Quran every day. At the end of the day, they would be paid the same as the wages for a day's labour. This was Maulana Ilyas's way of countering the Shuddhi campaign. It made the local Muslims more aware of Islam, brought in more believers to mosques and gave them a new social bonding, all acting as a possible bulwark against future conversions.

It worked for many decades. However, as the Tablighi Jamaat became too embroiled in ritualistic Islam, and internecine fights in order to head the body became a frequent occurrence, some of the poorer sections of Muslims felt alienated and left out. The successors of Maulana Ilyas failed to exhibit the same spirit in taking the poor along. Many in far flung villages remained untouched by the Jamaat's self-awareness campaign. These groups were probably the ones to feel the pinch of the lockdown and the pandemic the most. They were the ones who were converted to Hinduism in Jind and Hisar during the pandemic, bringing life full circle. Significantly, according to no law was their conversion said to be under duress or illegal. No questions were raised about the agency of women or about men being evil tricksters.

As for the rest of India, much of the country stayed quiet. Newspapers did not devote space to these developments on page one. Television channels did not have space for the Jind or Hisar conversions on prime time. Ghar wapasi was a problem only for the Muslims, not too different from an occasional interfaith wedding. A case in November 2022, for instance, demonstrated this when an interfaith couple in Mumbai called off the proposed wedding reception because a television channel head tweeted their reception card, virtually instigating the masses to stop the event. Reported The Quint, 'Hours after Hindutva proponent and Sudarshan News editor-in-chief Suresh Chavhanke tweeted out details of an interfaith couple's wedding reception invitation and linked it to the Shraddha Walkar murder case (Walkar was in a live-in relationship with Aftab Poonawala who allegedly murdered her in a brutal fashion in Delhi), Imran and Divya were forced to call off their function in Vasai, on the outskirts of Mumbai.'[22] Even as other channels kept quiet on Chavhanke's attempt to intrude into the personal life of the couple, he wrote, 'Aftab is a native of Vasai, he is the same man who chopped Shraddha into 35 pieces. Even after such a heart-wrenching crime, how can an interfaith wedding like this happen there?' The wedding reception was quietly cancelled. Nobody raised a voice about two consenting adults (who had already had a court marriage) not being allowed to celebrate their wedding with family and friends.

The quiet, almost simultaneous move from a supposedly anti-conversion campaign called love jihad to ghar wapasi was, to the Hindu Right, one of a journey from being anti-national to national, from being a foreigner in India who could stay here on condition of good behaviour to one completely at home with all attendant privileges. Of course, that 'good behaviour' did not include the right to celebrate even a court marriage!

24

Hijab and Hindutva

In EARLY FEBRUARY 2022, VISUALS of bedlam in several colleges of Udupi and other districts were beamed into people's living rooms through television news channels and social media. The videos showed saffron-wearing college boys confronting a hijab-wearing Muslim girl with slogans of 'Jai Shri Ram'. The girl, later identified as Muskan, was clearly outnumbered but not intimidated and was seen shouting back 'Allah-u-Akbar' at the crowd. Some scholars found fault with the girl's response, arguing she should have just walked on or responded with the slogan of 'Jai Hind'. But the critics forgot that this was a teenage girl faced with a hostile crowd, falling back on her faith for moral support.

However, the events did not start with Muskan. It started with a bunch of teenage girls who returned to the campus of the pre-university government college in Udupi in December 2021 after more than a year of online classes due to Covid-19. When the six hijab-wearing girls entered their classroom, the teacher told them to seek the principal's permission to attend lectures. The principal had apparently banned hijabs in the classroom. The girls could thus wear a hijab on the campus but not in the classrooms. The girls did not give in and instead cited precedence—their seniors had also worn hijabs to the college and inside the classrooms. For the next few days, the girls were not allowed to attend classes. Word spread. Soon, several other colleges imposed a hijab ban, and we saw disturbing visuals of even teachers being asked to take off their hijab on the road near the gate of the institutions. In addition, there were also videos of boys wearing saffron scarves and shawls heckling the black hijab-wearing Muskan with cries of 'Jai Shri Ram'.

The state government threw its weight behind those seeking a hijab ban. Invoking Articles 133 (2) of the Karnataka Education Act, 1983, the government insisted that 'a uniform style of clothes has to be worn compulsorily'. It directed the colleges to ensure that 'clothes which disturb equality, integrity and public law and order should not be worn'.[1]

The colleges, meanwhile, drew a false parallel between hijab-wearing girls and saffron scarf-wearing boys, while banning both—the latter was worn merely to browbeat and intimidate girls who wore the hijab as part of their regular religious practice. Unlike the hijab, wearing saffron scarves had no precedence on the campus. Plainly speaking, the colleges shut their gates to hijab-clad Muslim girls. The state's message was plain and clear: If Muslim girls wanted to access public education, they would have to conform and leave their hijabs at home; they did not have a choice. The girls, with their innate belief in the Constitution of India, quoted the Articles of Freedom of Religion to buttress their contention. Then they went to the state High Court, seeking redress. It was not to come their way.

A three-judge bench headed by Chief Justice Ritu Raj Awasthi upheld the state government's ban on wearing hijab in educational institutions. The 129-page verdict held that 'wearing of Hijab by

Muslim women does not form a part of essential religious practice in Islamic faith' and 'the prescription of school uniform is only a reasonable restriction constitutionally permissible which the students cannot object to'.[2]

Barely a few hours after the Karnataka High Court judgment, AH Almas, a student of the Government Girls Pre-University College, Udupi, who was one of the petitioners in the case, was clearly disturbed while speaking to the Press.'We are citizens of this country, and we are not treated equally. What more do you want us to say,' she said on a note of anguish.[3]

Soon after the verdict, Yashpal Suvarna, a local BJP leader, called the hijab-wearing girls 'terrorists trained by a terror outfit'.[4] *Frontline* fortnightly analyzed the repercussions of the High Court verdict:

> The judgement has led to the further marginalisation of hijab-wearing Muslim students, groups of whom were turned away from colleges in the districts of Yadgir, Raichur, Hasan and Bengaluru Rural on March 15 and 16 and not allowed to appear for their international examination, which precedes the crucial Pre-University College, or Class 12, final exam. This has caused real concern for the future of the girls' education. There is also an apprehension that private educational institutions and degree colleges could also devise guidelines restricting the hijab from classrooms.[5]

The High Court verdict was criticized, with legal commentators holding that it had struck a blow against liberty, equality and fraternity. It was, however, left to M.A. Siraj of News Trail to convey the Muslim community's sense of anguish and betrayal. Speaking to *Frontline's* Vikhar Ahmed Sayeed, he said,

The sense of alienation among Muslim community is acute. They are economically deprived, educationally backward and politically under-represented. The RSS–BJP dispensation is now targeting them for social exclusion through its hate-mongering campaign. All measures that could sharpen social fault lines within society are being taken and exploited to tap political benefits accruing from communal polarisation. The latest to be weaponised is hijab and uniform.[6]

The hijab controversy was to Muslim women what cow slaughter and love jihad allegations were to Muslim men. Through lynching, poor Muslim men were denied their right to food and livelihood; through love jihad they were denied the agency of choice. Following allegations of cow slaughter, more than 40 men paid with their lives, and in some cases, FIRs were even filed against the victims or their families. The idea always was to intimidate the Muslim men and send a message to the women: if the men could be lynched at a public square, women were more vulnerable than ever before. In love jihad cases, scores of young Muslim men were accused of either concealing their identity to marry a Hindu woman or converting her through deceit. Either way, they were attacked for loving a Hindu woman; many were thrashed in public spaces, some were jailed. And a number of states, including Uttar Pradesh, Himachal Pradesh, Uttarakhand and Madhya Pradesh, framed laws against conversion, the belief always being that the Muslim men were deceitful and forcing marriage upon gullible Hindu women to augment their population. If the men were tamed through lynching and accusations of love jihad, the women had to be put in their place through allegations of their hijab being against uniformity and equality, a threat to discipline in schools, or as Suvarna alleged, the hijab-wearing girls were just plain 'terrorists trained by a terror outfit'.

Like in the case of 'love jihad', where Hindu women were denied their agency of choice—it was always lustful Muslim men on the prowl with gullible Hindu women falling for their charm offensive—in the hijab commotion, Muslim women were denied their right to education besides their ability to choose. It was all in conformity with Hindutva politics, which often reduces women to child-bearing machines, restricting their role to the kitchen or the bedroom. In the case of hijab-wearing Muslim women, the motive was even more sinister; the idea of Muslim women being the Other was reinforced in the public mind. 'They look different, they dress differently, they are not like us', was Hindutva bodies' driving mantra in the whole issue. Again, the unspoken principle being that there was only one way of being an Indian: one language, one dress, one culture, one food, one religion.

The directions to outlaw the hijab were part of a pattern to erase all shades of difference beyond the lopsided notions of majoritarianism. They were aimed at the fulfilment of all that Savarkar and Golwalkar stood for with their concepts of pitrabhu and punyabhu (fatherland and sacred land), a country where Christians and Muslims, with their sacred lands being abroad, deserved no rights, no consideration. Indeed, later, when the hijab case was heard in the Supreme Court, Justice Hemant Gupta refused to see a parallel between a pagdi worn by a Sikh or a Hindu man and a headscarf worn by a Muslim woman. While hearing the batch of petitions challenging the Karnataka High Court's judgment, which upheld the ban on hijab in colleges in the state, Justice Gupta orally remarked that 'a "pagdi" was not equivalent to a "hijab" and the two could not be compared'.[7]

As academic-author-activist Apoorvanand, a professor of Hindi at the University of Delhi, said, the hijab controversy was part of a larger project whereby 'Muslim identity markers are being declared as sectarian and undesirable in public spaces'.[8] 'It is telling Muslims and non-Hindus that the state will dictate their appearance and their practices,' he said.

The same report concluded with these eloquent words: 'On Monday, some students in hijabs were allowed into the government pre-university college in Udupi but were forced to sit in segregated classrooms. "We were made to sit in a separate room and no teacher came to teach us," said one student. "We were just sitting there like criminals."' Treating practising Muslim girls as criminals is to put it mildly. It was social apartheid being practised in Karnataka, India, 2022.

Later, in October, the two-judge bench of the Supreme Court hearing the case gave a split verdict. Justice Gupta upheld the Karnataka High Court ban while Justice Sudhanshu Dhulia spoke in favour of allowing hijab-clad girls to attend school, stating, 'A girl child has the right to wear Hijab in her house or outside her house, and that right does not stop at her school gate… The thing that was most important in my mind while deciding this case was the education of a girl child. It's common knowledge that already a girl child, primarily in rural areas and semi-urban areas, has to face a lot of difficulties. She is often required to help her mother in daily chores, in cleaning and washing, before she goes to school. There are other difficulties as well. What I asked is, are we making her life any better'. Well, certainly not. Justice Dhulia's words reminded one of the fate of well-known Tamil writer Rajathi Salma who was forced to quit school by her parents when she reached puberty. Born Ruqaiya, she had to take the pen name of Salma to even dare to write; the idea being to hide her identity not just from the larger society, but her own family.

Meanwhile, even as the hijab case is to be heard by a three-judge bench of the Supreme Court after the two-judge Bench's failed to pronounce a unanimous judgement, a number of Muslim girls lost a year in their academic careers for their refusal to take off their hijab and appear for the final examinations in March 2022. The loss was not only theirs.

25

Of Halal Meat and Food Fascism

FIRST, MUSLIM MEN WERE ATTACKED under the suspicion of cow slaughter. Next, they were lynched for merely transporting cattle, even milch cattle. Soon after, an orchestrated campaign started against halal food. People who had never touched meat in their lives suddenly became part of the campaign. In Bengaluru, the Hindu Janajagrithi Samiti, a Right-wing organization, started a campaign against halal meat.

> 'During Ugadi (considered the New Year for Kannadigas), there are a lot of purchases of meat, and we are starting a campaign against Halal meat. As per Islam, Halal meat is first offered to Allah, and the same cannot be offered to Hindu gods,' Mohan Gowda, the Samithi spokesperson claimed astonishingly, adding 'Be it Halal meat or Halal economy, the money that comes from this is used for anti-national activities, terrorist activities. By using Halal meat, it would be akin to a call and support for anti-national activities.'[1]

News18 reported online, 'The fringe outfits have already forced several hotels and restaurants, including a Biryani joint in Bengaluru, to remove the Halal tag from their menu. Protests to ban Halal meat were witnessed in Nelamangala, Mandya and Mysuru districts as well.'[2]

This bid to outlaw or at least enfeeble halal business followed a concerted attempt at getting rid of Muslim shopkeepers from in and around temples in Karnataka. In March 2022, a banner urging temples not to lease stalls to Muslims appeared outside the Bappanadu Durgaparameshwari temple in Dakshina Kannada. A similar banner was then put up in Chikmagalur, announcing that Muslim traders would not be allowed at the Subramanyeshwara temple fair. *The Telegraph* reported,

> What had begun at a Shimoga temple and was followed by more in Dakshina Kannada and Udupi has spread to shrines in Tumkur, Hassan, Chikmagalur and other districts. Among these temples are the famed Belur Channakeshava in Hassan, Siddhalingeshwara in Tumkur and even the 800-year-old Bappanadu temple, built by Muslim merchant Bappa Beary of Kerala and a symbol of communal amity that drew many non-Hindu prasada seekers. This season, for the first time ever, the temple banned Muslims from bidding for the leases to set up temporary retails at its festival venue.[3]

In Mumbai, Yashwant Killedar, president of the Maharashtra Navnirman Vyapari Sena, wrote a letter on saying 'no to Halal meat'. Unabashedly, he equated halal meat with terrorism. 'In a way, we are funding terror at our own expense. We should stop this in Maharashtra by saying "No to Halal". We require people to create a movement around this cause, and we request people to join this cause', the letter read.⁴ These repeated noises against halal meat in Karnataka and Maharashtra were good enough for the BJP National General Secretary CT Ravi to call the practice of selling halal meat and products a part of economic jihad.

Meanwhile, in Uttar Pradesh, Haryana, Delhi and Gujarat, Muslim eateries were forced to shut down during Navaratri, the nine-day Hindu festival when many people from the majority community abstain from certain kinds of food, including meat. In Delhi, the South Delhi Municipal Corporation (SDMC) directed its officers to take action to ensure the closure of meat shops during the nine-day period of the Navaratri festival observed from 2 to 11 April 2022. The SDMC Mayor Mukesh Suryaan said that in the future, licences for running meat shops would only be issued if they agreed not to operate during the Navaratri festival. Around the same time, the East Delhi Municipal Corporation Chief Mayor Shyam Sundar Agarwal tweeted, 'We give licenses to slaughterhouses with rules; they should be closed on Saptami, Ashtami, Navami, Diwali, Guru Nanak Jayanti, etc., which is why we closed them.'⁵ The issue was big enough for foreign papers to devote considerable space to it. Screamed a headline in *The Independent*, 'India's opposition lawmakers condemn Delhi's "meat ban" during Hindu religious festival Navratri.'⁶

Prime Minister Narendra Modi's home state, Gujarat, went one step further by banning not just meat but also eggs! And not just during Navaratri but during the Hindu month of Sawan, too. *The Times of India* reported,

A big order from the Rajkot Municipal Corporation (RMC) where there has been a ban on meat, mutton, egg and fish selling in Gujarat from 29th July because of Sawan Somwar. The Municipal Corporation has also banned non-veg selling on 1st,

8th, 15th, 19th and 28th of August. From 30th July, the month of Sawan will start in Gujarat. In North India, the month of Sawan begins 15 days in advance. As per the RMC rules, strict action will be taken against the person who will (not) abide by the order. It seems like after Rajkot, Gujarat's other districts and municipalities such as Ahmedabad, Surat, Vadodara etc. will also implement such rules.[7]

In the satellite township of Noida in Uttar Pradesh, post-2017, when Adityanath was sworn in as the BJP chief minister, no meat shop is allowed to operate during Navaratri and Sawan. The shopkeepers, mostly Muslims, feebly complained about the denial of the right to earn their livelihood. It was to no avail. Recalling the first imposition of meat curfew in 2017, a meat-seller explained how the ban on meat came to be enforced in the township:

> The workers of Hindu Yuva Vahini came here. They said, shut your shop, else you will see the consequences. To tell you the truth, nowadays, you cannot even buy eggs in many sectors of Noida. Then why to talk of this place only? You cannot buy meat in Ghaziabad, no beef, no mutton, no chicken, no fish... We have got two times vacation in a year. Earlier what you ate was your wish... But now we have this Yogi government. The government does not want anybody to eat meat during Navaratra time. You must remember, it is this government that showered rose petals on pilgrims coming with Ganga jal during Shivratri, and cut the Hajj subsidy. So, people compromise on these nine days. Nobody would like to be killed for selling fish or chicken.[8]

Against the backdrop of a vicious campaign against halal meat and the imposition of the dietary preferences of a section of the majority community, especially during Hindu religious festivals, Parvesh Verma, a BJP MP from Delhi, took the socio-economic apartheid a notch higher. Verma, son of former Chief Minister Sahib Singh Verma, was no fringe element. At the time of his alleged hate speech, he was by far the tallest Jat leader of the BJP in Delhi. At a public gathering in east Delhi, he gave a call for complete boycott of a community, without naming it but with enough hints in his speech. Reported Citizens for Justice and Peace, 'Controversial BJP leader Parvesh Sahib Singh Verma has fired yet another salvo against members of a particular community, urging people to boycott them. Though Verma did not specifically name the Muslim community, he was speaking about an alleged case of murder, where the victim was Hindu and the alleged perpetrators all hailed from the Muslim community.'[9] Verma said at the gathering, 'If you want to set their minds right, if you want to cure them, there is only one solution—complete boycott.' He then asked the audience to take an oath with him, 'We will boycott them completely. We will not buy anything from their shops and establishments. We will not pay them any wages.'[10]

Though Verma later claimed he was referring to those families whose members were involved in the killing of the Hindu youth, Manish, the video of the incident exposed him; every word he uttered was, however, lapped up by audiences who cheered after him and happily repeated the pledge not to buy from or sell anything to a Muslim or even employ a Muslim as a labourer. Verma's words proved all lingering suspicions right. He was not operating in a social vacuum.

Later in the month (October 2022), in neighbouring Haryana's Manesar township, the VHP held a meeting where efforts were made to intimidate the Muslim populace with calls asking for an economic boycott and a possible migration. Said a leader, 'I want to tell those maulvis, pack up your belongings or else the people of Manesar will not leave you... Ye Hindu rashtra tha, hai aur rahega,' he added.[11] This event was held a little over a week after Verma's thinly veiled call for boycott, and some three months after a panchayat organized at a Manesar temple by members of the Bajrang Dal and the VHP called for an economic boycott of 'Muslim shopkeepers and vendors'.

Things turned worse in July 2023. Until then, restrictions were imposed on selling meat during Navratri festival. Now, meat sellers were forced to down their shutters during the Hindu month of Sawan. And the month extended to almost two months, as the shopkeepers were told in Noida. Wherever the meatsellers went, to local police or administration, they heard only one reply, "Aage se aadesh hai" (Order from high above). No seller was shared a copy of the order, yet nobody could sell meat for full two months. Reported News18:

> The Uttar Pradesh government has decided to stop sale of meat in the open along the routes fixed for Kanwar Yatra. Sawan or Shravan is being considered unique this year as the festival is being celebrated for 59 days after 19 years. There will be eight Sawan Mondays instead of the usual four every year... Adityanath said this year due to Adhimas (additional month), the month of Shravan is of two months duration. The festivals of Shravani Shivratri, Nagpanchami and Rakshabandhan will be celebrated during this period, he said.[12]

No questions were asked by the media about providing an alternative source of earning to the meat-sellers or giving them temporary space away from the Kanwar Yatra. Nor did the government deem it necessary to think of the livelihood of those who do not observe the Shravan protocol; could be practitioners of another faith altogether. The meat-seller and the daily wage earners at their tiny shops suffered untold hardships.

These actions together proved that be it the campaign against halal meat or Muslim shopkeepers in the vicinity of a temple or coercive shutdown of meat business during Navaratri, it was never about Hinduism. It was never about the sacred cow. It was never about animal rights. It wasn't even about Hindu festivals. All along, it has been about denial—that of food and livelihood to Muslims, to push an embattled and a largely impoverished community further into a corner, strip the weak of their dignity. It has all along been a campaign to destroy a community financially and at the same time, practice social apartheid. A psychological genocide, if ever there can be one. Food fascism is just another one of its manifestations.

PART 6
Looks and Beyond

26

'You Look Like a Muslim'

BEING A MUSLIM IS DIFFICULT enough but looking like a Muslim? Well, it is risky too as Deepak Bundele, a lawyer from Madhya Pradesh, discovered. Based in Betul, Bundele, who sports a luxuriant beard, had stepped out to purchase medicines a little before a nationwide lockdown was imposed in March 2020 to prevent the spread of Covid-19. He is a patient of diabetes and hypertension.

On the evening of 23 March, a little more than 24 hours before Prime Minister Narendra Modi's televised address to the nation about imposing a lockdown from midnight, Bundele was stopped by the police for not wearing a mask as he headed to a government hospital for procuring medicines. Incidentally, wearing a mask at that time was optional. Soon, a policeman slapped him. When Bundele cited the Indian Constitution to stop the cop from beating him up, other police officials gathered to rough him up even more.

'I need constant medication and life-saving medicines to survive and I told the policemen everything while they were assaulting me. But, they kept hitting me, even after I fell,' he said, adding, 'I bled for almost a 2–3 days after the incident,' he was quoted as saying by the portal Newsclick.[1] In the same report, he also raised serious concerns about the communal angle of the incident, saying, 'It's a matter of grave concern that the police is turning communal and targeting a particular community.'[2]

Bundele, who has been a journalist too, approached the district superintendent of police to register his complaint. The real face of the police, though, was exposed just a few days later. Following Bundele's letters to the State Human Rights Commission, besides the chief minister's office, the police pressed upon him to take back his complaint, telling him they were willing to apologize and that he had been a victim of mistaken identity. A police official named BS Patel came to his residence to prevail upon him to take back his complaint.

'"Police, whenever there are Hindu-Muslim riots, always sides with the Hindus, even Muslims know it. But this happened, it was a mistake," one of the policemen is heard in an audio clip Mr Bundele recorded. "So you are saying they thrashed me thinking I am a Muslim," he asked them, to which one of them replied, "Yes, that is the case, your beard is long too," explained the police officials to Bundele on a note of apology.' Bundele recorded the conversation.[3]

'The police officer is a staunch Hindu,' added the official in the recording, referring to the man who had raised his hand at Bundele. He added that as a mark of accomplishment, the man had 'tortured' many Muslim prisoners. He was probably hoping to win Bundele's favour by talking of the police's partisanship. And went on to state how as a lawyer Bundele needed to work in sync with the police. The underlying message was collusion was needed between police and lawyers.

The Wire commented on the clip, 'Patel, in the audio clip, admitted that the accused police official, Kapil Saurashtriya, mistook him to be a Muslim because of the beard. Saurashtriya is a "staunch Hindu" and "tortured" many Muslim men who are in his custody, Patel proclaimed. While requesting Bundele to withdraw his case, the official admitted that the state police always favour Hindus during communal riots.'[4]

Bundele did not give up. He went to the state High Court to seek relief. It did not come his way. He plans to go to the Supreme Court. As he did not agree to take back his complaint, the Madhya Pradesh Police charged him with manhandling policemen on duty, and produced as witness three men of the Rashtriya Hindu Sena. The men claimed Bundele's injuries were self-inflicted. The Wire reported, 'According to them, the police officials spoke to Bundele very politely and tried to make him understand the enormity of the coronavirus pandemic. Yet, the Rashtriya Hindu Sena members said, Bundele lost his cool and created a scene, forced himself down and started beating himself up.'[5] Their statements specifically mentioned that Kapil Saurashtriya, who Bundele had identified as leading the police officials there, did not beat him up at all. The statements of the three Rashtriya Hindu Sena members were identical and even the language used was the same. Maybe, men with a similar ideology of hate and falsehood use similar language too!

If looking like a Muslim can be so traumatic, imagine actually being a Muslim, particularly somebody manifestly so—a man with a beard and a skullcap, a woman in a traditional black burqa! In the summer of 2019, the BBC put out a video showcasing the experience of a man in Assam, a devout Muslim, with a beard, being accosted by a mob, which then forces him to kneel and eat pork. All along the masses watched approvingly. It was as if every blow on the Muslim man's body was a collective one. In the video, the man called Shaukat Ali was accused of being both a beef-seller and a Bangladeshi.

The BBC reported, 'It happened just days before the first phase of voting in the Indian elections. A Muslim trader in the northeastern state of Assam was leaving work when he was accosted by a mob. Shaukat Ali was surrounded by the group, forced to kneel in sludge as he was attacked.'[6]

In the video uploaded along with the report, a man was reportedly heard shouting at Ali, 'Are you Bangladeshi? Do you have your name in the NRC?' The incident, reported by First Post,[7] reinforced a certain political section's oft-repeated claims of Muslims in the state being Bangladeshis. For the man who made the attack, sporting a beard and wearing a tehmat (an unstitched skirt which folds at the front) was the equivalent of being a foreigner! Incidentally, after an elaborate NRC exercise, it was discovered that the state had a little under two million people who failed to provide their citizenship papers. Most were found to be non-Muslims.

'"Why did you sell beef here?" asked another as he jabbed his finger at Mr Ali. Instead of stepping in to help, the crowds that gathered filmed the incident on their mobile phones,' the BBC reported.

More than a month after this attempted lynching in the Biswanath district in the state, Ali struggled to walk when the BBC correspondent met him at his residence. Describing the incident, he called it an attack on his entire faith.

'As the 48-year-old sat cross-legged on his bed, his eyes filled with tears as he recounted the horror of what happened. "They beat me with a stick, they kicked me in the face," he said, showing me the injuries to his rib cage and his head… "I have no reason to live now," he said as he broke down, "This was an attack on my entire faith,"' the BBC reported. As part of the hate attack, he was made to eat pork; the aim being to humiliate him and the tenets of his faith—pork, as it is well known, is prohibited in Islam. And most

Muslims do not eat it. The dehumanizing video showing a blood- and sludge-soaked Ali kneeling on the ground and being force-fed pork sparked social outrage. Of course, there were political leaders who chose to let their silence speak. It was disquieting.

For many years, Ali had been selling beef curry for a living. Beef is not prohibited in Assam. The state follows the Assam Cattle Preservation Act of 1950. It permits the slaughter of cattle over 14 years of age. If the animal is incapacitated for life due to injury or health issues, a 'fit-for-slaughter' certificate is to be obtained from the state husbandry and animal welfare department. Importantly, the legal injunction does not differentiate between buffaloes, cows and bulls. So, Ali had not faced any problem in his trade. Everything went normally. But then these are not normal times. Rather, these are dangerous times to be a Muslim.

Biswanath district is separated from Betul by more than 2,000 kilometres, yet things remained the same for 'Muslims', whether they were practising Muslims or non-Muslims who merely looked Muslim, as in the case of the Betul lawyer.

Nothing, absolutely nothing, changed even when one travelled all the way to India's capital. There Mohammed Zubair became the first victim of the north-east Delhi violence. His fault? He looked like a Muslim. Zubair was a practising Muslim who was going back home after attending a religious congregation. Speaking to the author from his bed in Delhi's Inderlok, where he was recuperating, and too scared to step out even two weeks after the incident, he recalled the mob attacking him, 'They raised cries of "Jai Shri Ram". They shouted, "Mulla ko maro... bolo Jai Shri Ram (Hit the Muslim, say Jai Shri Ram)"... They did not attack me but my Muslim identity. I was wearing a skullcap and a salwar kameez at that time.'[8]

If Zubair was attacked for being a Muslim, in the same violent incident, poor Qamar Jahan's husband risked his life and limb to go back to his home, which had been torched by the mob, only to recover her Aadhaar card. Thankfully, Qamar Jahan, showing great presence of mind, had hidden the card amidst the waste material lying on the roof of her house. It was too risky to take along, just in case the mob attacked her and took away the document that she believed would prove her citizenship if the government decided to go ahead with an NRC. Later, speaking about the violence and the palpable tension preceding it, she told the author,

> I left the house. I was about to take a piece of jewellery my husband had gifted me. I thought the crowd might try to lay its hands on me to take the gold chain. I left it at home under the mattress. But I ran to the roof of the house. Some waste material was lying there and a broken tricycle. I hid my Aadhaar card there. I thought nobody would think of burning the trash. Four days after we left, my husband went back home. Everything was charred. I told him to go to the roof. He found my Aadhaar card, his card and those of the children lying safely there.[9]

But didn't she, as a woman, try to take her gold chain at least? 'See, if we get to live then I can have another gold chain. But if we do not have an Aadhaar card, the government can throw us into a detention camp. Then what will be the use of the gold chain?'[10]

In the targeted violence, almost every lane of north-east Delhi had a tale of sorrow to tell. Qamar Jahan's story, though, was a scathing indictment of a state that had instilled fear in its citizens; a large section of it, anyway.

I, too, discovered just how widespread the fear was, much to my chagrin a couple of years later. Towards the end of September 2022, I was headed to Bisada village in Dadri in western Uttar Pradesh to visit the house of Mohammed Akhlaq, who had been lynched there in 2015. First, Akhlaq's brother, Jaan Mohammed advised me not to go, or if I did, to do so during the daytime. Then, similar advice came from Mohammed Qumar, a local who had taken part in Akhlaq's funeral. Finally, an autorickshaw driver, Pravesh Kumar, said almost the same thing, 'Hawa kharab hai. Woh Thakuro ka gaon hai. Apka wahan jana safe nahi hai (Circumstances are adverse. That's a village of Thakurs. It is not safe for you to go there).'[11]

From the crime of looking like a Muslim, as in the case of Bundele, to being a Muslim, as Zubair and others discovered, it has become clear that there are no guarantees of life on the streets of India anymore.

27

Firoze Khan, the Sanskrit Man

GHAFFUR KHAN WAS A WELL-KNOWN bhajan singer in Rajasthan. He was often invited to perform at various temples in and around Jaipur. He sang the works of Tulsidas, Mirabai and Surdas. He told his son, Munna, stories from Hindu mythology. When he grew up, Munna studied Sanskrit at the Government Shastri Sanskrit Mahavidyalaya. Life moved on an even keel. Governments changed very five years in Rajasthan. Invitations to Ghaffur remained unaffected by political vicissitudes.

It was inevitable that Munna would step into the shoes of his father. He had been trained for it since childhood. What's more, he loved it. Munna too sang bhajans with zest and fervour. He, too, was invited regularly to perform at temples. He even maintained a gaushala (cow shelter) even as he continued his study of Sanskrit. Over a period time, he became a rare Muslim, one who was regular with his prayers, but was as much loved at temples and bhajan festivals. He had read the classics of Kalidas, and could quote from Ramcharitmanas freely as he knew the text like the back of his hand. No Muslim objected to his quoting Tulsidas or

Surdas. No Hindu objected to a Muslim singing Krishna bhajans in temples. When he was awarded the Padma Shri, it seemed an acknowledgement of a life spent in devotion. Life was beautiful.

Like Ghaffur earlier, Munna too brought up his son Firoze Khan in an environment of epics, mythology and Sanskrit poetry. Firoze, it seemed, had divinity in his blood. Munna hoped that Firoze too would carry on the devotion, maybe even take it to a higher plane. His joy was understandable when Firoze was appointed assistant professor at Banaras Hindu University's Sanskrit Vidya Dharam Vigyan department. What more could a Sanskrit scholar and a singer of bhajans seek than to be at Kashi! However, Firoze's joy was short-lived. The students at the university, at least a vocal section of them, objected to Firoze Khan, a Muslim, teaching vidya dharam vigyan (science of religion)! According to them, he was not capable of teaching the subject. After all, he was not a Hindu. Times had changed. India had come a long way since the time when the Muslim deity Bonbibi was worshipped by Hindus in Bengal. Or when a bhajan of the Hindi film *Baiju Bawra* (1952), 'Man Tarpat Haridarshan ko aaj', was written by Shakeel Badayuni, sung by Mohammed Rafi, composed by Naushad and loved by millions of Hindus and Muslims alike.

Speaking to the author, Firoze Khan expressed both surprise and anguish at the protests against him,

> I am surprised. All my life has been spent in learning Sanskrit. It is part of who I am. It has given me my identity. Nobody ever objected to me, a Muslim, learning the language. But now, when I am qualified to teach it, there suddenly seem to be issues with people. My Muslim identity has become paramount over my academic credentials. My family has been involved with Sanskrit learning for many generations. My father used to teach the

language too. He has written bhajans in praise of Krishna and is a gau sevak himself. My grandfather used to sing bhajans in public places. We have studied Hindu scriptures. Nobody ever objected. Never did I face any discrimination or problem. This is the first time I am made conscious of my Muslim identity. I am told as I am a non-Hindu I cannot teach the language.[1]

Here the critical sentence is, 'I am made conscious of my Muslim identity.' This is the first time since Independence when being a Muslim closes many doors, even those of learning or teaching Hindu scriptures. In the past, there have been allegations about discrimination against Muslims at the time of job interviews or even in procuring seats in schools and colleges. Though these claims were seldom backed by proof, they may have been a by-product of a nation just stepping away from the shadow of Partition. What we are witnessing today is the demonization of an entire community, with no exceptions. Whether a Muslim dresses in a sherwani and quotes Mohammed Iqbal or moves around in a dhoti–kurta and quotes Mirabai, the objections, the ridicule, the sarcasm flow endlessly. It is alienating, unsettling; words are uttered to drive home a single point: You do not belong here. Much like the Savarkars and Golwalkars said in the past.

The Banaras Hindu University gave in to protests and transferred Firoze to its Faculty of Arts. Firoze could only quip, 'I feel alienated. I would not have applied for the job had the university mentioned in the advertisement that only Hindus could apply. I passed through a proper interview process. I would say, Sanskrit belongs to us all. It is my language, too.'[2]

His is a lonely cry of protest. Much of India failed to stand up for him. The nation in which people customarily paid obeisance at a mosque on their way to Lord Ayyappa's shrine has forgotten much about pluralism. Not long ago, Shashi Tharoor wrote about the shared traditions, stating,

> Hindu pilgrims, after the steep climb to the shrine of Lord Ayyappa at Sabarimala, first stop at the idol-less shrine dedicated to the Lord's Muslim companion, Vavara Swami. Even the richest Hindu temple, at Tirupati, has a Muslim connection. One legend has it that Lord Balaji's second wife is Muslim, Bibi Nanchira, the daughter of a sultan who was enamoured of the Lord, much to her father's dismay, until Balaji appeared in the Sultan's dreams and informed him that He wished to marry his daughter.[3]

Bibi Nanchira's father acquiesced, and today, she, as Balaji's second wife, is said to live in the town below, at His feet, while Padmavati, the first wife, stays on Tirumala hill, in His heart. That was in south India, where it is still possible for a Raziya Mohammed Kutty, a schoolteacher, to teach Sanskrit to students at a school in the morning and give a Quranic lecture to adults at a religious centre in the evening. It is mainly in north India where our shared traditions are being cast aside, where Muslims are being made aware of their distinct identity, and through it, are being forced into socio-economic exclusion. 'Not people like us' is a constant refrain they have to deal with. It is in this part of the country where names of cities are changed because of their association with Muslims. It is in this part of the country that vendors were driven away during the pandemic because of their religion, just as others were forced to fly a bhagwa dhwaja (saffron flag) on their carts and roadside shops. Exclusion for some, familiar identification for others. Firoze Khan's fate is a product of a society which no longer has space or time for syncretism. Gone are the days when many would proudly talk of Raskhan and his Krishna bhakti. Or the Mughal court being a patron of translations of Hindu religious texts from Sanskrit to Persian. Today, vast multitudes swear by the Hindutva hegemony. In this relentless even violent bid for supremacy, there is no space for peaceful dialogue, for appreciation of differences. The Hindutva practitioner, in his mind, is sorting out the equations of the past. The result is an attack on a mosque in Ayodhya, a Muslim teacher in Varanasi, or even a dairy farmer in Alwar. The assailants are always Hindutva chauvinists, the victims are either symbols of India's Islamic connection or followers of Islam. As Khushwant Singh put it, 'The juggernaut of Hindu fundamentalism has emerged from the temple of intolerance and is on its yatra. Whoever stands in its way will be crushed under its mighty wheels.'[4] Demolished, destroyed, displaced for being a Muslim. Fascism has arrived.

PART 7
Finding Their Voice

28

Jihad at Every Step

JIHAD IS NOT XENOPHOBIA. IT is not about lustful killing, but about looking within. It is a constant, peaceful cleansing, overcoming your own foibles, your own elasticity of morals. Once, the companions of the Prophet came back from a battle in which they had conquered the enemy. They heaved a sigh of relief. Just then the Prophet reminded them they had merely come from a smaller jihad to a bigger one—an incessant peaceful strife. It was time for internal jihad, fighting oneself.

The besieged Indian Muslim community had sought to do likewise. Instead of being drawn into a game of one-upmanship with purveyors of hate and exclusion, it decided instead to focus on internal cleansing, concentrate on education, participate in open competition in the market to nudge ahead, bit by bit, step by step. It is early days, but the results are beginning to show as the community strives to make a mark for itself and increase its contributions to the nation. The Indian civil services provide a forum, an opportunity to make a mark, for self, for the community, and the nation.

Overcoming years of lethargy and a feeling of being discriminated against by the system, the community, in recent years, has taken to appearing for secular competitive examinations in a big way. We have had the case of the Rahmani-30 classes, through which more than 300 students have been sent to IITs across the country over the past 12 years. A brainchild of Wali Rahmani, former speaker of the Bihar Assembly, the Rahmani-30 classes have been gaining traction with each passing year.

On the same lines have been the efforts of the Zakat Foundation of India (ZFI), Jamia Millia Residential Academy and other similar though admittedly smaller ventures of Jamia Hamdard, the Haj Committee in Mumbai and sundry mosques in Chennai, Hyderabad and Bengaluru. They have all striven to increase the representation of Muslims in civil services. Except in cases like that of Jamia, they have used community resources, financial and manpower, to prepare students to take on the toughest examination in a level playing field without the benefit of any reservation. Just helping prepare better-informed, better-guided candidates. Young men and women born in the 1990s were often told about the success of Amir Subhani, just as those who entered college after 2010 were informed of the success story of Shah Faesal. They were just two men who topped the civil services, but for the youngsters in the community they became icons and role models. For middle-class Muslims, just like for those from other religions, the government job offered a security of tenure, a regular income and the promise of social dignity. The civil services added to it by its undoubted lustre and was an aspiration point for anyone looking for upward mobility.

Thanks to the efforts of ZFI and Jamia, the representation of the community in the civil services began to increase, though very slowly. In any case, it was never likely to be a T-20 cricket kind of instant gratification; it was most like a five-day test match, calling into question both powers of patience and skill. Every summer when the final results of the civil service exams were declared, not only the candidates who had taken the examination but also the community elders waited with bated breath to find out how many Muslim candidates had cracked the civil services. Felicitation ceremonies followed. Attended by many youngsters preparing for the exam, these events helped instill hope and dreams by inviting the successful candidates and presenting their success stories to the next batch of aspirants. Slowly but surely, the community was breaking free of the hold of the semi-literate clerics and trying to shed the tag of being the community of no-good biryani-eaters and puncture repair-wallahs. Except that some read in this relentless effort to do better, join the mainstream of progress and contribute to nation building, a threat to the nation!

The 'threat' was aired by TV channel Sudarshan News whose editor Suresh Chavhanke posted a 45-second-long promo on Twitter in 2020 about an upcoming episode of *Bindas Bol* scheduled for daily relay from 28 August 2020 at 8 pm.[1] The promotional clip showed Chavhanke claiming that the number of Muslims appearing for and clearing the Union Public Service Exams had suddenly recently increased. 'How has the number of Muslim IPS [Indian Police Service] and IAS [Indian Administrative Service] officers increased recently?' he asked, and wondered aloud, 'What will happen if "Jamia ke jihadi" rise to positions of authority in the country?' The insinuations, the bigotry, the overweening hatred were all there. Backed by visuals of ISIS members and other men with beards and skullcaps, it sought to show the community in a certain light—not only negate its efforts to progress in a pluralist democracy through hard work but also put a question mark on its motives, on the candidates' funding, etc. That even Jamia, a central university, was not spared, said it all. Terms like 'Jamia ke jihadi' and 'UPSC jihad' were loosely bandied around, much like a huge section of the media carelessly and irresponsibly used terms like 'corona jihad' and 'Islamic insurrection' following the Tablighi Jamaat episode. The provocation for Chavhanke to make his show was the recruitment of 42 Muslim candidates—up from 28 the previous year—by the Union Public Service Commission through the Civil Services Exam (CSE) for the 2019 batch. There was, however, only one candidate, Safna Nazarudeen, ranked 45, who secured a place among the top 100.

NC Ashtana, former Indian Police Services officer, wrote about this in The Wire:

> I have not had time to get details of the religions of the candidates from the UPSC through RTI or any other means. However, the religion of the candidates can be made out approximately from their names in the official results, even as it does not guarantee accuracy. A little inaccuracy does not affect our conclusions significantly. In the 2019 examination, 35 out of 829 selected candidates were Muslims. That comes to 4.22%, whereas their percentage in the population of India, according to the 2011 Census, is described as 14.2%. Since they are way below their percentage in population, this busts the charge of disproportionate selection. If anything, there is under-representation. In the 2018 examination, out of 759 successful candidates, just 2.64%, or 20, were Muslims. In the 2017 examination, out of 810 successful candidates, 41, that is 5.06%, were Muslims. There are four Muslim candidates amongst the first 100 candidates. For all these three years, there are zero, 2 and 4 Muslims in the 1–100 rank…This busts the 'maximum marks to Muslim candidates' allegation.[2]

Not renowned for his attention to detail or background research, in his hate-filled show Chavhanke did not bother to talk of the Sachar Committee report (2006) that had pointed out the abysmal representation of Muslims in civil services and found that against many social and economic parameters Muslims ranked below SCs and STs. According to the report, 'Their share in IAS, IPS and IFS is extremely low as compared to other religious minorities. Muslim representation in the bureaucracy was about 3-4% in 2006 which has reportedly been stagnant in the last 14 years.'[3] A marginal increase in the number of Muslims in civil services in 2019, taking their representation to about 5 per cent of the successful candidates, was still way below the percentage of their population in the country (Muslims, according to 2011 Census, account for approximately 14 per cent of India's population). A couple of years later, out of the 933 candidates who were declared successful in UPSC CSE 2022, only 29 belonged to the Muslim community. In 2021 exams, the figure was 25 while in 2020, the number of successful candidates from the community was 31. In 2023, 32 candidates were successful. That this small increase was possible without the crutches of reservation should have been a cause for muted celebration rather than relentless hatred.

The fact that religion and region have no bearing on selections to civil services did not strike the *Bindas Bol* anchor, keen as he was to portray an entire community as trying to destabilize the nation. The Wire wrote,

> A civil servant's religion is her personal matter. According to the Government of India's decisions under Rule 3 of the All India Services (Conduct) Rules, 1968, civil servants should so conduct themselves in public as to leave no room for an impression that they are likely, in their official dealings, to favour

persons belonging to any particular religion. In addition, they must uphold the supremacy of the constitution and democratic values. The Supreme Court had held in the famous Kesavananda Bharati case and reiterated in S.R. Bommai vs Union of India, that secularism is inherent to the basic structure of the constitution.[4]

Jamia and ZFI both took recourse to the judiciary for redressal of their grievances against Chavhanke. Meanwhile, when a section of citizenry sought a ban on the telecast of the episodes, the Supreme Court commented, 'A message needs to go out to the media that it cannot make a religious minority the target of its attacks. The dignity of a community is as important as journalistic freedom.'[5]

As reported by *The Hindu*,

Justice Chandrachud said the channel had no business to make sweeping comments about the entire Muslim community. It crossed the Rubicon when it implied that civil services aspirants from the community had terror links. Not every child can afford to enrol for elite UPSC coaching classes. They may be helped by organisations to enter civil services. These students may also be from other religious communities... 'Is it right to imply they have infiltrated UPSC and have terror links', Justice Chandrachud asked. Justice Indu Malhotra said such content was 'plainly hurtful'. The Sudarshan TV show has smeared an entire community.

Justice Chandrachud said, 'Flames come up on the screen, bearded people in skull caps and the colour green are featured when a reference to a Muslim is made in the show. Every time you refer to the UPSC, you show ISIS and jihad. You suggest a deep-rooted conspiracy.'[6]

On the same bench, Justice KM Joseph made some important observations about various communities running coaching institutes to aid their candidates. 'Communities run institutions for their children to attempt civil services. These attacks will marginalise people who want to come into mainstream... You may end up driving them into the wrong hands. Every community strives to have a voice in the bureaucracy. Every community wants to have a slice of power. What is wrong in that?'

The community got the message. Barely hours after the Supreme Court judgment, this author got phone calls from young men and women in places like Moradabad, Asansol and Begusarai asking for the details of the ZFI entrance examination. The show, rather than sowing seeds of doubts in the community, told the youngsters that professional coaching for possible entrance to civil services was a sure shot way to upward mobility. As observed by the *Deccan Herald*, 'A noticeable shift has been in evidence among Muslim youth for several years now. They are no longer attracted by the emotive "Islam in danger" rhetoric frequently raised from religio-political platforms. They realize that there is much good in educating themselves, enhancing livelihood prospects and participating in nation building rather than engaging with religious zealots.'[7]

However, there is one small though significant change. In the past, the Muslim religious zealots in the form of sundry maulanas told the community members that secular education would take them away from Islam. Now, the Hindu zealots, symbolized by Chavhanke, were determined to keep the Muslim youngsters away from mainstream education and jobs. Two years after floating the UPSC jihad theory, Chavhanke continued in the same vein despite the Supreme Court's verdict. At a Hanuman Chaleesa and Jansabha in Haryana near Delhi in September 2022, he claimed, 'I am proud to be the Suresh Chavhanke whose show was stayed by the Supreme Court... The truth cannot be repressed by the powers that be or the court. I have a list of 100 such people who are IAS, IPS... but they work for Islam and not for the country.'[8] He continued with his bigotry. The Muslim community remained focused on the task ahead. After all, wartime jihad is easier. The internal jihad of peacetime calls for daily struggle, a control over one's impulses, mood swings and the rest to focus on the goal ahead. Just as one is required to do during the arduous preparations for the ruthlessly competitive civil services examination.

For the media, it will be 'love jihad' one day, 'UPSC jihad' the next, and 'corona jihad' on another day. For the Muslim community, life is all about a silent, peaceful jihad within, striving to make tomorrow better than today, everyone doing his bit to make sure the community focuses on the larger challenges of peace, and capitalizes on the opportunities that it throws up.

29

The Shaheen Bagh Women Show the Way

THE CAA OF 2019 GAVE legitimacy to discrimination and sought to turn tiered citizenship based on religion into a reality. What it offered and to whom were not as important as whom it denied. It denied Indian citizenship to Muslims from Pakistan, Afghanistan and Bangladesh, no matter how persecuted, even as it opened the doors to all Hindus, Sikhs, Buddhists, Jains and Christians, etc. Nowhere did it use the word, 'persecuted' for those allowed to seek Indian citizenship; just being the nominal adherent of any faith other than Islam was good enough to seek Indian citizenship. The addition of Christians seemed a little like an afterthought, more with a view to keep the West quiet. Otherwise, the CAA gave definition to what Savarkar and Golwalkar had preached nearly a century ago; India belonged to Hindus, and all others whose sacred land and motherland lay within its frontiers could stay here on condition of good behaviour, maybe even expect to be treated as guests, but they could never treat India as their home. It was a terrible responsibility to impose. And a disrespectful denial of self-worth.

As Savarkar wrote in his book *Who is a Hindu?*,

> A Hindu means a person who regards this land of Bharat-Varsha from the Indus to the Seas as his Fatherland as well as his Holyland, that is the cradle land of his religion. These are the essentials of Hindutva—a common nation (rashtra), a common race (jati) and a common civilisation (sanskriti). All these essentials could best be summed up by stating in brief that he is a Hindu to whom Sindhusthan is not only a pitrbhu but also a punyabhu. For the first two essentials of Hindutva nation and jati—clearly denoted and connoted by the word pitrbhu while the third essential of sanskriti is pre-eminently implied by the word punyabhu, as it is precisely sanskriti including sanskaras i.e. rites and rituals, ceremonies and sacraments, that makes a land a Holyland.[1]

Back in 1937, Savarkar in his presidential address to the Hindu Mahasabha had said, 'India cannot be assumed today to be a unitarian and homogenous nation, but on the contrary, there are two nations in the main, Hindus and Muslims, in India.'[2] The home minister offered a chronology, just in case the Muslims failed to grasp their station in social hierarchy. The CAA was to be seen in conjunction with the NRC, the National Register of Citizens. And the National Population Register (NPR), was the first step, the threshold of NRC, which in turn paved the road to CAA. A non-Muslim who failed to produce relevant documents at the time of the NRC census could hope to continue to enjoy benefits of citizenship under CAA; a Muslim who failed to do the same could be treated as a foreigner, worse, an infiltrator, or even a 'termite', as the home minister reportedly put it in a public address.³ The minister was referring to illegal immigrants from Bangladesh, but the allusion to a specific community was hard to miss. As Reuters reported,

> The head of Indian Prime Minister Narendra Modi's ruling Hindu nationalist party took his invective against illegal Muslim immigrants to a new level this week as the general election kicked off, promising to throw them into the Bay of Bengal. Bharatiya Janata Party (BJP) President Amit Shah referred to such illegal immigrants as 'termites', a description he also used last September, when he drew condemnation from rights groups. The U.S. State Department also noted the remark in its annual human rights report. 'Infiltrators are like termites in the soil of Bengal,' Shah said...at a rally in West Bengal, as voting in India's 39-day general election started. 'A Bharatiya Janata Party government will pick up infiltrators one by one and throw them into the Bay of Bengal,' he said, referring to illegal immigrants from neighbouring Muslim-majority Bangladesh.⁴

The Act went against the Constitution of India, the right to equality, the principles of fraternity. Political commentators, human rights activists, some lawyers and authors spoke out against the new, discriminatory law. Most political parties, barring a stray voice of dissent here or there, went on silent mode. It was too risky to raise one's voice for Muslims; the Hindu vote was in perennial danger of being lost. Not gifted with anything better than a selective conscience at the best of times, many of the Opposition parties almost disappeared from the scene when voices were raised against the CAA. For a hundred days, the common citizens protested—from 15 December to 24 March—in scores of places across the country. No Opposition leader deemed it necessary to speak up for them.

The resistance from armchair critics, commentators and human rights activists was on expected lines—totally predictable, easily manageable. What was not was the stirring fight launched by the gutsy students of Jamia Millia Islamia. They gathered in hundreds against the new law, coined slogans against it, organized a march Some male students marched naked waist upwards. It was a show of hyper masculinity meant to send a certain signal to opponents. In the chill of Delhi's December, it was a health risk. The students were sought to be silenced through tear gas and stun guns. Some were lathi-charged even as they sat with their books and notebooks in the library. One student lost his eye. Many were left to groan with broken bones and bruises. For days many were seen with a sling, a plaster and a bandage.

Yet the most potent symbol of resistance came in the visual of two girls in hijab protecting their male colleague from policemen who rained blows on the man who had fallen to the ground and was literally hiding behind his friends. The girls covered him with all their might even as they looked the policemen in the eye. The visual sent out a strong message of hope and defiance. Muslims had lost their sense of fear, and the timidity that had overcome their character due to the pressure to always be the one maintaining the peace. They would take this much, and no further. The visuals signaled to the government, too, that India's largest minority was not ready to succumb, not ready to accept the discriminatory law or resign to being browbeaten. They were determined to assert their right to be here as much as anybody else. They were not guests meant to be suffered for a while and then sent packing, and they would say it out loud. Then, social media went into a frenzy—on

15 December 2019—when unarmed students were targeted by the police.

The Jamia students soon had company from their Aligarh Muslim University counterparts, followed by students from Jawaharlal Nehru University. They went to the Delhi Police headquarters to protest on a chilly December night. Even non-students, advocates, academics and social activists joined in. The city seemed to be in the throes of a revolution.

By the next morning, the early shoots of the revolution became clearer still. And from the most unlikely of quarters: the women of Shaheen Bagh, located barely a couple of kilometres beyond Jamia Millia Islamia, rose as one. History has witnessed many a fightback by the oppressed; many revolts and revolutions were started by the young and the armed; many a rousing counter too was posed by unarmed youngsters on university campuses. There have not been many cases of housewives and unlettered, frail, old women speaking up, united not just as a community, but as right-thinking people and lovers of justice against the actions of an increasingly authoritarian government. This time they did, and the women sent a message of equality and freedom with such zest and fervour that even a historian as seasoned Romila Thapar came down to join the protest. As did famous author Arundhati Roy, with her limited Hindi and abundance of enthusiasm.

The women of Shaheen Bagh launched what became a call for revolution and azaadi—freedom from discrimination, freedom to live by the ideals of our founding fathers, by the Constitution of India. For the first time since Independence, Muslim women were out on the streets, holding the tricolour aloft; the same flag which had in the past been used to question the patriotism of the community by far-Right proponents. Under the same tricolour the women took shelter, and then rallied the nation around it. For more than a hundred days in the biting cold of Delhi winters, they sat at a public square, Shaheen Bagh, asking, pleading, beseeching the government to take back the discriminatory law. Cocking a snook at the high-on-Hindutva male, these remarkable Muslim women were articulate, brave and totally at ease talking of the Constitution of India. They spoke in public like they were born for it, quoting resistance poets, recalling freedom fighters. Many spoke only in Urdu, some in Hindi and English too. They decorated their protest square, which became a pilgrimage site of secular, egalitarian India, with photographs and cut-outs of Mahatma Gandhi, Dr BR Ambedkar, Maulana Abul Kalam Azad, Bhagat Singh and Ashfaqullah. They sang songs of resistance; they dished out poetry every evening; they stood up to mark their respect for the national anthem tens of times every day. They ushered in the New Year of 2021 the same way. Resolute and gutsy, they were unceasingly proud—proud of their Indian citizenship, proud of their Muslim faith. The two were in a happy fusion. Often, they sat with a copy of the Constitution in one hand, even as they counted the beads of a rosary with the other. There was no contradiction in being an Indian and a Muslim. They said their prayers every day; when they were joined in protest by sisters from other faiths, they made space for them, and like passengers in an unreserved compartment of a train, first they adjusted, then assimilated. They even organized an all-religion prayer meet. Soon, the Shaheen Bagh women could scarcely be recognized by their clothes, something they did not tire of pointing out. There was even a hand-drawn sketch at the place. It showed a woman, half of her face had a bindi and half her body was draped in a sari, the other half donned a hijab. It challenged the prime minister to recognize the protesters by their clothes!

This audacious stir, completely and absolutely peaceful, was too much to take for the pro-Hindutva male, used to imagining the Muslim woman as a meek, helpless being, living under the fear of marital violence, used as a child-rearing machine, and dumped with the pronouncement of triple talaq. Brought up on a regular diet of prejudice and disinformation, this is not what he had hoped to see. The Muslim woman with a flag in one hand, the Constitution in the other, singing songs of love, aspiration, patriotism and shared joys was unimaginable.

For the hate-filled morons, there was only one way of silencing this brave dissent. First a message was sent by the powers that be. The slogan 'Desh ka gaddaro ko, goli maaro...', coined by a union minister in the run-up to Delhi Assembly elections in 2019, caused multilateral damage. On the one hand, it made dissent against the government akin to treachery, good enough to be put down with a bullet. On another, it gave the man on the street or the mob on the road the licence to do as they pleased with anybody not falling in line with the government. The difference between the government and state disappeared. Almost on cue, a young man, Kapil Bainsla appeared in Shaheen Bagh, a pistol in his hand, ready to shoot down protesters. He was arrested by the police. The Shaheen Bagh women responded to this belligerence with flowers and more songs of love and brotherhood. Much like the way they responded to filthy allegations of being professional protestors who sat on dharna for Rs 500 a day and a plate of biryani. Far from being dismayed, they invited the men making such allegations to send in women from their families to join them over biryani even as they took recourse to the judiciary for justice.

Within four weeks of the protest at Shaheen Bagh, almost every part of Delhi resonated with its cry, every part had its own Shaheen Bagh. From Hauz Rani to Inderlok, from Khureji to

Khajuri Khas, from Kardampuri to Jor Bagh, there was a Shaheen Bagh everywhere. At one place where the women sat near a busy lane, they put up a placard: 'Sorry for inconvenience. A revolution is underway!' The women sat on an indefinite but totally peaceful protest against the CAA–NRC–NPR trilogy. For 24 hours a day, they occupied small parks, street corners, even open spaces next to public drains. They imparted education to the young, honed the painting skills of their children in weekend competitions, were seen knitting sweaters and pullovers, but they refused to backtrack. It was a completely, intimately female protest, and a very Muslim one at that. They worked like a well-oiled engine. *Frontline* observed,

> When Shabana feeds her six-month-old baby, there is a Nabeela or a Shah Jehan to lend a shawl to cover her. 'If we do not sit here today, we might have to sit in a detention centre tomorrow. So we will fight for our rights here and now. We will not allow Modi to change our Constitution. People of all religions cooperated to give us this Constitution,' Shabana says. Rehana Khatoon, with her 20-day-old baby in her lap, says: 'If I do not protest, when my child grows up, he will ask me, "What were you doing when India was protesting against the CAA?" What will I say? I do not want my child not to respect me or think of me as a coward.'[5] When Salma has to go home to check on her ailing mother-in-law, her neighbour of many years in Abul Fazal Enclave, Suraiya, stepped in. Rifat, who teaches at a school, joins the protest in the afternoon. 'They have awakened a sleeping giant. They call us Pakistanis. It is our land. Kisike baap ka Hindustan thode hi hai [India belongs to nobody's father]. You tell the world it is Muslims versus the government. It is not true. Yes, I am a Muslim. And I am proud of being one. Why should I hide my Muslim identity to be accepted as an Indian?

They all realise that today it is the Muslims, tomorrow it could be them. You want to divide us. We will not let you.'[6]

Whenever a woman had unavoidable domestic responsibilities, another stood up for her; when one went home to cook and bathe, another occupied her place at the protest site, which by itself became an advertisement for egalitarian strains of democracy. Often one saw domestic workers and their employer 'madams' sitting at the same protest, on the same rug, under the same pandal. Their economic and educational statuses were different, but their concerns and fears after the CAA were common.

Laudable as these sidelights were, Shaheen Bagh was made well and truly memorable by its remarkable grandmothers—women in their late 70s and 80s who had never taken part in any social uprising or even a rally until now. Some had never even been to elementary school. Yet, at Shaheen Bagh, they stood and fought like tigresses for their grandchildren, for their education, their jobs and businesses, and above all, their right to be considered Indians. At the height of the protest, Bilquis Dadi and others like Sarwari and Asma Khatoon were invited by the studios of NDTV to present their reason for the protest to a wider audience. On the live show, they challenged the prime minister to reel out the names of seven generations of his ancestors even as they gave out the names of the male members of their family tree. It was no idle banter. It was a strong message to the powers that be that they belonged here, have lived here, and would die here. Once back from the studios, and fussed over by fellow protesters, they told the author, 'Yesterday, we went to a video wala. They made video with us.' This was their description of a television studio! Sarwari, the youngest dadi at 75, gave a reality check to those who framed the CAA–NRC–NPR trilogy, stating,

We have grown up in India. And suddenly we are asked to give proof that we are Indians. My parents were from Deoband. I lived there before marriage. Then I came to Delhi after marriage. But my husband died some fifty years ago. I have been a widow since then. How do I prove my husband was an Indian? I know he was an Indian but how do I prove it on paper? He is long dead. Does the government have no sensitivity?

The presence of these old women who attained fame as the 'Dadis or Grandmothers of Shaheen Bagh' gave an altogether different dimension to the movement. The world sat up and took notice of how unarmed, uneducated, grand old women were on the streets, protesting against a new law in India and shaking a whole nation up from its slumber. At a time when many institutions stood compromised, the doughty women sent out a signal of hope. David could still defeat Goliath.

The BBC reported, 'The protest has drawn women of all ages. "I won't leave this country, and I don't want to die proving I am Indian," says 70-year-old Aasma Khatoon, who hasn't left the protest site for days. "It's not just me. My ancestors, my children and grandchildren—we are all Indian. But we don't want to prove this to anyone".'[7] The government, though, insisted that the CAA was not about them or Indian Muslims. It was about foreigners. Nobody bought the official line. A protestor captured what was on everyone's mind when she asked, 'If that is indeed the case, why has the home minister repeatedly linked the CAA with the NRC and NPR? We were sitting at home. Who forced us to come to the street, sit and protest?'[8]

By the end of 2020, the women of Shaheen Bagh were being celebrated for taking on the government, standing up for principles of equality and fraternity. *The Time* counted Bilquis Dadi among the Hundred Most Influential People of the World. In an irony of sorts, for in the issue, she shared space with the prime minister of India. The essay of *Time* read,

> Bilkis gave hope and strength to activists and student leaders who were being thrown behind bars for standing up for the unpopular truth in a democracy that was sliding into authoritarianism, and inspired peaceful copycat protests across the country... She said to me as a parting note: 'I will sit here till blood stops flowing in my veins so the children of this country and the world breathe the air of justice and equality.'[9]

The 82-year-old grandmother was happy to be recognized but conceded that she would have been happier had her demands been met, the CAA been repealed.

The Act united the women like nothing else. After all, they had the most to fear with the CAA–NRC–NPR trilogy taking shape. Most had no property under their name, the gas, the electricity, the landline phone connections were all under their husbands' names. All they had were their voters' identity cards, their Aadhaar cards and passports—proofs not considered good enough to be regarded as bona fide Indian. So, out they came in droves, in hundreds, in thousands. From Delhi to Gaya, from Jaipur to Kolkata, from Chennai to Bhopal, and Lucknow to Bengaluru, they made their own little Shaheen Baghs, giving the nation a ray of hope, and a community under endless siege a little launchpad for a future struggle.

30

Muslims Move Past Their Clerics

THE DATE 20 DECEMBER 2019 will go down in history as the day the Muslim community broke the shackles of self-serving clerics. It started at Delhi's Jama Masjid, the unlikeliest of places for a revolt or even social engineering to begin. For decades, the Shahi Imam of the Jama Masjid had had a firm grip over the community. His writ ran the area. He was as feared as he was respected. Never had the imam been defied publicly by the residents of the walled city. In the lanes around the red sandstone mosque—built by the Mughal emperor Shah Jahan in the 17th century—the word of the imam, who hails from the family of the first imam from Bukhara, was respected and obeyed. He was called 'Shahi', a royal, simply because his predecessors were appointed by the royalty! When he stepped out of his house to proceed to the mosque, lesser mortals made way. When he walked down to his hujra (room) everybody went quiet. Except for Fridays and special occasions, he seldom led the way. There were, however, a few occasions when he gave his customary Friday address but refrained from leading the prayers soon afterwards.

It all changed that 20 December, a Friday, as thousands marched across the streets of Old Delhi protesting against the NRC and CAA, passed by the Parliament earlier that month. The young men and women in the Walled City were pretty agitated about it. Their identity, their very existence seemed under challenge. They had already heard of a number of protests against the CAA at Jamia, Shaheen Bagh, Jantar Mantar, Jor Bagh, India Gate and the Delhi police headquarters. They were itching to be part of the action. They too had a voice, they too wanted to be heard. Some of them had gathered at the historic mosque one evening expressing open opposition to the new Act passed by the Parliament. Then Imam Ahmad Bukhari had spoken to community members, sought to allay their fears about the CAA and the NRC. 'It [CAA] is not against the minorities. It is not against Muslims of India. They [Muslims] need not fear. Nobody is asking them to prove their identity. They will not be deported,' Bukhari told a few hundred people who had joined the protest near the mosque. 'First understand the CAA. It is not about Indian Muslims,' the imam said.[1]

The protesters heard him out, but they were disappointed. For many of them, his words seemed a reiteration of what the home minister had been saying. They had come looking for a shoulder, a voice loud enough to drown all other voices. All they got was some solid backing for the CAA. It was enough to shake their faith in the imam. So bitterly disappointed were the faithful that old fears and apprehensions about his business interests being paramount behind his decision-making came back to the mind of the young; they had heard their parents voice something similar some 30 years ago.[2] Some even vowed not to return to the masjid for prayers. They dispersed only to return the following Friday. Thousands gathered to speak in one voice against the CAA. From the lanes of Urdu Bazaar and Matia Mahal, from Chawri Bazaar and Chitli Qabar, they came in droves, then hundreds, and thousands. They occupied every inch of the mosque. There was no stool left to perform ablutions at the hauz, hardly any to do the same with the running water from the taps. There were men, men and more men. Then there were women and women. Like always, they too had gathered at the mosque for Friday prayers. The congregation that Friday was much larger than any other Friday. It reminded old-timers of the days of Emergency when Ahmad Bukhari's father Abdullah enjoyed hypnotic control over the masses; each sentence he uttered was lapped up by the listeners. On 20 December, though, Imam Ahmad Bukhari saw that the writing was on the wall. He avoided the burning topic in his speech, which preceded the Friday prayers. There was no mention of the NRC–CAA in his sermon. He knew there would not be many people to believe his defence of the new Act. His credibility was at stake. Gauging the mood of the worshippers, he even stepped aside for another imam to lead the prayers. Bukhari prayed behind him. Once the prayers were over, the faithful ignored Bukhari and rallied behind the Dalit leader Chandrashekhar Ravan, who planned to lead an anti-CAA rally from the Walled City soon after the Friday prayers.

The youth leader, clad in white with a blue jacket to go with it, addressed the faithful from the steps of the mosque, waving a copy of the Constitution of India. He read out the Preamble, in English and Hindi. The crowd read after him. As he raised slogans and pledged to uphold the Constitution, the law of the land, the crowd roared behind him. As he walked down the steps, men jostled with one another to touch him, hold his hand, embrace him. Together, thousands of men, their heads still covered with skullcaps, tricolour held aloft in their hands, raised their voice against the CAA. Chandrashekhar could as well have been a popular Muslim leader. It reminded old-timers of the address of the staunch

Arya Samaji leader Swami Shradhhanand, who too had spoken about Hindu–Muslim unity from the mosque in 1919 during the freedom struggle. Clad in saffron, Swami Shradhhanand had begun his address on 4 April 1919 with a Vedic mantra and the crowd roared 'Amen' at the end of his address, during which he called the masjid a 'Rashtriya Mandir' (national temple). A century later, another Hindu leader addressed the Muslims from the ramparts of the same mosque. Then the call was against the colonial masters, the British. Now, it was all about rallying the masses against a new divisive law. And uniting people of all faiths all over again. It was a stirring spectacle, a lone Hindu leader, yet unproven in the crucible of elections, being loved and applauded by hundreds and thousands of Muslim devotees at a historic mosque in India.

Incidentally it was also from the same mosque that Maulana Abul Kalam Azad, back in October 1947, had beseeched the members of the community not to leave India for Pakistan. In an impassioned speech, recorded for posterity, Maulana Azad had said,

> Where are you going? And why are you going? Behold, the towers of this historic Masjid bend to ask you: lift up your gaze and see. The dome of this Shahjahani mosque asks you where you have lost the pages of your history. The sacred relics of your ancestors ask you, in whose care you are leaving them? The sounds of 'Allahu Akbar' echoing from this mosque, ask you, on whose mercy are you leaving them? The walls and doorways of this mosque call out to you, again and again. O! those who are leaving, a time may come when you could lose your identity… Don't you remember that it was only yesterday that your caravans had performed 'Wuzu; (Ablutions) on the banks of Jamuna. And today you are afraid to live here… Remember that you have nourished Delhi with your blood.[3]

Nobody reminded the faithful of Maulana Azad's words that day. If somebody did, maybe, just maybe, the masses would have retreated, convinced, India was their home, CAA or no CAA. In the charged atmosphere of that Friday in December 2019, the believers who gathered at the masjid remembered they had nourished Delhi, and indeed India, with their blood. They were not ready to give in to anybody seeking to change its pluralist ethos. A 30,000-strong crowd of Muslim men and women rallied behind Chandrashekhar Azad 'Ravan'. Imam Bukhari, meanwhile, cut a forlorn figure as he watched from the ramparts of the mosque with only a handful of his aides by his side. He peered from behind the curtains of the window of his hujra. It was a moving picture. The man who had once virtually ruled over the gigantic mosque was confined to a small room. He did not dare step out; such was his fear of the men who until then longed to pray behind him every Friday.

The vast multitudes followed the Dalit leader. They could not have enough of him. He was taken into custody by the police but managed to slip away and come back two hours later to address the crowd. He asked the faithful to offer their Asar prayers, then march with him to New Delhi to uphold the Constitution of India. The masses did as advised, and rows of faithful could be seen praying on the roads of Old Delhi on the remarkable day. The prayer was brief, not more than five minutes. It was followed by another round of sloganeering and pledge-taking as thousands and thousands of men and women mingled on the roads, vowing to fight for every inch to protect the Constitution. By then Bukhari had retreated to the confines of his private room, preferring to say his prayers all alone. The faithful dumping the imam for the Bhim Army leader Chandrashekhar was more than symbolic. The community had decided to break free of leaders who could not be trusted. The imam was supposed to lead the prayer, not be a politician, was the message.

This was in stark contrast to 1975, when from the same ramparts of the masjid the present imam's father and predecessor, Imam Abdullah Bukhari, stood up to the dictates of Prime Minister Indira Gandhi, who had declared the Emergency. His word counted. At that time, he saved many a house from being demolished and many a man from being subjected to a coercive vasectomy. The masses rallied behind him. His popularity rose so high that no subsequent election could ever take place without a fatwa, or at least an appeal, issued by Imam Abdullah Bukhari. In 1977, he was a much sought after man by politicians and common people alike.

If there was any consolation for Ahmad Bukhari, it was that he was not the only religious leader whom the community members defied. Similar was the fate of the likes of the popular Shia leader Kalbe Jawwad and the Ajmer dargah dewan Sayed Zainul Hussain Chishti, who too had urged the community not to link the NRC and the CAA. The masses refused to buy into their defence of the Act. 'Muslims of India should not be scared of this law, and it will not take away the citizenship of any Indian Muslim,' Chishti said a day before the Friday prayers on 20 December 2019.[4] Muslims of Ajmer, Jaipur, Tonk and other areas joined Hindus, Sikhs, Christians and others as they marched behind Rajasthan Chief Minister Ashok Gehlot, forming a 3,00,000-strong contingent of the Samvidhan Bachao Rally against the CAA in Jaipur. Chishti's counsel was ignored; Gehlot's words were applauded when he said: 'They want to divide people in the name of religion. What is their agenda? Their agenda is the making of a Hindu Rashtra.'[5] To avoid forming a Hindu Rashtra, and to retain their Indian citizenship, the community was ready to leave its imams behind. The imams either had to walk with the masses or be prepared to be dumped by the community. The imam of New Delhi Jama Masjid felt the pulse of the community. Next Friday (27 December 2019), he drove down to Jor Bagh to stand with those opposing the CAA. Climbing a makeshift stage, Imam Muhibullah Nadwi left his chaste Urdu behind, and in a speech with a smattering of English and good Hindi, he told the masses that what the government wanted was not a Hindu Rashtra but a Hindutva Rashtra; one where the Dalits will not stand on par with the upper castes, one where Muslims and Christians will be reduced to second-grade citizens; the fight was between Ambedkar Rashtra and what the proponents of Hindutva projected the nation to be. 'We want Ambedkar Rashtra where Dalits, Muslims, Hindus and all others have the same status,' he said, before proceeding to the prime minister's residence to hand over a memorandum.[6] The imam and other protesters were prevented from going much further by the police. Yet, in the few steps they took, a piece of history was written. The masses, not the imams, called the shots.

A couple of days after the Jaipur march, the Ajmer dargah head was compelled to write to Prime Minister Narendra Modi to reconsider the decision to implement the CAA. He wrote: 'No law that even remotely hurts the sentiments of any religion should be framed.'[7]

Meanwhile, the Shaheen Bagh women proved smart too. Not only did they keep their protest entirely apolitical, but they also opened their stage to many an amateur poet, many writers and journalists. They invited artists to perform, orators to deliver their talk. They made space for theatre troupes. They listened to TM Krishna and Shubha Mudgal perform. And stand-up comics were much loved and admired. They listened to Rihai Manch's veteran activist Mohammed Shoaib. Harsh Mander's speech was lapped up, Prashant Bhushan much respected. As was the case with the Supreme Court-appointed interlocutors. The women expressed themselves lucidly, forcefully, asking many a question about their democratic right to protest. Yet there was no space for imams and maulvis and muftis. The women did not cede their stage to an ideologue from the Jamaat-e-Islami Hind or Jamiat Ulama-e-Hind. They gave no concession to any representative from the Nizamuddin or Ajmer dargahs. The presence of the imam of the Shahi Jama Masjid was a no-no. Other imams understood and kept a distance from the largest women-led movement of post-Independence India. It was an assertion of secular Muslims who believed in the Constitution of India and fought for their rights as equal Indians. They did not want a conservative maulana to be either seen with them or to let them hijack their Gandhian protest and give it any secessionist hue. The community had not only lost faith in their so-called leaders, but was, in fact, ready to leave them behind.

The common Muslims, men and women, had found their voice, and, for a change, led their leaders! They had had enough of the semi-literate, conservative clerics, who were easily available for a price to political parties. Call it a case of the tail wagging the dog, but on 20 December 2019 the community proved it was no longer willing to live in the past or be led by divisive leaders with their own agenda to advance. It was time for the masses to be heard. And the imams to listen.

The night is still not over. It is dark, very dark still, as the subsequent violence in north-east Delhi proved. Yet, the tiniest ray of light seems to be coming through. It is early, but a new dawn may just beckon.

Acknowledgements

A BOOK OF THIS NATURE can be both physically exhausting and emotionally draining for the author. Keeping a tab on each new crime, every instance of denial of justice to the innocent is deeply disturbing. My family's support made coping with the constant news of death and destruction less painful. My wife Uzma did her best to keep me calm and focused. She kept her head whenever I lost mine! My daughter Maryam added some fresh insights and even read some to help me with the chapters. Aliza, Juveria and Mishal lit up many a dark moment with their sunshine smiles. Most importantly, they gave me the space and peace of mind I needed to write. The same goes for my sisters Muslima and Sajida, their spouses SM Zakir Ali and Dr Sadaqatullah Khan and my bhabhi Nazish Jalali. Their prayers have helped me immensely. Much like the good wishes of brothers Tausief, Tauqueer and, of course, Ammi. Not to forget my nephew Umair, who was always keen to know the progress of the book, and happy to help. And my niece Rida, whose love gives me great energy.

I have enjoyed, too, the selfless support of Chhoti Maa (Natasha Ma'am to the world) and Robin Bose, my 24x7 friend. Then I had the calm presence of Anjana Rajan to bank upon. She took a trip with me to north-east Delhi in 2020, when people needed help desperately. She lent them her ear when they needed it and helped me photograph the destruction in and around Ashok Nagar and Mustafabad. Veteran author Humra Quraishi helped by sharing with me a copy of her book, *The Indian Muslims*. Some of my wonderful colleagues, especially Sudha Vemuri, Sandeep Phukan, Anand Mishra and Anando Bhakto, also helped at various times in this long journey. And dear Sriram, can I ever thank you enough?

Of course, it was such a reassurance to have brothers Iftikhar Hashmi, Masroor Mian, Rashid Ali, Mushtaq Ahmad, Mansoor Ansari, Syed Asad Ali and Irfan Ahmed around me.

Then there was Husain bhai, far from the madding crowd but never short of a good word, warm vibes and long-distance hugs!

For all the support of my family and friends, this project would not have reached fruition without the faith shown by Swati Chopra, associate publisher, HarperCollins India. I am grateful to her beyond measure. Swati and her colleague Anju Christine were amazing! Every morning would probably begin with a fresh manuscript in front of them. Yet to be able to give this book their sustained attention shows the kind of professionals they are, and the values they stand for. So, thank you very much. Swati, this book is as much yours as mine.

Notes

The detailed notes pertaining to this book are available on the HarperCollins *Publishers* India website. Scan this QR code to access the same.

About the Author

Ziya Us Salam is a noted literary and social commentator. A former student of history from the University of Delhi, he is currently engaged in building bridges of commonality between communities by turning to the Quran and the Vedas. He has been associated with *The Hindu* for more than 23 years and has been its features editor for the north Indian editions for 16 years now. Currently, he is its Associate Editor and writes on minority and sociocultural issues.

A prolific and an acclaimed author, Ziya released *Of Saffron Flags and Skullcaps* in 2018, in which he took on some of the key challenges to the idea of India. His other book released in the same year, *Till Talaq Do Us Part*, was a study of the various divorce options available in Islam. In 2019, he published *Lynch Files,* which raised the issues of victims of hate violence, and *365 Tales from Islam*, a book that aims to introduce Islam to children. His book *Women in Masjid: A Quest for Justice* (2019) has been much talked about in relation to women's rights in Islam. Ziya has also authored *Inside the Tablighi Jamaat* (2020) and co-authored (with Dr M Aslam Parvaiz) *Madrasas in the Age of Islamophobia* (2020) besides *Shaheen Bagh: From a Protest to a Movement* (with Uzma Ausaf in 2020). His most recent release is *Nikah Halala: Sleeping with a Stranger* (2020).

HarperCollins *Publishers* India

At HarperCollins India, we believe in telling the best stories and finding the widest readership for our books in every format possible. We started publishing in 1992; a great deal has changed since then, but what has remained constant is the passion with which our authors write their books, the love with which readers receive them, and the sheer joy and excitement that we as publishers feel in being a part of the publishing process.

Over the years, we've had the pleasure of publishing some of the finest writing from the subcontinent and around the world, including several award-winning titles and some of the biggest bestsellers in India's publishing history. But nothing has meant more to us than the fact that millions of people have read the books we published, and that somewhere, a book of ours might have made a difference.

As we look to the future, we go back to that one word— a word which has been a driving force for us all these years.

Read.